MY WEDDING DRESS

True-Life Tales of Lace,
Laughter, Tears and Tulle

Edited by and with contributions from
Susan Whelehan and Anne Laurel Carter

Foreword by Stevie Cameron
Afterword by Amy Cameron

Vintage Canada

To Francis, who was the reason for the dress,
To my mom, who would have loved it all.

S.W.

To Craig

A.L.C.

———————————————

VINTAGE CANADA EDITION, 2007

Copyright © 2007 Susan Whelehan and Anne Laurel Carter
Notice of copyright of each contribution shall be in the name of its Contributor.
Foreword © 2007 Stevie Cameron
Afterword © 2007 Amy Cameron

www.randomhouse.ca

Pages 335 to 336 constitute a continuation of the copyright page.

Library and Archives Canada Cataloguing in Publication

My wedding dress : true-life tales of lace, laughter, tears
and tulle / edited by Susan Whelehan and Anne Laurel Carter.

ISBN: 978-0-676-97846-9

1. Wedding costume. 2. Women—Canada—Biography. I. Whelehan, Susan II. Carter, Anne Laurel.

GT1753.C3M9 2007   392.5'40820971   C2006-904469-4

Text design: CS Richardson

Printed and bound in the United States of America

10 9 8 7 6 5 4 3 2 1

STEVIE CAMERON

Foreword

As I read many of the stories you'll find here, the same thing happened: my eyes prickled with tears and I would pause for several minutes, engulfed in memories of my own wedding and all the hope and joy and worry I felt so many years ago. These stories, each so different, each so beautifully written, describe the same emotions—hope, joy and worry. But not all of them. A few also recall irritation, usually driven by a family's demands or expectations, or panic, coming from a bride's knowledge that this marriage was going to be a mistake. Some of the stories are simpler—funny, even slapstick. But most of them share three common themes: the complex relationship between a mother and a daughter, the longing for a perfect wedding outfit and the hope for love.

And even when their mothers were impossible and their husbands worse, almost every one of these brides remembers every detail of her wedding outfit, whether it was a traditional white dress with a veil or a trim pantsuit or a silk sari shot with gold thread, or even just something thrown together in a last-minute fit. She remembers how she found it—the store or sister's closet or grandmother's attic, the price, the anxiety. But so many of these writers also tell stories of their mothers' weddings and their mothers' dresses, showing how family memories and traditions, for better or for worse, end up tangled in their own experience.

Some of the stories illustrates some of the rules surrounding weddings when I was a girl: pregnant brides, previously married brides or widows and, yes, "older" brides (i.e., anyone over, say, thirty-five) almost always wore suits or cocktail dresses, usually pale beige, pale blue or pink, usually at small family weddings held at City Hall or a country club, restaurant, hotel or a large living room—almost never in a church. But when Jackie Kennedy went to Valentino for the short, cream-coloured lace dress worn at her wedding to Aristotle Onassis in 1968, five years after her husband's assassination, it was considered exactly right. Marrying the froggy Onassis for his money—she required twenty million dollars up front—shocked the world, but she did much to rectify her mistake with a perfect outfit. Not frilly, long, or in any sense bridal, but pretty and celebratory.

Maybe that's when things began to change. Jackie made it okay to wear white or at least cream for a second wedding. Odd, isn't it, this whole white wedding thing? For women in most North American and European cultures it seems to have started in the early 1800s, although most women still wore coloured dresses at that time. It was only when Queen Victoria married Albert of Saxe-Cobourg in 1840, wearing a dainty white dress with a little bustle and a lot of lace, that women settled on the colour that remains dominant to this day. Three other wedding dresses have had almost as much influence: those of American actress Grace

Kelly, British aristocrat Diana Spencer and American socialite Carolyn Bessette. Kelly married Prince Rainier of Monaco in 1956 wearing twenty-five yards of white taffeta, one hundred yards of silk net and an antique rose-point lace veil, a dream outfit with a high neck and long sleeves designed by Helen Rose and given to Kelly by her studio, MGM. The prince wanted a big dowry, so Kelly's father gave him two million dollars; Kelly herself had to agree to a fertility test.

Royal weddings have always inspired wedding fashion, even Princess Margaret's wedding in May 1960 to her second-choice groom, commoner Anthony Armstrong-Jones, who was only slightly preferable to the Royal Family over her true love, divorced commoner Peter Townsend. Poor Margaret, always slightly frumpier than her steadfastly frumpy sister, Queen Elizabeth, had her dress copied all over the world.

Until 1981, Grace Kelly's dress remained the ultimate for many brides. But that year the sight of Lady Diana Spencer emerging from a carriage at Westminster Abbey in the pouffiest of pouffy cream silk taffetas and, at twenty-five yards, the longest train in British royal history, led to a huge demand for enormous puffed sleeves, vast skirts and lashings of lace. In all, the dress, designed by David and Elizabeth Emanuel, had a hundred yards of tulle for the crinoline, a hundred and fifty yards of netting for the veil and ten thousand mother-of-pearl sequins and beads. Like Grace Kelly's, the dress showed nary an inch of Diana's skin except her smiling face. Even her hands were covered in white gloves.

Everything changed when Carolyn Bessette married John Kennedy Jr. in 1996. Her bias-cut crêpe silk slip-dress, designed by Narciso Rodriguez, was held up with thin straps and showed plenty of skin; only a woman as tall and thin as she could have carried it off. Even her feet were bare. And after the wedding hundreds of thousands of women wanted to look just like her. A dress as unforgiving as Carolyn Bessette's was impossible for most brides, so many turned to strapless, backless numbers instead and today it is almost impossible to find a wedding dress that isn't strapless. Not the best choice for many brides, but they persist.

Well, as they say, in my day such a thing was unheard of. Back in the 1960s we all wore modest dresses, usually with sleeves, high necklines, veils and trains, often with white kid gloves, always with white shoes and pearls. Weddings, especially in churches, were considered sacraments and anything that showed too much back or front was . . . *highly inappropriate. Well, embarrassing, really.* My own always stylish mother, despite the six-week interval between her meeting my father and marrying him, and despite wartime scarcities, found an organdy and chiffon gown with a high square-cut neck, a full, sweeping skirt and a big picture hat; she carried the most beautiful bouquet I have ever seen. Ever. I went upstairs to look at her picture just now and to my surprise she was as gorgeous as I had thought she was and *most appropriate.* I still have the recipes from the wedding supper party held at our cottage and they still work. The marriage, however, was a disaster.

In my own case, I had a disastrous wedding but a pretty good marriage. I can't begin to count the number of things that went wrong: all the hurt feelings because we could only invite forty people; having to cancel my hair appointment so I could vacuum the pigeon feathers out of the university chapel that had been vacant all summer; the wedding bouquet arriving crammed with orange roses instead of cream ones; getting to the church late because my mother and brother went hunting for better flowers; my mother getting the photographer to carve the ham instead of take pictures—and getting him drunk in the process, so that I wound up with only one or two pictures, all black and white; the cake icing that cracked off in cement chunks because the baker forgot to slap egg white between the marzipan layer and the royal icing; my husband's uncle, the one who had a bad heart, fainting at the reception because he was mixing booze and the tranquilizers he had slung back to recover from running late for the wedding (so late, in fact, that he had hauled on his underpants back to front); being hustled out of the reception by my mother, who told me we should leave before David's uncle died. Well, you get the idea.

The only thing that worked out okay turned out to be the dress. Unlike most of the brides in this book, my mother had nothing to do with it, as she was in Vancouver and I was in Ottawa when I got engaged. I had a couple of weeks more to plan than my mother did, but unlike her, no money. I could sew, though, so I thumbed through Vogue pattern books (my mother sewed too, and had taught me that Vogue patterns were the only ones that worked because they never forgot a step in the instructions), looking for something . . . *appropriate.* We were having a tiny wedding—no money, so I was paying for everything, no time, no cheer from my groom, who wanted no guests at all—but I did long for a white dress and a modest service in the Presbyterian chapel at the University of British Columbia, where I'd attended services for years. I wanted to come down the aisle on my brother's arm to "Praise, My Soul, the King of Heaven," be married by John Ross, our much-loved minister, and go out on my new husband's arm to the bell pealing in the tower. As long as that worked out, I'd be fine; I wouldn't ask for anything else.

I found a pattern for a simple little dress with a tight waist, long sleeves, high neck and long, bell-shaped skirt. It was a Dior pattern and called for a wide band of thick lace to go down the front and around the hem: perfect. Then I needed a going-away outfit. Although we didn't have a dime for a honeymoon and

spent most of it in my mother-in-law's basement suite, cur-
tained off with an old bedspread, I wanted to observe the pro-
prieties: a girl had to have a going-away outfit. It was September
and we were soon moving to England to go to graduate school,
so I found some fine, tawny wool and stitched up a skirt and
jacket, following another Vogue designer pattern, doing all the
interfacing and linings by hand. It was very smart, especially
after I found a pair of matching Italian snakeskin shoes and a
silk shirt, both on sale. For the dress, I went to Montreal; at that
time, Ottawa didn't have fabric shops good enough for the Dior
pattern. I didn't want pure white—I wanted ivory or parchment
silk, which I thought would suit my hair and skin, and I found
the perfect yardage on St. Catherine Street. I also found a roll of
cream-coloured Point de Venise lace that cost far more than the
silk for the dress itself.

But when I got the yards of silk and lace home, all those pay-
cheques' worth, I was too nervous to cut into them. A friend heard
of a good seamstress who wasn't expensive; she was married to the
caretaker at the German embassy a few blocks from my Centretown
apartment. She took me into their flat in the embassy, poured me
coffee, looked through the bundle of stuff and the pattern and
then lifted her eyes to mine. "Beautiful," she said. "It will be
beautiful." And so we worked together, me finishing my suit and
bringing bits to show off—"Ah, yes, nice work on the sleeve, my
dear"—and she fitting and tucking and shaping the dress.

We drove to Vancouver in four days in David's Austin Mini-
Minor, with David's brother as chaperone and extra driver, the
trip timed to allow us to stay with relatives across the country.
I sat in the back, sharing the tiny space with the big cardboard
box that held my dress, the long tulle veil embroidered with bits
of the cream lace, and matching shoes. I wouldn't let the boys
near it; I knew they would sit on it or smush it against a window.

It was, I have to admit, a little girl's party dress, but in so many ways I was still a little girl. I was twenty-one, a university graduate and a junior officer at External Affairs; I had lived all over the world with my errant American father and patient mother and had even worked for nearly a year in Ottawa's ultra-secret electronic eaves-dropping headquarters called, at that time, the Communications Branch of the National Research Council. I had studied Russian language and code-breaking there and now hoped for a career in diplomacy. I felt grown up, but to the dressmaker and, deep in my heart, to myself as well, I was still just a girl. And as a girl, desperately in love, I believed in this marriage. The fact that the wedding was small didn't matter. I was getting the boy—he was only twenty-four—I knew was perfect for me. And so he has proven to be, for forty years now.

When you're reading these wedding dress stories, you'll also be reading about marriages—good, bad and indifferent. But the stories, as mine does, all come from the heart. We have all gone back and thought hard about our weddings. We've looked at pictures of ourselves as we were, canvassed others' memories, filtered that day through all the things that have happened since. Some details may have blurred over time, but I think we have all told the truth about our lives.

STEVIE CAMERON is a Toronto journalist who has worked as a spy, foreign service officer, food editor, political columnist, antiques colum-nist, host of the *Fifth Estate* on CBC and investigative reporter for the *Globe and Mail* and *Maclean's*. She was the founding editor of *Elm Street* magazine. The author of four books about Canadian politics, she is now working on *The Pig Farm*, a book about the Pickton murder case in British Columbia, for Knopf Canada. Her marriage has lasted a happy forty-one years and her wedding dress is in her hall closet.

Introduction

A few years ago, a group of women friends who love to write sat around the table in my home and took turns calling out topics and writing for ten, fifteen or twenty minutes. Then we read our pieces aloud. At one point I called out, "Your wedding dress. Go!" Twenty minutes later, pens were set down, the pieces were read one by one, and we laughed and cried and were amazed at the memories that flowed out.

There is a place where you go when you put pen to paper and write without pausing. It is a place of sights and sounds, feelings and fantasies, exact words and ecstatic ramblings. It is a place of surprises. It is the reason my friends and I get together to write every so often. We love going to that place. It is not the place you would go if you were to call out a subject and then have a conversation. Oh no. Some say the truths of the heart flow down the arm and out the pen.

A few months later, I went through this process again with a group of women who are not used to writing. They were quite taken with the exercise, and again, truths, insights and long-forgotten details flowed out.

I knew then that using "My Wedding Dress" as a door into a memoir was a wonderful basis for a book. I collected pieces, put them in a folder, kept them safe in my office and went on with my life.

It was not until Anne Carter called a couple of years later, full of energy and enthusiasm for the project, that it came to life. She had been one of the women around the table that first day. If she hadn't called, the pieces might still be living quietly in a drawer. We had great fun making lists of people we wanted to approach for stories. We had great faith in the project and were blessed to find Deirdre Molina of Knopf Canada/Vinage Canada, who believed in it as well.

It was an honour to read the many pieces that were sent in from women around the country. The selection process was agonizing at times. We have tried to include as many different voices and experiences as we could, and we know there are so many others worthy of being told.

Susan Whelehan
Toronto, July 2006

SOMETHING OLD, NEW, BORROWED, AND BLUE . . .
AND A SILVER SIXPENCE IN YOUR SHOE

Bought in exclusive London salons or borrowed from a friend's closet, a wedding dress tells a story. No other piece of clothing causes so much angst, and happiness, as this one gown. I marvel that a dress worn for a particular day in a long, complex life manages to capture the essence of a woman. Maybe it's because marriage is a rite of passage. Our choices reflect our emotions, beliefs, dreams, intimate relationships, even the politics of our communities. We want the day, the dress, the partnership to mean something, *everything,* and so it does.

I placed calls for submissions around the country, asking writers to weave their family history into the memoir of the dress. We received over eighty submissions and chose twenty-six. Some hold poignant echoes of Canada's history. They speak of prairie hardships in the thirties, the Second World War, immigration, even Joey Smallwood's controversial resettlement program. Some touch on the importance of a parent, usually a mother. All tell a love story—even the gay artist who never intended to marry.

The memoirs fell easily into sections using the well-known Victorian rhyme. Only a few of us chose to honour *something old:* ancestors and traditions. Full of dreams for a better future, most of us, myself included, opted for *something new.* What if a *borrowed* item from a beloved friend or sister would bring us the same measure of good fortune? *Blue* (or peach, striped or floral)—this section was for the non-traditional woman who had dramatic reasons for not picking white.

I happen to love the white wedding dress, although it's not universal or timeless. In Asia, brides love red—the colour of luck. From biblical to medieval times a Christian bride chose blue, the colour associated with the Virgin Mary. Puritans picked grey. On a frontier homestead, a woman considered herself lucky to have a "good" dress that didn't show dirt or wear. As Stevie Cameron writes in the foreword, Queen Victoria is credited with starting the white wedding dress craze. She married her handsome cousin and appeared before her subjects in an unusual choice of colour. She did not intend her dress to be a fashion statement. A strong nationalist, her focus was on having her bridal attire made completely in Britain. Over two hundred workers in Devon were employed for months to make the lace flounces for her skirt, sleeves and veil. What did the public pay attention to? How the plain-faced woman stood out from the crowd in white.

As for the last line in the rhyme, "And a silver sixpence in your shoe," none of us married for money. We're writers! We tend to like bare feet and, better yet, to be swept right off them.

Whether your dress or story is old, new, borrowed, blue, we wish every reader an abundance of love and a very good read.

Anne Laurel Carter
Toronto, July 2006

PART ONE

Something Old

Bridal Pink

A few hours after my wedding I was locked in the bathroom of the honeymoon suite of our hotel. I had been there for more than an hour, in tears, scrubbing my breasts and upper arms with a soapy hand towel, surveying myself in the mirror with increasing hysteria and cursing my decision to wear a shocking pink sari for the ceremony. If I had worn a white silk sari with a red and gold border, the traditional colour for brides from Karnataka, the part of India to which I belong, I would not have been in this wretched situation. I would have had a white blouse stitched to match the sari, and our wedding night would have passed into pleasant memory. Instead, it would end as one that was literally and figuratively written into my skin.

My frantic scrubbing was interrupted by a tentative knock on the bathroom door. "What's going on?" Madhav, my husband of two hours, asked, his voice muffled through the door. "Are you all right?"

"Yes," I called back. The marriage was doomed from day one, I thought morosely. I knew I should have called it off. "I'm fine. I'll be out in a couple of minutes."

A quarter of an hour later, Madhav knocked again. "Are you sure you are okay?" He sounded nervous now. "What are you doing in there for so long? Should I call a doctor or something?"

I gave my skin one last ineffectual swipe and slipped on a cream chiffon negligee. I wished now that I had bought one of those thick cotton nighties instead, the ones that looked as if they were made of sailcloth. It would have enveloped me more thoroughly than the sheer negligee, through which my upper body shone a fluorescent pink. What would my new husband think when he saw me looking like a street artist's version of a sunset?

I had known Madhav for eight months before our marriage. He lived in the neighbouring city of Madras and made the three-hour journey by train most weekends to spend time with me. He was shy around women and, to my annoyance, on our first date had invited his best friend along. Unlike my noisy, opinionated family, his was low-key and gentle. We were extravagant with our spending and our emotions, while Madhav's people were cautious to the extreme. And yet I liked him precisely because we were so different. We wrote each other long letters every week. For the first six months or so Madhav's letters were affectionate and interesting, full of opinions on books he had read, movies, politics, jokes. They took the edge off my uneasiness about being engaged to a man I barely knew, about having agreed to an *arranged* marriage, of all things. I wasn't sure whether I loved him, or for that matter whether he loved me, but with my usual optimism I was sure that we could make the relationship work.

In the last two months before the wedding, however, I grew less sure of this. Madhav had changed unaccountably. Once an open, charming young man, he had become silent, almost dour.

I did not know what the matter was, and all attempts to find out met with more silence or impatient dismissals. His letters, too, became a source of anxious uncertainty. Their tone changed from a chatty informality to something darker. They read like religious lectures, interspersed as they were with long passages quoted from the Hindu scriptures, with which I was completely unfamiliar as I had been brought up in a zany, ultra-liberal household. My father was agnostic. My mother believed in God but not in rituals, celebrating only one of the thousands of festivals in the Hindu calendar because it was "so pretty with all those lights and fireworks and all," and because it gave her the opportunity to invite friends and relatives for a boisterous party. What if my future husband was really a religious conservative like the man my best friend, Anu, had married recently? What if he refused to let me wear my sleeveless cholis, or the halter-neck blouses that went with my favourite green chiffon sari? And lipstick? Would he, like Anu's husband, ban makeup? I couldn't imagine life without lipstick. Or backless cholis, or sleeveless blouses, or saris worn low on my hips. And would Madhav prevent me from working or studying and curtail all the freedoms I was used to? And what if he had no sense of humour? My father, who had died a couple of years before, had often said that laughter was one of the main requirements for a happy married life.

Two months before the wedding, I began to consider calling the whole thing off. But how could I do so without hurting or offending or embarrassing not just my mother but our extended family as well? An Indian wedding is nothing if not a family wedding. To break my engagement at this stage, for no real reason other than that my future husband was writing religious letters, would be considered grossly selfish and inconsiderate.

I decided to stay engaged and hope for the best. The doubts did not subside, though. What did I really know about the man

I was marrying, except that he was a "good boy," as my great-aunt Lakki had put it. Years ago, in the tiny coal-mining town of Dhanbad, where her husband and Madhav's father worked as scientists in the fledgling Indian Scientific Research Council, she had been his grade-school English teacher.

"He was a good boy who never got into trouble of any sort," she wrote to my mother. "Very respectful and an excellent student. He always came first in the class spelling tests, and his grammar was impeccable. Since Anita likes books and reading, I think it will be a good match." Lakki Aunty was obviously of the opinion that a mutual fondness for words and the English language was an adequate foundation for a long and happy married life. "Also, I know his family well," she continued. "His father and my husband were classmates in high school and later shared rooms when they were studying engineering in London. I am told that they wore each other's clothes, that close they were. In fact, my husband still owes Madhav's father five shillings from their student days, and if this match comes through, he says that he will consider his debt repaid!"

I was twenty-two years old and worked as a copywriter in an advertising agency. Like most young Indians, I still lived in my mother's house, perfectly happy to let her pamper me when I came home after creating silly jingles for mattresses and refrigerators, cough syrups and face creams. I had no thought of marriage, although, since my father's death, Mummy, under pressure from various elderly members of our large and interfering extended family, was making noises about finding a suitable boy for me.

"That is, if you cannot find one for yourself," she added in a conciliatory way when I protested the idea of an arranged marriage. I had romantic notions of meeting the perfect man at a party, or a friend's wedding. Our eyes would meet across the room, and wham, love would hit us both at the same moment.

5

It had not happened yet. There were a few men I knew and liked, but they were only friends. None of them had the exact combination of attributes I wanted in a husband: attractive, naturally, tall so that I could indulge my passion for high-heeled shoes, bespectacled because I thought men with glasses were sexy in an intellectual sort of way, an engineering school graduate like my beloved father, someone who read as avidly as I did and wrote elegant prose and, above all, had a sense of humour.

In the meantime, my mother issued a global alert to all our friends and relatives that she was on the lookout for a groom for me. Suggestions poured in and were sifted through. Lakki Aunty's "boy" was the only one who appealed, mostly because I liked this particular aunt a great deal. Despite her status as a great-aunt, she was actually several years younger than my father, and I had always admired her for the pieces she published regularly in newspapers. They were beautifully written, ironic and often very funny. I trusted her judgment. I could not imagine her suggesting anyone other than the perfect man.

Two months later Madhav and I met and decided to get married. My mother was delighted—she had not expected me to give in to an arranged match so easily. The lines of grief and worry that had settled on her forehead after my father's death disappeared. She threw herself with her old vigour into the business of organizing the grandest wedding she could afford for me, her oldest child and the first of my generation from her side of the family to be getting married. A wedding date was selected by our family priest after duly considering horoscopes, the positioning of stars and more earthbound matters such as the dates on which the wedding *chhatra,* or hall, that we wanted was available. I was to get married in early October at the ridiculous but highly auspicious hour of 5:00 a.m. Cooks were hired and menus selected, invitations were ordered for the five hundred guests who would be arriving from all over the country and from abroad as well, hotel rooms were booked and musicians were selected for the live music that would be played right through the day. Once these details were taken care of, it was time to shop for my wedding trousseau. In addition to the light printed silk, chiffon, cotton, Kota, Chanderi and Mysore crepe saris, I would need at least six heavy Kanjeevaram silks with gold thread weaving for the variety of ceremonies that would precede and follow the main wedding, and one wedding sari. I insisted on an abbreviated version of the Grand Indian Wedding, which could easily carry on for three or four days, refusing point-blank to sit cross-legged on the dais while priests from both families chanted interminably in Sanskrit.

My mother and I wandered around the city, looking for the most beautiful, most unusual saris available. We spent many pleasurable hours examining flowing jewel-toned yards of Kanjeevarams, Tanchois, Pochhampallys and Ikkats. Salesmen patiently pulled out stacks of green and gold and purple, red and blue and magenta. They tossed the shimmering lengths of cloth over their shoulders and strutted around modelling the saris. Their faces seemed to alter under the caress of silk; they began to look almost feminine. The saris we liked were set aside, and then it was my turn to drape the silk over my shoulder and see how the colour looked on me. This was invariably accompanied by rapturous sighs from the salesmen, exclamations that my approaching nuptials had already tinted my face with a bridal glow, that therefore any of the saris suited me. They would tut warningly if I set a sari aside, insist that if I did not purchase it I would never be able to find anything as perfect again. And so on and on until I was persuaded and then, mission accomplished, they would turn their attention to the next customer, abandoning me and my mother at the cashier's desk.

Finally, all my clothes except for a wedding sari had been bought. I did not want to wear the usual white sari with the red and gold border. I wanted to wear pink. My grandmother Mammaji, who was known for her parsimony, had, surprisingly, offered to gift me my wedding sari. She had agreed enthusiastically with my decision to wear pink instead of white, and it was only when I asked her when she would be coming with me to shop for it that I realized why. I was not getting a new sari but her old one—a hot pink Benaras silk with large gold roses scattered over it—which she had worn for her own wedding. It was a tradition, she declared, which she was starting with me.

"Am I supposed to return the sari after my wedding?" I demanded, angry that she had found a way to wiggle out of her promise. "If this is to be a tradition?"

No, my grandmother said magnanimously. I could keep it and pass it on to my own daughter, and granddaughter too, if I wanted. I hated the sari. I thought it was hideous and old-fashioned. I told my grandmother this. She allowed tears to swim into her eyes.

"Well, it isn't bad," I added reluctantly, well-mannered girl that I was, taught never to insult anyone, not even Mammaji, who was the supreme queen of drama and could turn on the tears at will. "But I want a new sari, something with a newer design."

It will bring you good luck, my grandmother argued, changing tack. It would ensure that Madhav and I would have as peaceful and loving a relationship as she and my grandfather Pappaji did. I thought about the quarrels that my grandparents had almost every day, and how Mammaji chased my grandfather around the house waving a heavy stainless steel ladle at him when she was angry, and how he reciprocated by piling all his shoes on her side of their bed, and wondered whether it was really a good idea to wear that sari. But Mammaji, like all the women in my family, was a determined woman. She had decided that I would get the sari as one of my gifts from her. That way she saved money and could tell people she had given me my wedding sari. She came up with new arguments. Was it not a pink sari? And was it not my idea to wear pink instead of white? Would it not save my poor mother some money? And since the wedding was at the unearthly hour of 5:00 a.m., did I really imagine any of our guests would turn up for the moment when I circled the sacred fire with Madhav? No, they would all show up in time for lunch, by which time I would be wearing something else. So what did it matter if I wore an old-fashioned sari that I did not really like? It would be for only an hour or so, and then I could change into one of my newly purchased saris. Was it so difficult to humour an old lady who would be dead in a few years anyway? No fears, I wanted to say. Mammaji was sixty-two years old but looked about forty-five. She was perfectly healthy except when she wanted her way, at which point she developed high blood pressure or a fit of wheezing. Her hair was more black than white, her skin was relatively unwrinkled, her eyes were bright and sharp. I had seen her chasing some urchins who had tried to steal the mangoes from one of the trees in her compound and knew she had the lungs of a person half her age. She would be alive for longer than any of us! I gave her a sardonic look. She ignored it and wrapped me in the sari. Pinched my chin and pushed me in front of the mirror.

"And look," she said. "Look how well it suits your skin." Guilt, flattery, force—my grandmother used an entire battery of weapons to get me into that sari, and I had no choice but to be persuaded.

Now that my trousseau was ready, all that was left to do was to find matching material for petticoats and cholis. For the silk blouses it was necessary to purchase lining made of inexpensive cotton, which would be stitched inside the silk to prevent it from sticking uncomfortably to my skin and tearing from the stress. Another day was spent shopping for the exact shade of blue or red or pink material, and finally it was all delivered to Rao-ji, a cantankerous prima donna of a tailor who maintained a poky little shop on posh Commercial Street and took anywhere from three to five months to execute his orders. He measured me for the cholis, arguing over the length of the sleeves (too long, he thought), the dip of the neckline (too low, he insisted) and the tiny scrap of material holding the back together (shameful, he declared). I hoped he would stick to the measurements I wanted and not alter them to suit his own prudish soul. The tailor gave me a scornful glare and reminded me that he had been sewing blouses for several generations of brides. And for famous film stars too. He pointed a sharp-nailed finger at the dim wall of his tiny shop, where photographs of alluring beauties from Bollywood cinema were tacked up. Apparently, Rao-ji Tailor was responsible for the impeccable cut and fit of those skimpy little blouses.

At last it was the morning of my wedding. In the wedding photos I look serene and lovely, Madhav looks serious, the sacred fire leaps before us, and we are surrounded by loving family. In reality I was miserably hot in my grandmother's pink Benaras with the fat gold roses. The tiny choli felt like a vice around my breasts. I could barely breathe. I wished that I had listened to the tailor and had had it stitched a little looser. Sweat trickled down my back and into the hollow formed by the taut silk-reinforced-by-cotton stretched across it. My armpits felt horribly sticky. I had been sitting cross-legged for what seemed like a whole day, and my thighs were beginning to cramp. I wished that the priests would hurry up with their chanting and declare me a married woman. The physical discomfort was compounded by the certainty that I was making a huge mistake getting hitched for life to the man sitting solemnly beside me, automatically repeating Sanskrit phrases as instructed by the priests.

The chanting gathered momentum. It was time to get to our feet and circle the sacred fire seven times—one of the last of many rituals that mark a Hindu wedding. At the far end of the marriage hall the musicians beat thunderously on their drums and the flautists and the sitar players, the pipers and the cymbalists reached a crescendo. Madhav and I walked around the fire, the end of his shawl knotted to the end of my sari pallu, both of us symbolically bound together. The five hundred guests threw rice in blessing towards us. I saw my mother and my aunts weeping into their handkerchiefs. I spotted my sister, whose face, I thought with vague surprise, seemed to match the yellow of her salwar kameez. I wondered for a moment whether I was hallucinating from the heat and the exhaustion and the uncertainty of my feelings, but discovered later, with some relief, that my sister had been suffering from undiagnosed jaundice. I felt damp and miserable and not at all sure of what lay ahead of me.

The seventh circle was completed. Madhav and I were now joined, if the symbolism was to be believed, for seven lifetimes. I glanced at his tense, unsmiling face and wondered whether our marriage would survive even one.

And now, hours later, in our honeymoon suite, I stood before Madhav in my sexy negligee, feeling anything but sexy. Instead, I felt like a fiasco, and wretchedly mortified.

"What *happened* to you in there?" Madhav asked. His eyes fell on my bright pink skin, clearly visible through the transparent cream of the negligee.

I burst into tears. "The blouse," I sobbed. "The colour . . ."

Madhav gave me a puzzled look. I explained, through my tears, that the tailor was supposed to wash the coarse cotton lining material in salt water to shrink it and set the colour. Obviously he had not. And I had not thought to check.

A look of dawning realization spread across my husband's face, and then he grinned. "Is it permanent?" he asked. "Are we stuck with shocking pink boobs forever?"

I glared at him and then the absurdity of the situation hit me as well. I giggled and caught sight of myself in the dressing table mirror.

"But I look so awful!" I wailed. "What must you think of me?"

"I think you are beautiful," my new husband assured me. "I will always think you are beautiful—for seven lifetimes." He laughed and added. "A shocking pink beauty."

Needless to say, the rest of the honeymoon passed in a haze of happiness. I discovered the reason behind the sudden piety in Madhav's letters, the silences, the gloominess. He, too, had been filled with doubts about marrying a woman he had known for such a short period of time. He loved me for my noisy ebullience, had grown fond of my quick-witted, nutty family, was enchanted by my low-slung saris and halter-neck cholis, but wasn't sure whether I would be happy with a man like him—quiet, sober, low-key. He had been afraid that I might be too much for him and he too little for me.

"But you are tall and you used to come first in the spelling tests and you wear glasses," I teased him. "And most of all, you know how to laugh." There was nothing for either of us to be afraid of. We would be fine together, for seven lifetimes if it came to that.

We will have been married for twenty-two years come October. My grandmother's sari lies in the bottom of my chest, carefully wrapped in tissue paper, with a sliver of sandalwood in its folds to keep the moths away. The blouse is there as well, in another piece of tissue. It does not fit me anymore, but I cannot bear to throw it away.

We have had a wonderful, laughter-filled life together. And any dark clouds that have dared to cross our sky have always been lined with bright pink.

ANITA RAU BADAMI is the author of three novels. She lives in Montreal with her husband. They love books, life and laughter and have an abiding passion for the colour pink.

ALISA GORDANEER

Green Silk and Black Leather: The Official Story

I feel cocky, telling my new boss that I'm taking the afternoon off, but from the way he smiles and shrugs, I can tell he doesn't mind. I may have worked here for barely a month, but already I've proven myself—this time by finishing the week's tasks before lunchtime on Friday.

"Nice dress," a co-worker comments as I prepare to leave the office. "Green is a good colour on you."

I smile at her confirmation that I've chosen a flattering outfit, and pull on my favourite old black leather coat. I know it's muggy outside, but the office's air conditioning has given me a chill that's taken hold, made me shiver. Or maybe I just have an uncharacteristic case of jitters.

"Thanks," I say. "Think I'll go get married or something."

By the way she laughs, I can tell she thinks I've made a joke.

14

She's well aware that I went home to the West Coast to get married, just a few weeks ago. She shakes her head and waves me off, and I imagine she thinks I'm sneaking off for a hot weekend with my new husband.

If she only knew.

As I dash down the stairs of the office building, I wish I knew her better, wish I knew someone here in this city well enough to invite them along with me this afternoon. But I'm new here, and

know that well is right now standing on the
e, holding a gorgeous, embarrassingly large
He kisses me as he presents the bundle of
hery proteas, heart-shaped anthuriums.
blinking away tears. The flowers make me
is a florist, and who not long ago arranged
orchids I carried at our first wedding
's concerned, I'm already married.

ost of the flowers in the car, and choose
protea to hold. It's a bizarre flower, with
d soft, furred petals. Its sturdy stem is
thick as a bone.

"Shall we?" Marc asks, and I nod.

The August breeze picks up, flipping the hem of my dress smartly against my knees as we walk the four blocks from my office to the Detroit City-County building. We're hot and sticky by the time we reach the white stucco monolith that acts as city hall, county administration and even courthouse for the city of Detroit, seat of Wayne County, state of Michigan, United States of America. Over the past several weeks, I've become unwillingly familiar with the industrial carpeting and clunky escalators of this particular building. As we walk through its revolving glass doors, it reminds me of a downtrodden shopping mall, or an especially grimy

15

university—not exactly a setting for romance. But, as Marc reminds me, when has bureaucracy ever been the stuff of romance?

Bureaucracy indeed. Two weeks ago, when we first visited this building, we waited for nearly an hour in a stuffy room, simply to apply for a marriage licence. We took a number, stared at the clock, hoped to get done before my lunch break was over. When we finally got our turn at the wicket, the clerk seemed friendly in that way that only city workers on a Friday can.

"Welcome to America," she said in a down-South accent, noticing the fiancée visa stapled into my Canadian passport. "You gotta take the health course."

Health course?

"It's mandatory. All couples gettin' married in Michigan need to be educated about AIDS."

"I thought when you got married you got away from all that," I said.

"Y'all don't have AIDS in Canada?"

So one morning a few days later, I told work I had a doctor's appointment. Marc and I sat along with a half-dozen other embarrassed couples in a weakly air-conditioned room down the hall from the City-County building's parking fines office. A bored civil servant explained the bare bones of the matter: AIDS is spread through sex. Straight people can get it. If you're getting married, you're probably straight and planning to have sex. Any questions?

Stifling a giggle, I looked at my husband-to-be, who was struggling to contain a yawn. "How ridiculous is this?" I whispered, and he rolled his eyes. I'd already passed an HIV test to get my immigration visa.

"Just one more hoop," he murmured.

When the lecture was over, the city official munched a sandwich as he stamped and signed our forms. Now prepared to navigate the dangerous waters of AIDS and, presumably, other hazards of marriage, we swam against the tide as hundreds of workers returned to the building from their lunch breaks.

It was another level of bureaucracy that had brought us here in the first place. If we hadn't been worried about adhering to the letter of the immigration law, we could have been done with the whole wedding thing three weeks ago, like we'd planned. The photographs of our big day would have been proudly displayed on our bookshelves already, instead of tucked away in storage as though we feared an immigration official might drop by for a surprise visit. As it was, we were pretending to each other that we were married. But just as importantly, as far as the government was concerned, we were pretending *not* to be married yet at all.

Three weeks ago, our "real" wedding had gone almost as planned, with a gathering of family and friends on a sun-soaked Victoria Day in a friend's waterfront backyard. It was marred only by a call, early that morning, from the American consulate in Ottawa. "I can't tell you not to have a *wedding*," the official said. "But I can tell you that for your fiancée visa to be valid, you must be *officially* married *in* the United States." Emphasis on the "in."

So it went ahead, almost as planned. I arrived at the ceremony, accompanied by Elizabeth, my matron of honour—a close friend the same age as my mother who had, at my mother's insistence, urged me to wear a floral headpiece even though it was a tradition I had planned to ignore. Rona, my other matron of honour (why not have two?), met us at the gate—it was her house, after all—and made me take my dad's arm. "He wants to walk with you," she whispered in her British accent. "You really should."

Tradition, it seemed, was stronger than my irreverence, and I felt tears prickle as my dad gave me a kiss on the cheek. Then

I took his arm and, following my two attendants down the "aisle"—a grassy path winding through my friend's lush garden—I arrived at a ribbon-covered cherry tree on the edge of a bank overlooking the ocean, where Marc was waiting.

The marriage commissioner said a few official-sounding words, and then, instead of a full set of marriage vows, Marc and I—along with my brother and two matrons of honour—gave a full-length, twenty-four-minute-long reading of T.S. Eliot's long poem *The Wasteland,* from a slim volume that I'd kept since high school. Thus we avoided, in the most absurd way we could think of, making the binding promises the American consulate official had warned us about. I carried a bouquet of orchids that my mother had arranged, and wore, after discovering it fit me better than it had the time I wore it to a high school dance, her wedding dress—a knee-length party dress in creamy beige satin, hand-sewn in 1961 by my grandmother. Its one drawback was that it had no pockets in which to carry the book.

"Why *The Wasteland*?" someone wanted to know. "Isn't all that war imagery kind of grim for a wedding?"

Marc and I glanced at each other, smiling co-conspirators.

"It's our favourite poem," we replied.

So here I am, several weeks after our "real" wedding and its unsigned paperwork, getting officially married. Thousands of miles away from my friends and family, my parents and the city I still think of as home. The moment, like my bizarre protea, seems distinctly unreal.

On top of it all, I feel ridiculous carrying even one flower. But the busy clerks and city officials who breeze past us barely glance, and when we get to the queue in the second-floor office where we're to pick up our now-processed marriage licences, it begins to dawn on me why a woman holding a bouquet isn't an unusual sight around here. There are dozens of couples with us, and it occurs to me for the first time that Marc and I aren't alone in our mission to marry today.

And yet—is this really the right place? One couple looks as though they just got back from camping. He's in a plaid work shirt, she's in a pair of grey sweats with a college logo across the bum. Another man looks old enough to be his bride's grandfather, with his grizzled moustache stained yellow from tobacco. She's got her hair in a casual ponytail, her unfashionably large glasses riding low on her nose. A young couple looks as though they've just been dropped by limo from the senior prom. And another young woman is in a full white satin wedding gown with a train; a friend in pink is twittering away at her in Spanish as she waves a florist-made bouquet of silk flowers. The groom looks as though he's been caught out trying to shoplift a bag of chips from a convenience store.

"Everyone, when y'all have your paperwork, go on up to the courtroom on the thirteenth floor an' wait in the hallway," shouts a clerk.

Clutching our papers, we shuffle into an elevator. "I thought they didn't put thirteenth floors in buildings," I say, but nobody answers.

We pour out into the appointed hallway, where several of us women make a quick dash to the nearby washroom, crowding into a counter space meant for two at a time. The girl in white satin is still giggling with her pink-dressed friend, and I smile at them in the mirror. It's a big day, after all. They've got a dozen family members lined up in the hallway, moms and dads and aunts, all dressed for Sunday at the finest church in the city, not Friday afternoon in a government office.

As I wash the sweat off my palms, I wonder how we'll do the ceremony. Will we take turns, couples filing in two by two to say "I do" and kiss? How will they determine the order? Does the plastic number we took at the licence office door—*You will be served in the order in which you arrive*—apply here? Or will it be alphabetical, by last name? His or hers? How do they decide?

One woman, dressed in a white silk pantsuit, gives me a curious look, sidelong. Maybe it's my flower? My hair, which is short and spiked? Or the fact I'm the only white woman in the room?

Or maybe it's because I'm still wearing my black leather coat. In the mirror, I notice that its elbows are scuffed with age and its sleeves permanently creased. One of the buttons is missing. I haven't fixed it because I don't know how to sew, though Marc does—he's already repaired the pocket lining and softened the jacket with neat's-foot oil, his sworn remedy for old leather. The heat of the room makes the oil's scent rise above the mingling perfumes and hairsprays, and I want to take off the coat, if only for a minute. But it holds me like an embrace.

I was in grade twelve when my dad's belly grew too big for him to button this coat around it. He told me a story about how he'd bought it in Paris, from a vendor along the Seine, when he was studying painting there as a young man. Then he handed the leather over to me. "It's done me for thirty years," he said. "See what it can do for you."

Now I'm glad for a coat that reminds me daily of my dad and his paintbrushes, his smell of turpentine and the scent of oil paint. But at the time, I was simply glad for a coat that gave me the instant look of a brooding intellectual. I wore it daily, with a copy of *The Wasteland* tucked into the left pocket as reading material for the bus ride to school. It was a poem I'd recently discovered, or rather, had been introduced to by a friend I barely knew, a boy I'd met briefly that summer while on vacation. I was infatuated with this pen pal, who wrote to me about poets and music and communism, and I would carry each new letter folded into the Eliot book, taking it out to read from time to time. The book fit perfectly in the coat's pocket, and I imagined the boy seeing me, somehow, carrying his words along wherever I went.

"Ol' Eliot, he's a good guy," my dad would say, and I'd wonder if I was being teased. But the book had originally come from my dad's collection of poetry and books about art, just as the coat came from his closet, and I felt as though I was somehow following in honourable footsteps.

"What are you thinking?" Marc asks when I come out of the washroom, wiping my fingers under my eyes.

"About my dad. I'm about to get married in his coat. I don't think he'd ever have imagined that."

"Good thing you didn't try to wear it three weeks ago," he replies. "It was such a gorgeously hot day, you would have roasted in it."

"I'm roasting now."

I long for the fresh ocean breeze, sure I've sweated through the thin green silk beneath the coat. I consider ducking back into the washroom to check—I don't want to get married with enormous armpit stains showing, do I? Does it matter? It isn't like anyone is here to take pictures. But I don't want to ruin the dress. Even on sale, it cost more than I could afford.

I chose the dress this morning from among the many in my closet, wanting something nice to wear, but not so nice as to make my co-workers wonder why I was dressed up. Even though we're following the rules to a T, I'm still a little worried that someone might wonder why I'm getting married again. For the first time. It would be so hard to explain.

It was a choice made in the semi-consciousness of early morning, but as I thought back to the day I bought the dress, I realized it had a nice symbolism. Exactly a year before, on another hot, sticky day, I was in Paris with a childhood friend for the occasion of her own wedding celebration, a grand dinner

21

party thrown by her groom's parents at their country house. There was no "official" wedding there, either, as she and her husband had visited the Copenhagen city hall for a quick and private exchange of vows several months before they moved back to be with his family in France. Kia and I had gone shopping: I needed an outfit to wear to the party, having arrived on the red-eye with nothing more formal than a sundress in my backpack.

"I'm so glad you're here," she whispered. "I have nobody else from my side."

As we strolled through myriad dress stores, each more lovely than the last, she told me how strange it felt to be married, in another country, far from home. I told her about how I'd lost touch with the one man I thought I could ever marry, the one who had been my pen pal for years when we were teens, even through university. It had been five years since he and I had had a falling-out when his live-in girlfriend started hiding my mail to him, refusing to tell him I'd phoned. If she was still there, she might be his wife by now.

Kia pointed out that she and I had lost touch for ten years, but when she finally got up the curiosity to write to me it was as though we'd never been apart.

"You're right. But there's a lot of water under the bridge," I said.

She laughed and pointed down. I was so involved in thinking about him, I hadn't noticed we were crossing the Seine.

I chose the emerald-green silk from the sale rack at a trendy boutique in Montparnasse. A plainly cut knee-length dress, smooth in its fitted lines, it had short sleeves and a row of covered buttons from scooped neckline to hem. It was sleek and fancy, but informal, the kind of dress I could wear to a party—or to work. Kia approved. She had the same one in a delicious ochre yellow.

"You should write him," she said. "You never know."

I chose a postcard at the Louvre gift shop and wrote out a message twice in my notebook before I had perfected it enough to copy onto the card. I tucked the card into an envelope and, fearing his girlfriend might dispose of any letter from me, I wrote his work address on the outside, feeling my pen scratch the familiar city name: Detroit. I put no return address, hoping the foreign postmark alone would pique his curiosity enough to make him open the envelope.

I dropped it in the mailbox. And hoped.

"What will be, will be," Kia said with a shrug.

Three weeks later, back home in Victoria, I found a message from him in my email inbox. The girlfriend was, as I feared, still living with him. But they had broken up. She was about to move out. And he was glad, so glad, to hear from me.

I flew back east to visit him for a weekend that fall, and we decided within minutes that we couldn't be apart. But I was Canadian and he was American. It would be virtually impossible to ever just live in the same city. We'd get married to simplify the bureaucracy, we decided, and got engaged. "Just like that," I'd tell friends, snapping my fingers. We agreed to apply for jobs in each other's city, and whoever found work first would move. My American employer was pleased to hire me, even though I hadn't sorted out my immigration papers. I explained that I'd be getting married soon, and would need a week off to fly home for that. No problem, my boss had said. I was amazed by how easily things came together, and thought back to the quote from the German poet Johann Wolfgang von Goethe that my dad had written out for me years before. It said, in effect, that once one is fully committed to an idea, everything else will fall in place.

"We're gonna do this in two groups," a clerk says as she strides down the crowded hallway, numbering off the couples, *one, two,*

23

one, two. Marc and I fall into the first group, and we line up to walk through a metal detector and into the courtroom. "One at a time," instructs the clerk, as though we're at the airport.

"Yo, does it detect rings?" asks one joker.

"Only ones over ten karats," shushes the woman following him. "Don't worry, you're safe."

We don't have rings to exchange. We're already wearing the silver ones we put on at our "real" wedding. I'm quickly starting to think of this as our surreal wedding.

I look at Marc and shrug. "Don't need 'em."

The clerk tells all the brides and grooms, twenty couples in all, to line up along the front of the courtroom. Friends and family—the hooting best man, the church-outfit grandmothers, the prom-queen bridesmaids—all shuffle into the audience seats, black vinyl chairs with chrome legs. Everyone stands for the judge, who breezes into the room as though she's just been called off her coffee break.

"All right," says the judge. "Anybody object to these marriages, better step forward now. We got a lot of people to get hitched today."

I'm almost surprised when nobody does. No shotgun weddings, no jealous and jilted lovers? Then, with relief, I remember the metal detector.

"All right. Brides, repeat after me: I, state your name, take this man in matrimony."

The women parrot along. I feel ridiculous, wonder how many others are repeating "state your name" instead of saying their own names. I state my own. I'm going to do this right.

It's the grooms' turn. Marc speaks the words to me, more self-conscious than he was the first time we traded vows. We're alone in a crowd, facing each other only, feeling ridiculous. We could be reciting *The Wasteland* instead of the prescribed words, and nobody would bear witness to our transgression. Nobody but us, a shared secret. Would we really be married if we mocked the vows? They feel like a mere formality, to give a sense of occasion to the signing of papers, the stamping of official seals, the collection of the thirty-five-dollar official fee, plus an obligatory lecture on AIDS. I reach into my pocket, my fingers searching for a copy of Eliot, and think about the painting my dad gave us as a wedding present. It's a portrait of Eliot he painted especially for us.

"By the power vested in me by the state of Michigan, I now pronounce you all husbands and wives, from this day forward. You can kiss each other, and pick up your signed certificates down in the second-floor office in twenty minutes."

The prom queens, the pantsuits, even the sweatsuited couples are having their pictures taken, smiling for flash-lit snapshots in the hallway. "Move along," shouts the clerk. "We got another group to go."

Nobody takes our photograph. Nobody we know has come to see us be officially married. In the second-floor office again, we line up for our signed certificate, jostling between couples who are whooping it up, waving champagne bottles and exchanging long, probing kisses. "Save the booze for outside," a security guard says sternly. "Yo, you two, honeymoon's not on yet!"

It's three o'clock in the afternoon as we walk back to the car, holding hands, clutching papers. I'm glad for the cool breeze, which blows around my overheated neck. "What now?"

"We're officially married," Marc says. "Let's go prove it."

I have the sudden awareness that I'm living a moment I've dreamed of ever since those bus rides to school with Marc's letters folded inside *The Wasteland*. But I never could have dreamed us driving along East Jefferson Avenue to the immigration office, where I get my passport stamped, changing my status from visa holder to resident alien. Then on to the Secretary of State office, where I get my new driver's licence, declaring me a legal driver and resident of Michigan.

The only photograph taken of me on my official wedding day is a one-inch-high mug shot. In it, you can barely see the collar of my dad's black leather jacket.

ALISA GORDANEER can't remember exactly what she and her new husband did after visiting those official government offices. But she does know that their son was born exactly nine months and four days later.

JOANNE ARNOTT

Wedding Clothes and Marriage Blanket

In December 1999, I was a single mom on welfare, in Richmond, British Columbia. I had joint custody of my four boys, ages three to thirteen, and they lived with me half of the time. The other half of the time they lived with their father. For me this meant, in practical terms, that some weeks I was a very busy woman, and some weeks I languished.

Over the preceding three years I had, one by one, dropped all of my old community involvements. Many friendships, relied upon through crises, had since become inactive, in part due to my relocation, and in part as a natural process as all of us moved on to pursue the activities that people do, with work and school, family life, creative and spiritual pathways reabsorbing us. Single now for almost four years, I enjoyed many elements of my independence. At the same time, I was done with spending so much of my time managing loneliness.

The idea of advertising myself on a singles line, as encouraged in the back pages of the newspapers, intrigued me. How would I describe myself? A poet? Intelligent, barely educated? A Manitoba emigrant of French, Scottish, Cree and Irish ancestry, not much for drinking, not into bingo? "Single mom on welfare" was both true and in my face; I could hear myself making excuses: *I can't get together on Tuesdays, I have to go to the food bank. I can't afford to buy a coffee, sorry. Would you like to meet outside the public library?*

Ready to move out of hibernation, I found myself baffled at how to communicate my virtues.

From time to time throughout the fall, there in my basement apartment, I found my thoughts and feelings returning to a fellow I'd travelled with—and promised to marry—almost twenty years before. Maudlin songs of remembered love, on television ads and the radio, brought unexpected tears.

Nick and I had first met at university in Windsor, Ontario, when I was nineteen. He was a foreign student from Indiana, completing a master's degree in fine arts, and I was a hungry undergraduate, honing my poetry. The combined intrigue of his oversize, vibrant paintings and his shy, unobtrusive self caught my attention. Through the round of New Year festivities in 1980, we became a couple.

Over the course of our few years together, I'd twice travelled to visit him at his parents' home, in Evansville, Indiana, and together we'd visited my parents' homes, in the west. Dad was living with my stepmom and youngest brother in the town nearest to the land he'd grown up on, and where I'd lived for a half-dozen years of my girlhood. The Assiniboine River passes just outside of town, and of all the places I have lived, this place looks, smells and feels most like home. Ma had a tiny room in Vancouver. While visiting her, we stayed in my sisters' apartments and spent

29

time with my grandparents in East Van. We travelled the width of the continent together that first summer, hitchhiking all the way across southern Canada, coast to coast.

Our relationship had often been jeopardized by poverty, the combined forces of hunger, homelessness and Nick's diabetes undermining our various plans, and we'd traded disappointments in a quick succession of breakups and reunions. But I remembered singing together late at night and teaching him songs at the side of a hot summer highway. I remembered his hand on my belly in sleep. These natural comforts were more compelling, it seemed, reflections of a greater truth than past failures.

We hadn't seen each other since the early eighties. We hadn't had contact since the early nineties, when Nick was living in Seattle, just a few hours' drive from where I now lived. I wasn't sure what kind of reception I might get, should I make contact again, but it cost me nothing to check with directory assistance in Seattle. So, in early December, I did.

There he was.

The lure of all that had been sweet between us, tempered by our history of near-misses, joined with the goad of loneliness. I waited a week, maybe two, but I did call. We promised to exchange Christmas cards, but he forgot to ask for my address or my phone number. So, a week or so later, I called again.

Nick wrote me a letter, acknowledging the power of our past relationship and expressing his anticipation of much more happiness to come. Even before it arrived, however, I was aquiver at what might well be under way.

My friend Greg Scofield, recently returned to the Prairies, listened to me on the telephone as my emotional world began to tumble and cascade. Greg and I had met in Edmonton while giving a flurry of poetry performances together. While our growing-up years had been quite different and Greg's ties to Metis cultural life were more firm, we clearly recognized one another and the worlds evoked by each other's words. Our families' roots grew from the same prairie soil. In the following years, while we both lived in Vancouver, we met periodically to visit and to play poetry. Now we talked on the phone.

I answered Greg's question "How are you?" with the truth, and when gusts of joy signalled the liberation of a long-buried wish and flashes of fear stopped me in my tracks, I tried to articulate them. Greg encouraged me to enjoy myself, however it might turn out. He added an essential piece of advice that December: "Put those feelings into a poem."

Nick and I soon began spending time together on a regular basis. Sometimes he visited with my boys and me in Canada, and some-times I stayed in his art-filled apartment in Washington. Nick bought a van, a blue Caravan, to ease the cross-border visiting. Almost immediately, again at Nick's initiative, we started to plan a journey.

In the late spring, we drove down the coast together, some nights camping, some nights staying in a bed and breakfast, some nights sleeping in a motel. We traded stories of our years apart, checking one another out more deeply. We compared dis-crete versions of shared memories.

Driving away from the seaside highway in early June, turning east from the beach and climbing up the side of a mountain, we arrived at snowbound Crater Lake. We stood enchanted in the snowfall, in our summer clothes, feeling the wild presence of that ancient place. Later, in the interpretative centre, we heard for the first time the story of the crater's formation, of how Coyote, desperately in love with the Moon, filled the lake to the brim with his tears.

As the story goes, Coyote fell in love with the Moon. Coyote's

31

love was complete, all-involving. But Coyote's love was also exclusive, like greed: Coyote wanted not just to love the Moon, but to own the Moon, and to keep the Moon as a solitary pleasure, for himself. He failed. The Moon is, of course, for everyone.

Nick and I, in years past, had both played Coyote, and we'd taken turns embodying the elusive Moon. Once we were reminded of the acknowledged foolish reaches of love, the possibility of enacting a different story opened up for us.

As Nick drove north through Oregon on our return journey, I sat beside him with my thirty-nine-year-old bare feet propped on the dash. I felt more than satisfied. A spark had been lit inside me, an inexorable process of life, newly begun. It would be weeks before science could confirm it, but I felt the new child's presence. I welcomed this child's presence with primordial enthusiasm.

How to think about our past was a topic of many of our conversations. The litany of misconstrued intentions made it clear that we both needed to ask a lot more questions of each other before making life-altering choices. But to say it was all a mistake seemed disrespectful. I wasn't about to sweep the intervening decades away, along with my four young children. What felt right for me was a longer view, passage through difficult terrain: Nick and me maturing towards a possibility glimpsed, grasped and lost in the earliest moments, and now trying again.

We now prepared to conquer some of what had proved difficult in the past. The presence of the international boundary passing between us made marriage a necessity, just so we could be together. Although neither of us had married or immigrated before, we were prepared to take on the bureaucracies with all of the patience and persistence we could muster.

Shopping for our wedding clothes in the following months was not a departure from our now usual ways of passing time together.

Nick, a visual artist, enjoyed visiting second-hand shops in search of lace and other fabrics to use in his paintings. I had yet to develop an enjoyment of clothes shopping but, in Nick's company, it became for me, too, a light-hearted venture.

I found a creamy white dress, clean and undamaged, with cascades of gauzy fabric, seed pearls across the bodice and beautiful sleeves, in a trendy shop in the University District of Seattle. Nick picked up a blue suit and a dress shirt in the same shop. As this was my first and probably only wedding, I decided to go for the whole dress-up party.

At Clothes Encounter, a Richmond consignment store, I found three colourful vests, three white shirts and three pairs of pants in good condition for my younger sons. At the Salvation Army store, I bought a blue suit, a white dress shirt and black shoes for my first-born son, Stuart. My only unused purchases, from a discount shoe store at a Richmond mall, were three pairs of soft leather walking boots for my younger boys, each with an embroidered motif at the ankle, two pairs black and one brown. Nick's only unused purchase was a lovely little diamond ("brilliant, like you") set in a white gold band. I called it my "rainbow blaster." I used it to amuse my children and, as time went on, to fend off the sometimes bemused stares of strangers.

I called my friend Flo Robertson after a decade of lapsed contact. We'd lived in a housing co-operative in the Downtown Eastside of Vancouver, and we'd become friends while making policy together, sharing life stories as mothers and daughters over cups of hot tea. Although Flo is of the Nlaka'pamux people of British Columbia and I am a Winnipeg-born mixed blood, we were both urban persons of mixed race, with—at the time— palpably weak connections to more traditional communities. We shared a family feeling from the start, and plenty of humour.

33

I told her once, "If I have a daughter, I'd like to name her after you." She laughed. "The poor kid! Why would you want to do that?"

My heart was swollen by this reunion as well. Through the years of our separation, Flo had worked steadily to re-establish her ties with traditional communities, both the relations she'd left behind as a very young woman and the local people, elders of many nations and the Sto:lo people for whom she now worked. We spent many hours on the phone, she in the valley, in Mission, and I at home at the mouth of the same Fraser River. We started visiting again, and the wedding formed only a part of our conversations.

Besides her decades of work in child care and as a social worker, Flo has great expertise in beadwork and in the making of cakes. When I asked if she would make the wedding cake for us, she agreed happily, and we discussed designs and styles of cake, looking at photos from her album and sample pages torn from a cake supplier's ordering brochure.

Flo suggested that we consider a marriage blanket ceremony. Gifts of blankets, and their ceremonial use in weddings, funerals and other rites, is a practice continued by the Sto:lo, the Cree and many other modern First Nations people. Once upon a time, these blankets were handmade, sometimes woven from indigenous plant life or from animal hair, in other regions made from skins. Today the role of these gifts is largely symbolic, usually filled by colourful store-bought blankets. As I had been wrapped in a blanket in healing ceremonies in the past, I was deeply aware of the power of the gift she was offering, and I felt honoured. By providing us with a blanket, Flo was taking on the role of a family elder.

Greg continued his role as long-distance confidant/adviser. Because his knowledge of Metis traditions was greater than mine, Greg was a good person to consult about specifically Metis matters, to ensure, for instance, our respectful handling of our Metis sashes.

The traditional sash weaves together five colours—red, green, blue, yellow and white—symbolic of the four directions, plus the self. There is no end to what these five colours can represent, from the five petals on the Metis beadwork flowers to the source cultures that fed into the birth of the Metis Nation. What comes to mind for me are the different ways that my immediate family has found to get close to our roots. I have most identified with the indigenous and Metis elements of our ancestral inheritance, my brown skin and Aboriginal cheekbones identifying me to strangers from the mountains of Kentucky to the parks of Vancouver. My years in my father's home country, with the green pump in the kitchen and mixed-blood relations around me—albeit with no one acknowledging race—helped. One of my sisters, more urban, white-skinned and green-eyed than I, has studied old Irish, both as a language to speak and for its wealth of traditional songs to sing.

Like many mixed-race families—though by no means all— earlier generations of my family bowed to pressures to assimilate, and no material representations of culture have been preserved or passed on, to my knowledge. Thus, my Metis sashes, like so much else in life, I acquired second-hand. When I brought them home, I cleansed them with smudge, and I prayed to restore their sense of purpose, to rehabilitate the cast-off regalia in the same way that I attempt to rehabilitate my family members and myself.

After further discussions with Flo, I asked Amy Wuttunee Eustergerling to lead the ceremony. Amy is a respected Cree woman who, having spent many years assisting elders in the Lower Mainland, would soon be called upon to perform the role of elder for the community herself. Amy agreed, helping us with our plans to incorporate the sash and the marriage blanket into the ceremony, and generously adding elements from her own traditions and knowledge.

Nick and I also hired Clare Ash, a local marriage notary, to perform those elements of the ceremony that would satisfy the government of Canada so that Nick could gain status as a landed immigrant and a permanent resident. Clare was happy to take a shared role in the ceremony, and concise in coaching us on the steps we would be expected to take. He sent us home to collaborate on a set of vows that expressed our intentions, our commitments.

Once these two representatives of different communities had agreed to perform the wedding for us, in intertwined but distinct roles that would satisfy all of the necessary aspects of the wedding—spiritual, emotional, legal and social—the planning moved into a new phase. For a venue, we settled on the Eco-Pavilion, in Strathcona Community Gardens, a spacious and comfortable garden shed harbouring drying plants and implements, along with the tables, chairs and gathering space required.

Friends joined in to the spirit of the wedding, gathering many small items from second-hand shops on Vancouver Island, from costume jewellery to high-heeled shoes to lacy lingerie and a small purse, and provided me with a shimmering honeymoon dress, bought along with tablecloths, thank-you cards and a guest book. The handmade invitations featured a playful little painting by Nick: a version of us standing in a distinctive West Coast landscape, under an arch made of lace, with the words, "Welcome to Forever/ Joanne and Nick" painted across the sky.

As the months passed and our plans were finalized, it became clear that the gestating child I carried would not be accommodated by the wedding dress come the wedding day. I brought the dress to a Filipina tailor who owned a little shop in central Richmond. She listened to my pleas, frowned over the calendar, the dress and my belly, and agreed to take on the job. She also agreed to put together a simple veil, compatible with the materials and design of the dress.

When I returned for a fitting, I was delighted. Her careful, painstaking hours of work had rendered the dress a comfortable fit, useful once more. She told me, because she knew I didn't have the skills to recognize it for myself, "I want you to know this is a *miracle* I performed here! I made a miracle for you!"

Nick's parents travelled up from southern Indiana to be with us. The Zenthoefers are an old German-American family, one time owners of the local tavern, the kind of family that gathers gladly at every opportunity. Warm-hearted and highly social people, Carl and Doris were easy to be with, and it was good to see them again after so many years. We shared burgers and laughter in Seattle, and sat on beds in a motel room, sipping beer. They reminisced about my husband—their first-born child—as a greedy breastfeeding infant, much to my delight. As they talked, the years dropped away, and Nick caught a glimpse not only of his unexpected past, but of what the near future held for him with the birth of his first child.

In the evenings before the wedding, my son Stuart and I prepared for the ceremony by making tobacco ties together. Tobacco opens communication with the Creator and with the Grandmothers and Grandfathers, and the small cotton twists of tobacco-filled cloth are a necessary part of many ceremonies. We discussed the changes underway in our family, the upcoming ceremony and the gifts for the family and friends who would soon gather. At our final sitting, Nick joined us, and we taught him as we had been taught the how and the why of making tobacco ties.

37

The night before the wedding, Nick's mom, Doris, told us that her family, like mine, is of mixed blood. I remembered how, many years before, when I was a nervous girl visiting her home, she had tried to start a conversation with me about race. I was so afraid of what she might say about my worth or lack thereof that the conversation had ended prematurely. Nick said later that he'd always thought she was Irish; he couldn't say if he'd been told the truth and forgotten or had never been told at all.

On the west coast of Canada, with our protracted seasons of rain, a community garden in November is a damp and interesting place.

At the Eco-Pavilion, I waited nervously, instructing my children in hushed tones and greeting our guests as they began to trickle in. Out-of-town guests and local but rarely seen loved ones arrived. Flo arrived early with the cake, and it was perfect: a tiny couple stood below an arch decorated with rings and birds. Flo had carefully wrapped them in a marriage blanket of their own.

Amy began the ceremony with an opening prayer, with voice and with drum. Clare then oversaw the ceremonial exchange of rings and vows. My elder sister sang a traditional love song for us in Irish.

Amy performed a smudge ceremony, cleansing Nick and me with the smoke of burning medicine plants, wafted over each of us with strokes of an eagle feather. At Amy's sign, I extended the Metis family to include my new husband, encircling his waist with a sash.

With Flo's assistance, Amy smudged the blanket. Geometric patterns in five colours—red, turquoise, beige, blue and black—created a vibrant, earthy feel, and as the blanket was turned, a different combination of diamonds, triangles and arrows was revealed. To my eye, the blanket looked warm, durable and beautiful. Nick and I were called forward again, and the two women enfolded us in our new marriage blanket.

"Treat this blanket with reverence," Amy told us. "Treat it with respect, because it is your marriage. You were two, with two different lives, and now you are joining your lives together; now you are one. The blanket represents that. You have to respect yourselves and your marriage, and consider yourselves one now, in everything you do. This blanket covers you, in the same way that your marriage will cover you. Treat it with respect."

Amy lifted her drum again and sang two songs, one in Cree and one in English.

Then, after a few closing words, the ceremony was complete.

Today the marriage blanket is kept, clean and safe, at the top of our bedroom closet; it goes where we go. While most of the tobacco ties went home with our guests, a few still grace the family altar, a blending of indigenous and non-indigenous spiritual traditions. One tie, encompassing a small prairie river stone, I wear around my neck on a long strip of leather. It gently beats against my belly as I move through my days.

Our youngest children—blue-eyed Flora, dark-eyed Jules— romp around in the wedding veil, decorate themselves with the costume jewellery and toddle around in the high heels. Each weekday morning I tie the last of the new boots bought for my sons onto my smallest child's feet. The gold-embroidered purse that, just once, carried my cigarettes now dangles from a small boy's arm, stuffed with toy cars.

My friend Flo, retired now, sells her beadwork at conferences and powwows, and gives presentations about the big changes in our indigenous ways of life, as witnessed in her lifetime. We make the long drive to visit each other's apartments when we can, and talk on the phone in between.

From time to time, in the evening, Nick and I leave the youngest children in the care of their brothers. I put on my honeymoon dress, and we drive to some venue together. He sits in the crowd, sipping a drink, and I move to the stage, stand before the mike, feel the heat of the spotlight upon me.

To warm up the crowd and myself, I might ask, "Do you like my dress? Do you like my hair?"

I search for Nick's face through the crowd. When I find him, I retell my love of this person I married, as recorded in the poetry I wrote during the first twelve months of our reunion.

RETURNING

the creekbed shifts her hips
in anticipation and longing

for the salmon who will hurl
and spend themselves

on her rocks
in her cool waters

JOANNE ARNOTT's six children all live at home where, like inter-weaving tides, their comings and goings keep the house full and the place lively. Nick arrived as a landed immigrant in 2002, and he's made a place for himself, in the midst of all the busyness. Carl Zenthoefer, father-in-law, died in the summer of 2005, while Doris continues to live at home in Evansville, Indiana. Poetry that captures the ups and downs of the courtship year is collected in *Steepy Mountain: love poetry* (Kegedonce Press, 2004).

ELYSE POMERANZ

Knitted Together

It was October 1985. My boyfriend of six weeks, Amnon Buchbinder, and I were telling his mother that we intended to wed. "Why don't you just live together?" was the response from my mother-in-law-to-be.

It became clear to me immediately that "wedding" was one of those words that evokes something entirely different in every person.

At the time of my engagement, forty-four percent of marriages in the United States ended in divorce. In the Sunni Muslim community, the triple talaq was practised, where a man could say, "I divorce you, I divorce you, I divorce you," and voila, the wife was cut loose and cut off from many of the social supports she had before or during her marriage. Electronic matchmaking was on the rise, people comparing lists of requirements before agreeing to meet someone.

Actually, I had a list myself. I had written it when I was nineteen. It included all the qualities I was looking for in a mate, with only one prohibition: this man could not be a Gemini. The man I eventually married has the sun, moon and Mercury all within one degree of each other in the sign of Gemini. I have learned that what I want and what life wants can be vastly different.

To begin the wedding preparations, I hand-picked burgundy-coloured maple leaves and stored them in green garbage bags in my parents' garage. These would be spread generously on the floor so that autumn leaves would rustle underfoot when the guests entered the hall in mid-winter.

I combed the thrift shops for cotton sheets, then dyed them with a friend who was studying at the Ontario College of Art. We worked for almost twenty-four hours, dying forty sheets. Half were dyed pale blue to be made into a canopy representing the day sky, the other half were indigo to create a canopy of the night sky. Later, my friend created a beautiful silkscreen motif, which she printed onto the sheets that would adorn the central canopy, or *chuppah,* and border the whole room.

Out of discarded samples from designer showrooms, I made a quilted sun and quilted moon, each three feet across, which would hang from the day and night canopies. On the day side, eighteen origami seagulls (ranging in size from six inches to two feet, hung on nylon) would be flying into the quilted sun. I painted dozens of metal spirals made from the unwound springs of old clocks. These were hung to represent stars in the night sky. For the traditional *chuppah,* we suspended a tent in mid-air, with a crown of lit candles on top. Below the canopy was an altar holding a string of bells and a single candle. On either side of it were wooden stands supporting over a hundred tapers, which would be lit during the ceremony. Behind the canopy, a painting of a winter forest of birch trees, fifteen feet wide and seven feet high,

43

completed the setting. We hoped that when our guests entered the space they would find it so unfamiliar, surprising and beautiful that they might be opened to something entirely new.

We had rented a space in an elegant old building, recently refurbished and used for music performance. The ceilings were high and there were no windows, allowing us to create a space that was intimate yet open. The environment we built up vividly conveyed the elements and the seasons. The space was inner, in both senses: indoors, and somehow within the realm of the imagination. And it was outer: seeming to be outdoors, and within the realm of physical reality. The ceremony took place on December 22, the day after the shortest day and longest night of the year. It was the day the light began its return. Inside the candlelit space, the rulers of day and night held equal sway in the canopy above. The time was both day and night. Although the wedding took place in the dead of winter, the floor was strewn with leaves, and the painted winter scene was in the warm colours of spring or autumn pinks. This space was paradoxical, a threshold where we would die to ourselves as a single man and woman and give birth to our marriage. We thought of our marriage as something living. It would require warmth, light, nourishment, work, rest and joyful celebration! We were bringing into the world something new, something invisible yet very real, which would be created out of all of our thoughts and deeds in years to come.

The space required great care and planning, and so did the clothing we would wear as bride and groom. Knitting was a great love of mine. At sixteen years old, I bought mohair yarn, a pair of knitting needles and an instruction pamphlet. While my parents were away, I played hooky for three days in order to finish my first sweater. At twenty-three I started a business called Odd Ball Knits. I purchased yarn for my sweaters at discount prices from clearance houses and ordered wholesale.

44

One day, a few months before meeting the man I was to marry, I spent ninety dollars on a rich indigo textured wool. It was not enough to make a whole sweater, maybe half. It was an extravagant purchase. I generally tried not to spend more than twenty-five dollars for a whole sweater, and I often managed fifteen dollars or less. I got home and wondered what sweater would ever merit such rich materials, and who would wear it. The wool demanded to be knitted in a textured cabled pattern, creating a kind of chest plate, front and back. A sweater fit for a prince. Well, the prince showed up and, having decided to get married, we took a road trip that was meant to deliver my intended to Vancouver in time for him to teach the fall semester.

Our direct route from Toronto to Vancouver soon took a detour via Colorado. We pitched a tent, surrounded by mountains, and the temperature dropped radically. I surprised him by coaxing a good blaze out of the dampness, and he enchanted me with a delicious lentil and potato stew made from scratch. The next day we looked at the map and made an intuitive choice together. Amnon suggested that we go one of two ways, and asked me which one felt right. We closed our eyes, and Taos, New Mexico, seemed to be calling us. I had no idea that it would extend our trip by many miles.

The no-longer-unknown prince was at the wheel as I began knitting the indigo yarn into a sweater. As we drove into New Mexico, we stumbled upon a wool festival near Taos. There I found a few skeins of beautiful handspun wool that complemented the indigo well. At some point it became clear that my prince would wear this sweater for the wedding itself.

Our first evening in New Mexico, we almost lost our tent at twilight to fierce winds. We gave up on finding shelter for the night and instead wandered into town. We were in a charming store when Amnon recognized people he knew from Vancouver.

We were told that tonight was a special celebration at the temple, and Ram Dass was going to be speaking. Ram Dass, formerly known as Richard Alpert, had lived through experiments with LSD at Harvard and subsequent years of study in India with his guru, Neem Karoli Baba, writing many books, beginning with *Be Here Now*. We stayed up that night listening to his memories of his beloved teacher and warming ourselves by a sacred fire. Children ran by us, knocking cups of hot chai all over the cloth bag that held my knitting. I wondered how soon children would come and turn our lives upside down. I thought this knitting bag might do very well for carrying diapers. Many different thoughts and feelings were knit, stitch by stitch, into that sweater.

We discovered the extraordinary synergy of our combined intuitive worlds, and also the tremendous clash of our emotional and social selves. I knitted in so much hope, warmth and trust.

We arrived in L.A., landing on the doorstep of Amnon's cousin, who had just given birth and moved in the last three weeks. To top it off, her in-laws had come to visit, planting themselves firmly in front of the TV. Amnon and I quietly unpacked boxes, held the baby, bought groceries and cooked food. The knitting was put on hold.

I solved many problems, making design decisions as I went along. Some quick turns in the road took the stitches right off the needles. Once, with the stitches hanging dangerously in mid-air, I realized that I could weave a contrasting wool in between the rows. I faced what seemed like disasters and turned them into triumphs.

When the sweater was finished, my beloved really did look like a prince in it. For his pants I took a length of handwoven cloth that I had made several years before. In fact, it was the only handwoven cloth I had ever made. So his pants were made of beginner's delight and his top of leaps of faith.

I turned my attention towards my wedding dress. With my own hands I had already made so much; now I felt ready to be made. Made into the woman who could walk across the threshold and begin the work of marriage in the world.

In developing my knitting business I had tried to take the step towards machine knitting. I purchased an old knitting machine but failed to ever understand how to make it work. For a brief time I was in a little knitting group, and one woman wanted to learn machine knitting. She was a much more refined, patient knitter than I. I asked her if she would knit the sweater I would wear for my wedding, and I offered her my knitting machine as a gift of gratitude. She enthusiastically agreed. We designed a top that was simple, elegant and used three strands at the same time: one of wool, one of linen and one of silk. Together they made a fabric that was warm, supple and invincible—to me, it expressed body, soul and spirit. The sleeves were three-quarter, the back dipped down further than the front, which rose up. The whole sweater was made of tiny cables so that it was rich like brocade.

And now I must bring my mother in, for all marriages lead into the future but sail out of past marriages. My mother, an artist (she painted the winter mural) and lover of beauty, had seen an exquisite antique bedspread years before and bought it. It had been made in the nineteenth century from handmade Spanish lace. In her mind, she saw it as a wedding dress and produced it when I told her I was going to get married. A gifted seamstress who worked as a costumer for the theatre world took up the task. She made a linen underskirt and pieced and stitched the lace into a skirt made of layers, which fell gently around me. My wedding dress, made out of the mystery of life, love and destiny.

On our tenth wedding anniversary, we had a recommitment ceremony, at which we repeated our vows to each other; this time, I spoke the vows he had written and spoken to me and he spoke those I had written and spoken to him. After ten years of marriage, we wanted to be able to understand each other and see one another and life through the eyes of the other. We wore our wedding clothes.

When my brother-in-law got married (on our fifteenth wedding anniversary), I wore the sweater and skirt together once more.

We recently celebrated our twentieth anniversary quietly in our kitchen, where we looked at photos from our years together. We realized that, over time, so many individuals and families had befriended and inspired us. We looked back and remembered each relationship as a strand, a thread that over the years we had knitted into a whole, the life of our marriage.

This anniversary, our wedding clothes were tucked away, and, wearing jeans, we made packages to send to each person or family, including photos and a bookmark that read on one side "20 years of climbing the mountain" and on the other "GRATITUDE."

ELYSE POMERANZ is grateful for the rich and varied experiences life has allowed her over the last forty-four years. The knitting gave rise to felting, rug hooking, beading and soft sculpture; the sacred fire led to many sweat lodges, talking circles and rites of passage and celebrations. The stained knitting bag inspired a handmade diaper bag, and two sons arrived (1987 and 1992) to use it and to spill juice and joy all over her life. She followed them to the Waldorf School, where she became a classroom teacher, telling stories, writing plays, painting, counting and reading with the children in her class as they grew year after year from young children to young teens. She is now finishing three years of schooling at Arscura: A School for Living Art and is weaving together art-making, group conversation and conflict transformation. Her most recent knitting project has been underway for ten years. Maybe this year it will be finished.

The Art Project

What I wanted was the most traditional wedding dress possible.
I wanted white satin, tulle and seed pearls, a high lace collar and
puffed sleeves, a row of tiny buttons down the back. I wanted
long skirts and layers of crinoline and maybe even a train.

Unfortunately, the only dress at the Salvation Army that even
remotely resembled this vision was a size 2 at best, the waist so
small I could have worn it as a garter. But it would have to do. It
just meant that we'd have to change the script a little.

It was my first year at art school. Our class had been assigned
a project on colour and symbolism and, tired of endless gouache
colour scales and charcoal drawings, my friend Jan and I had
decided to do something different. We were ready to take the
performance art plunge. The colours we'd chosen were red and
white. Red was passion, temptation and danger. And what better
symbol of white's purity and innocence than the wedding dress?

Our original plan was that Jan, in something tight and red, would read aloud some suitably inflammatory quotes on the topic of women's purity (or lack thereof), things like, "Woman is impure by her very birth, but attains a happy state by exercise of her one eternal duty, the service of her husband," or "Of the woman came the beginning of sin, and through her we all die." Meanwhile, I would put on a wedding dress and start hanging out red and white lingerie on a clothesline, while slides of naked women were projected onto the skirt of the dress. In the closet of the apartment I'd moved into, I'd found an old copy of *Playboy* that contained some pictures of women wearing white stockings and nothing else. We thought they'd be perfect.

I'm not sure that we were entirely clear on our concept to begin with, and the performance wasn't helped by the technical glitches. The wedding dress didn't fit either one of us, so it had to be hung on the clothesline, and we never did figure out a satisfactory alternative costume for me. The slides had so much white in them that they barely showed up against the white surface of the dress, and I managed to hang all the lingerie we'd bought before Jan was even halfway through the quotes. But our efforts were received kindly enough, and afterwards I took the dress home with me, reluctant to return it to exile at the Salvation Army.

"What on earth?" said my housemate when he got home that evening and found it hanging on one of the hooks in the hallway. "You're certainly planning ahead, aren't you?"

That first year at school was an eventful one for me. I developed a crush on someone in my class, a skinny boy with long hair and a funny, smart, attractive girlfriend. It was the kind of safe and unattainable crush I was used to, the kind I'd been relying on for some years now to persuade myself that I wanted what I was supposed to want.

This particular boy proved not to be quite so unattainable after all, even with girlfriend. In fact, the girlfriend came as part of the package. And while it all ended predictably badly, with tears on all sides and an embarrassing photo-documentary, it did make one thing clear. I could no longer keep telling myself that all those safe, sweet, unattainable boys were what I wanted. I had to admit that it was the smart and funny girls I should have been looking at all along.

At the end of that year my housemate and I were packing up the apartment when he came across the wedding dress again, hanging under the coats in the hallway. "Should I add this to the garbage heap?" he asked. It occurred to me, for the first time, that this used and slightly tatty wedding dress might well be the only wedding dress I would ever buy.

"No," I said. "I think I'll hang onto it."

I was surprised to find that I cared enough to keep it. The Big White Wedding had never played much of a role in my fantasy life. As a child, I had assumed that one day I'd get married, because that's what people did, but I had given little thought to the wedding itself. As a teenager, I considered my parents' city hall hippy wedding—to which my mother had worn a brown paisley minidress—to have just the right degree of nonchalant coolness. I sneered at the girls who dreamed of a white wedding. If those white dresses stood for purity, my own goal was quite the opposite—as an overweight frizzy-haired girl with braces, my secret fear was that I was doomed to die a virgin, and I planned to shed my innocence as soon as an opportunity presented itself.

But the myth of the white dress was stronger than I had given it credit for. In that moment, it seemed to me to be a symbol of a different kind of innocence. It seemed like a symbol of a life with no hard questions, where your path was laid out for you in a series of safe and predictable landmarks: school, then work, love, then marriage, and finally a family. It wasn't even the life I'd have said I wanted for myself, but being denied it by circumstances outside of my control felt very different from simply not choosing it.

I spent the summer mulling things over. When second year began, I returned to Halifax newly equipped with a buzz cut and a pair of purple Doc Martens and posted a notice at the school looking for gay-friendly housemates. That was how I met Chris and Jenny, who needed a third housemate for the drafty old three-bedroom house Chris had found in the South End. They were both amused by the wedding dress, and we installed it in a place of honour, on the wall in the large kitchen that served as our common room. We were all taking at least one textiles course that term, and we joked about how much time the three of us—modern young feminists more likely to start a band than a women's collective—spent in that kitchen, sewing, drinking tea and exchanging gossip while the dress looked on. "Next thing you know we'll be talking about childbirth!" joked Chris.

Soon enough we were. A friend of mine from the city's gay and lesbian student group came over one evening and told us that she had just discovered she was pregnant. The father was the boyfriend she had left when she and her long-time best friend realized that they were in love.

"What are you going to do?" we asked her as we all sat around the kitchen table. She smiled. "Clara and I are going to keep it. My ex wants nothing to do with it, but we're going to move in with my brother, who has a house, and we're all going to help raise it."

They were planning a party to celebrate, a kind of combination baby shower/housewarming/engagement party, and under the eye of the wedding dress I stitched them a hanging for the wall of their new place. I cut a piece from one of the lacy underskirts of the dress to incorporate into it—I didn't think the dress would mind.

Bits of the dress started to appear in Chris's and Jenny's work, as well. Chris took some of the tiny satin buttons from the cuffs to use in one of her textiles pieces, a series of silkscreen prints based on photos of her mother and grandmothers that she was adorning with beads and buttons and small plastic baby dolls. She was starting to think about motherhood herself. She hadn't had a serious girlfriend in a while, but she'd always wanted children, and, as she put it, the sperm thing would have required some creative problem-solving in any case. She couldn't see any reason not to raise a baby on her own, eventually.

Jenny was a little older and had left a successful graphic design career to come back to school. She was taking a photo class, and started using the dress as a prop in a project she was doing on family photos. As her work progressed, she started to share with us some details of her own family, in which a picture-perfect surface hid tragic secret cruelty and neglect. Chris and I sat up late with her and listened, plying her with tea and red wine. As the year went on, it was a special pleasure to see her find a love she had never expected, with a sweet and satisfyingly attentive younger man.

And as for me . . . despite my new haircut and the LGB student group, I was still single, and just beginning to realize how many unquestioned assumptions I'd had about love. I'd thought I knew what it would look like—all airbrushed perfection and the kind of burning, love-at-first-sight glances that made awkward discussions and negotiations unnecessary. I'd thought I knew what it would feel like—a blinding passion that would cause me to effortlessly transcend my own limitations and self-doubts. And I'd thought I knew why love was important—that once I found that one perfect person, I'd have all I ever needed.

Now I was beginning to get an inkling of just how subtle and complex love could really be. Grudgingly, I was coming to accept that being forced to ask myself hard questions might have been a good thing after all.

At the end of that year, Chris graduated and Jenny moved in with her younger man. I moved into the bay-windowed house that was to be my home for the rest of my time in Halifax. Money was tight that year and, unable to afford a van rental, I moved what I could of my belongings in a shopping cart, leaving behind most of the things too big to fit in it. The wedding dress came with me, draped over the top of the final load of stuff.

The room that was mine the first semester in that house was so small it was essentially a nest, and so cold that anything I could hang on the walls, I did, less as decoration than as insulation. There the wedding dress watched over me as the hard questions and sometimes harder answers kept coming.

It saw the failure of the complicated dating protocol I attempted to negotiate with the only lesbian in Halifax who had more intimacy issues than I did. What, I was forced to ask myself then, could you expect from someone else if you weren't willing to risk anything yourself?

It witnessed the misery of the hopeless passion I developed for one of my straight housemates, when the universe answered me definitively that, no, wanting something that badly was still not enough to guarantee that you'd get it.

It looked on the night that one of my gay male friends from the student group turned up on our doorstep, in tears over the spectacular meltdown of his first relationship, and spent the night chastely cuddled into my bed with me for comfort. Which was when I asked myself whether one kind of love really was enough.

The dress didn't just stay in my bedroom, though. One of my housemates was a committed polyamorist who managed, through sheer force of personality, to juggle three simultaneous relationships. She wore it to a couple of the fetish balls that were the art-school trend of choice that year. Another day we squeezed a male friend into it and sent him to answer the door when the Jehovah's Witnesses knocked. If we had hoped that the sight of a goateed young man in a wedding dress would drive them away, we were wrong, but it had a different kind of effect on one of our housemates. She whisked him away to her bedroom, and they barely emerged for the next three months.

The wedding dress was looking distinctly the worse for wear by now, pieces of the skirt and most of the buttons missing, a seam in the bodice burst down one side and its whiteness yellowed and begrimed. "Perfect!" exclaimed the exchange student who lived with us for a term. "That's just what I need!" She used it in a video piece on how her mother's marriage to her father, a man outside her family's narrow fundamentalist faith, had inspired her grandmother to leave her abusive marriage and live proudly on her own for the first time in her life.

The wedding dress made its last appearance as my housemate's graduation gown. The full tulle and lace overskirts had been cut off completely by this point, leaving only the narrow-skirted satiny lining, and the burst seam in the bodice was mended with safety pins. Wearing her army boots, she proudly stomped up on stage and accepted her degree.

I stayed in Halifax for a few months following graduation. During that time, one of my best friends announced that she and her long-time boyfriend were going to get married. She was the first of my friends to officially tie the knot.

"If you'd done this last year," I joked, "you could have borrowed the wedding dress!"

"Thanks, but no thanks!" she laughed. "But would you be willing to act as my dyke of honour?"

I helped her write her vows, and a Universalist Unitarian clergywoman conducted the ceremony in the middle of a field in the country. My friend wore a dress embroidered with leaves and flowers. I wore a red zigzag-patterned sundress that showed off my cleavage and my tattoos. All of us, gay and straight, friends and family, wept buckets and got ferociously drunk. It was the best wedding I've ever been to.

Soon after that I moved back to Toronto. Today I'm single and co-own a house I've shared with two close friends for more than seven years. I didn't find true love at art school, and I certainly didn't advance my marriage prospects. But my travels with that white dress, and the various women and men I met along the way, taught me a different way to think about that white surface and what it promised. It taught me that the accepted forms and meanings are not the only possibilities open to us, and that we can inscribe that blank surface with our own definitions of love, of friendship and of family.

JESSICA RUTH HARRIS lives in Toronto. She is thirty-five, single, and owns no cats.

PART TWO

Something New

ANNE LAUREL CARTER

Sunday Dinner and Wedding Dresses

In a break with family tradition, my mother didn't involve herself with either of my wedding dresses. My first dress would have required tolerance to premarital sex and a mixed marriage, neither of which my mother was ready for. In the mid-seventies I made a bold step just by inviting her to the wedding. As for the dress I wore a decade later, unless death had ended my first marriage, second chances ("whatever you do, don't wear white!") were best kept private. No celebration required.

My mother struggled to keep and pass on meaningful traditions in a perplexing, changing world. The tradition she excelled at all her life was Sunday dinner. Her version was a formal family meal that followed church. My sister and I set the good china and silver for the six of us around the dining-room table. My mother's skills shone as she prepared a perfect roast and surrounded it with colourful vegetables. In August, the carrots, green beans and tomatoes would be fresh from her garden. The sweetness I'm sure she longed to create for us was served in desserts mixed from scratch, chosen from her box of favourite recipes.

When I was a child, there were things I couldn't possibly understand about her: certainly not the demon I diagnose from my armchair now. Like my three siblings and father, I tiptoed around her for decades, trying to keep her happy.

The summer I was seventeen I stuffed a few belongings into a backpack and left, seeking adventure in Scotland, France and Israel. Reluctantly, I returned home to complete two years of pre-med courses at the University of Toronto. Calculus, physics, chemistry . . . formerly a high school scholar, suddenly I was close to failing.

I lightened my backpack and left again. It would take me eight years to finish my undergraduate degree. During this restless period, I went to live in California with Ray, a young man I'd met on a kibbutz in Israel. My mother totally disapproved.

Ray finished his master's degree while I worked illegally in stores and restaurants. He had an uneasy relationship with his own mother. With the best of intentions, we decided to marry and move to Canada.

Twenty-two years old, without resources or sewing savvy, I stitched together our wedding clothes. I said "I do" to Ray, unaware I was really saying "You win" to my mother.

For the past year, Sunday dinner has begun when I pick up my parents, around 4:45. They live in a seniors residence a block from my house, in the west end of Toronto. If I arrive too late, they forget the invitation, or what day it is, and start to eat in the dining room. I moved them from their home in the east end, where they'd lived (and wanted to stay) for half a century. They needed care, and to stop driving illegally, and I needed them closer. When I moved them, my mother accused me of many unpleasant things—all of which she's forgotten. Memory loss has certain advantages.

My relationship with my mother has always been complex. She has a loving disposition, yet she spent most afternoons retreating from the world, asleep. The child of a misogynist world, she felt somewhat powerless to change her life and to become involved. She played a lot of solitaire at the kitchen table. Entertaining any-one outside her family was an ordeal best avoided.

Sadly, her love had conditions. As an adult I observed how these didn't apply just to me; disapproval kept others away too. Her life shrank to the size of a deck of cards on her kitchen table. Or the six of us around her dining room.

Her only sister wronged her once, and my mother never for-gave her, never phoned or willingly saw her for the next forty years. When my aunt died, my mother didn't attend the funeral with me.

Her memory is bad now. She forgets where she lives, who's alive and who did what to whom. Not a mere advantage—a blessing.

As we drive away from the seniors residence, she asks me for the third time, "Did I bring my purse?"

"You don't need it, Mom. There's no charge for Sunday dinner."

"Is it Sunday?" my dad asks.

"No. It can't be Sunday," my mother says. "We didn't go to church this morning."

"Yes, you did," I assure her. "I drove you. Guess what else?" I give her hand a gentle squeeze. "Craig put four beers in the fridge to get cold."

Inside my house, coats away—"Did I bring a purse?"—we pour drinks.

Clink. "Here's to growing old with the one you love!"

We are all cheerful. Craig finds the cards and we play a few hands of bridge. My dad's diagnosis is Alzheimer's. So is my mother's. They are happier now than they ever were. My mother's critical edge is mostly worn away. A smart woman, she was a frustrated housewife. My dad was the outgoing, successful executive. In the last decade of their lives, they've become equals.

There's a lot of table talk as we play the hands. Table talk is against the rules in bridge. My parents, once rule-ridden, now take turns asking, "What suit are we in? Are there any trump left?"

My husband teases them. In his view, family is much like a hand you've been dealt. Play it for all it's worth. He doesn't tiptoe around family foibles.

"Percy, your memory's awful," he says. "And don't laugh, Kathleen. Yours isn't any better."

I learned to play bridge before I reached puberty.

My parents had an unwritten list of taboo subjects. While we enjoyed a family game of cards, we didn't talk about problems or things that mattered. Sex was at the top of the list. I grew up never seeing my parents kiss or hug (they do so all the time now). When I turned twelve, my mother gave me a little book with diagrams showing the location of ovaries and womb. That was as close as we ever came to a conversation about sex. I shoved it in a drawer. Mor-ti-fied. She could have given me a Canadian Tire manual on engine parts, it was *that* weird.

Bridge was easy to talk about.

"Open one in your best suit. If you have thirteen points, then you have to say something. You can't keep quiet. Say 'one heart' if you have four or five hearts and a good top card like an ace or king."

"What if I have six hearts and they're all little ones?"

63

We could talk about bridge, although the rules got more complicated as we got older. Bids. Coded messages. That's what we were good at.

In the fall of 1974, I turned twenty-one and went to my parents' house for Sunday dinner. I'd been in primal therapy for a month. I could cry in a quiet room with my therapist. But I couldn't talk about my feelings in that Scarborough kitchen.

"I'm leaving next week," I said abruptly, between roast chicken and rhubarb crisp.

What I'd gone there to say, what I couldn't say was, *I'm quitting university again. I'm quitting piano. I don't know what else to do. The sky's grey and heavy and it's gotten inside me. I ride the subways and don't know where to get off.*

It sounded too stupid to say. So instead I gave information. I gave flight departure times and a destination. "I'm going to live with Ray in Los Angeles."

My mother left the table and threw her dishes in the sink. "Then you can call yourself a whore. Don't call yourself my daughter. If you go, I don't want to hear from you again."

She marched upstairs. The slam of her door was as loud as any shotgun.

They didn't mention any of this in the little book with diagrams.

In March 1976, twenty-two and disowned, I married Ray. We'd met in Israel after the Yom Kippur War. I'd completed a six-month study program of Hebrew and moved to the small kibbutz that allowed me, the blonde shikse from Toronto, to milk cows in the refet. Ray, the American Jew with a degree in psychology (what else do you study in California?), worked as an apprentice electrician. We were happy and in love. We explored a more elemental life, intense politics and communal living. He had a head of soft, black curls, loved John

Cheever stories and talked about feelings and ideas the way my dad and brothers talked about NHL scores and golf games. He was unlike any male I'd grown up with in Scarborough.

He cooked. He ironed his own shirts. He read poetry.

Oh. My. God.

We were married in his parents' backyard in the San Fernando Valley. Orange trees were heavy with fruit. We found a reform rabbi to marry us under a *chuppah*—the symbol of making a home together. In nomadic times, the bride was taken into the groom's tent and the marriage was consummated right then and there.

Before the wedding, my parents sent no money and no advice.

I remembered my mother's wedding dress. My grandmother had taken my mother shopping at an exclusive salon, where she could choose any dress she loved. Expense was not an issue. White, closed at the back by fifty tiny buttons, my mother's dress flowed around her as she proceeded down the aisle. She looked absolutely beautiful.

In Los Angeles, I had no money and no doting mother, and I wasn't inclined to fuss. But I believed in the transformational power of a dress. Cinderella's gown got her to the ball. I needed my wedding dress to take me home.

I hadn't discovered thrift shops, but I remembered some basic sewing. In Scarborough, home economics had been compulsory for girls in grade seven. I'd made an A-line skirt with a sloping hem that would have been in style today. I got a D.

No one was marking the wedding dress, right?

I bought a Simplicity pattern. Wedding dress for bride. Matching shirt for groom. I didn't know fabrics, but satin sounded like the right material for a wedding dress . . . or was it fancy bedsheets? White cotton sounded right for a man's dress shirt. Oh no. Maybe *that* was the fancy bedsheets.

A-line. Open neck. A few pleats down the front. I bought red tracing paper to guide me. How hard could this be?

My friends said it was lovely, but it *felt* like another grade seven project. I said my vows in a satin sack with puffed sleeves, fearful that the odd red line was showing faintly through the seams. I left it behind me in California. Bedsheets would have been more practical.

Nevertheless, my dress performed the much-needed magic. Saying my vows, I smiled—glowed—at the people who'd flown in for the event. My sister and brothers. My dad. Most important of all, my mom.

Ray and I moved to Toronto. I went back to university and finished my degree. I got straight A's. I loved language and teaching. I failed at marriage. We stayed together less than three years before I wanted out.

For the next five years I worked and wandered, mostly in northern Quebec, not understanding that I was looking for a way to feel good. There was always a heavy greyness, like a fog threatening to roll in, that I fought against. Music could lift it. A new man. A new job. A new world.

Ray and I had never been ready for children. The only complication in our straightforward divorce was finding me. I was learning French in Chicoutimi when a clerk from a law firm approached me to serve papers. He kept glancing at something in his hand to identify me: my wedding photo.

All this time I had a good friend, Craig, back in Toronto. I'd met him through university friends when I was twenty. We talked about everything. He knew my affairs; I knew his. We had fun together, and he laughed at the taboos in our families. His parents had divorced when he was learning to walk and talk. He was raised by a doting, bitter single mother.

Craig was like my dad: successful and comfortable in the business world of Toronto. He talked NHL and golf. But he also talked
ideas and feelings. He loved plays. Even more than Ibsen and
Shakespeare, he loved baseball.

In the spring of 1984, I received a fancy invitation to his
wedding and reception in August. I'd been teaching up north and
had just returned to Toronto to complete a master's degree. He'd
been living with a woman for five years. They were both over
thirty, and she wanted to get married.

Agreeing to marriage was a psychological hurdle for Craig. His
divorced parents had battled each other for years. Once Craig
jumped the bar, he realized he could risk the impossible.

Late in July he phoned me. He sounded terrible.

"I have to tell you something, Anne. I'm ready for marriage,
but I'm marrying the wrong woman. I think . . . I'm in love . . .
with you."

He went on to describe our friendship for the last ten years.
We knew everything about each other. We laughed and had
fun. He'd always been attracted to me. We'd never gone out.
We didn't know what we were like together. We should give it
a chance.

The phone was starting to steam a little. Hot little puffs
through the holes in the mouthpiece.

"What we're like together? Are you crazy? You mean in bed?"

"Yes," he laughed. "I guess so. Not right away. But yes, that's
where it might lead."

"You can't be serious," I said. "You're still nervous about the
commitment thing. We shouldn't be having this conversation."

"We should have had it a long time ago."

"We were always dating other people. We never would have
lasted."

"We might last now."

"You're getting married in three weeks! I am not going to date you now. No way. Don't call me again. Forget my number. Forget you ever knew me."

Four days before the wedding I got another phone call.

"Okay, the wedding's off."

On our first date we went out for wings and beer and jazz. We waited a week after the cancelled wedding. Part of me felt guilty. *We should wait longer.* What was right in this situation? Shouldn't there be a grieving period? Two weeks? A month? I knew the other woman. Somewhere in Toronto, a beautiful four-thousand-dollar wedding dress was being returned to a salon.

But Craig had opened a door between us that had been closed before. I *was* interested in him. Why hadn't I noticed? All that therapy and I was still blind to what I really felt.

Still, I couldn't imagine him touching me. I never had. I didn't think I'd respond to him that way. He was one of my best friends, and a confidant. I didn't want to lose that.

We walked back to the little house he rented off Mount Pleasant Avenue. In front of it, he told me to sit down on the curb. In the yards and gardens around us, the crickets were singing in the dark the way crickets do, rubbing their legs. They were speaking their own language, sending their coded messages, but I understood them perfectly. They said, "Breathe him in like summer."

There was a physical barrier between us. Craig sat beside me. I looked at him, feeling too wary to be hopeful. His fingers touched mine, and his eyes said, *Don't look away.*

"I've been thinking about kissing you for ten years," he said.

He leaned closer.

"You mean that time you came over to my parents' house in Scarborough . . ."

Craig's lips were incredible. The minute I kissed him I knew

I was home. I'd never kissed a man and felt this way. The searching was over.

When he pulled away, I said, "Don't stop."

He slapped his shoulder. "Mosquitoes are biting. Let's go inside."

I'd signed a contract to teach in Peterborough, a small city an hour and a half away from Toronto. We spent every weekend together. The following year I got a job near Toronto. Craig wanted us to buy a house. I resisted. I was afraid of my life becoming suburbia. My mother had never been happy. I was so sure that if I resisted my mother's fate, I wouldn't have her problems. Owning a house together . . . walls, closed doors, a kitchen . . . never!

Defiant, confused, resisting, I cashed in my RHSP savings—ten thousand dollars—and bought my dream: a beautiful piano.

His response? "I love hearing you play."

We rented an apartment in Brampton, and he commuted to his job downtown. Housing prices doubled in Toronto. Craig was a smart real estate lawyer, and he never said one critical word. We were happy.

His mother told him I was "used goods."

Craig told her she was entitled to her opinion, but not in our home.

We were in total control of our lives until late January, when life threw us a little curve ball. We'd been using a diaphragm and sperm-killers for birth control. Craig's sperm sent in a strong new rookie, who hit a home run.

I was thirty-two years old, unmarried and pregnant.

"Marry me," Craig said. "Let's have a family. Let's buy a house. Let's go for it."

"A shotgun wedding? My first one felt like that. I don't want to be judged or forced into this. I don't want it to be an opportunity for our mothers to criticize us."

"No one's forcing us. Our mothers will criticize us whatever we do. Forget them. This is between you and me. You know I want to marry you. We've talked about it."

He got out a calendar. "It's perfect timing. I can marry you on Valentine's Day."

Craig laid his hands on my flat belly. "We're going to have a baby," he said, awed. "We're going to be a family. Please, marry me?"

This man I loved had ways of surprising me. I'd underestimated his strong traditional streak.

I decided to risk embracing *some* of my traditional values. I agreed to a wedding. I agreed to buy a house. I had only two conditions. We would never live in Scarborough. And if anyone ever referred to me as a "housewife," Craig could shoot me. Or them.

The Anglican church my parents attended was available on the Saturday closest to Valentine's Day, February 16. So was the minister. We had three weeks. We phoned family and closest friends. My father offered to take care of a lovely reception dinner.

I wanted a real wedding dress when I stood beside Craig. Once again, my mother had no advice and did not involve herself in any way. Lunches, girl talk, planning a social event—these were not part of my mother's world.

I decided to peek into a bridal shop. I went alone. I was in a foreign country where I didn't speak the language.

"Do you have an appointment?" the saleslady said.

An appointment? I'd never heard of shopping by appointment. I shook my head.

She surveyed me critically. "What's your price range?"

I thought about what I had left in my savings account. "One hundred and seventy dollars."

She frowned.

"That's including the tax," I whispered.

She didn't say anything. She pointed to the back, where I found a very small, nearly hidden rack marked SALE. There were several I liked and tried on in the small dressing room. I was too embarrassed to ask for a turn in front of the big three-sided mirror where another woman was being fitted.

I think that's when the mother I needed spoke up inside me, as I looked in the mirror. We both recognized *the dress* immediately. It was white, mid-calf with a scalloped hem (something I could never have sewn), a zipper down the back and a narrow waist. Not fussy. The sleeves and upper bodice were sheer and weighed next to nothing on my skin.

I looked at my reflection and said, "Absolutely beautiful."

On my wedding day I said "I do" to Craig. I couldn't stop smiling. I felt a lightness of being.

Then I had four children and a miscarriage in less than five years. Three wild little boys exhausted me. It was hard to find anyone to babysit at our house. Craig and I were using the diaphragm, sperm-killers *and* a condom when the fourth was conceived. She turned out to be the miracle daughter. I quit teaching. Raising our hellions was up to me.

I was up all night with them. They had colic, ear infections, hip dysplasia and defiant natures. Two would be diagnosed with ADD. I started needing naps.

With almost every period I'd get a migraine. Those were the worst days. A migraine isn't a normal headache. Mine were thankfully short, lasting about eight hours. I'd lie on the sofa, wanting to die. I'd hear the boys fighting in the basement, my daughter crying, knowing I should move. We needed a moving, talking adult in the house, one who didn't want to die. I had to call someone for help—but who?

I thought of Craig and the stress he had at work. I thought of my mother and her closed bedroom door. I thought of Craig's mother and the critical things she said about me. I thought of my dad. He'd never played with us when we were kids. He didn't know how to turn on a stove. He'd always been at work, at Rotary, at the club, at church.

I'd throw up and dial the number I knew best.

"Dad, I'm sick. Can you come?"

He always came. He dropped everything and came immediately. It was a half-hour drive across the 401. He came alone and had no conditions.

Every night I read piles of books to my children. I fell in love with picture books. Forty years old, I began to write stories from an imagination I didn't know I had.

For a long time, writing saved my spirit. Every time I got restless, I could write a new story. I threw myself into it, keeping myself challenged. I didn't know I was also keeping the greyness at bay. Success gave me a temporary high.

My eldest son had problems socializing. He was ostracized at school and in our neighbourhood. I took it hard and found it more and more difficult to connect with other mothers. How could they be so mean? Without seeing what I was doing, I judged others, and myself, and began to withdraw. I quit my book club. I quit committees. I quit teaching night school. I quit teaching fitness. One by one, I closed the doors, shrinking.

I couldn't write. I'd sit at the computer all morning, eking out a sentence or two, then delete it and curl up on the sofa. There were piles of laundry everywhere. Messy rooms. No Sunday dinner.

If I went out, I'd come home and sit in the driveway for a long time, unable to get out of the car, dreading coming inside. I didn't feel close to Craig or my children. I thought the solution to my problem would be to rent, close by, a "room of one's own."

Craig wouldn't let me. "No leaving. I want you to stay."

I kept my distance, angry. It was his fault I was becoming just like my mother. "I'll stay if you sleep on the sofa," I said. "I can't sleep with you. I want some time alone."

"Okay. I'll sleep on the sofa. But as long as you know one thing: I like my marriage bed, and I like you in it."

For years I'd mentioned "fatigue" to my doctor. She'd tell me to get more help with the housework and kids. Then I switched doctors. The new doctor called it depression.

I said, "No way. It's my marriage. I've become a housewife. You'd be depressed too if you lived at my house."

"I want you to try some medication. I see a lot of depression, and I'm sure the right medication will help you. I'll also get you on a waiting list for counselling."

What did she know about it? I resisted. I tried prayer. I tried exercise. I tried chocolate, lots of chocolate, alcohol, meditation, vitamins and a naturopath.

Greyness. It was my word for it, a word I'd known since I was a teenager. It wouldn't lift. I relented and tried the drugs. A new one every four or six weeks. It took almost a year to find one that made the interior skies lighten.

I got *really* lucky when a spot opened up with a psychiatrist at St. Michael's Hospital. For a year, once a week, I visited her. I had to stay on the antidepressant. She challenged my assumptions and behaviours, giving me assignments from a book called *Mind Over Mood.* I'd describe my life and she'd challenge a behaviour. I'd always been so observant of others, but strangely my own depressed behaviours I hadn't noticed.

We started with the way I walked my daughter to school. I wouldn't enter the playground, where the other moms chatted in groups. Ever since high school I'd found groups intimidating. I hadn't noticed when all those mothers' backs became a wall that made my stomach knot. My first assignment was to cross the road and stand in the playground as if I belonged.

Sometimes it took weeks to complete these assignments. They were always self-rewarding. A breakthrough assignment was to smile at people. I wasn't to expect a smile back. I was just supposed to smile.

Progress was slow and steady. I started to write again. I felt connected to my family. The medication helped me sleep and the marriage bed became our intimate, shared space again.

Around the same time, one of my brothers called me. "I'm just calling to tell you I've been diagnosed with depression . . ."

We had a long talk. Not once did we mention the NHL or golf scores.

I saw my mother and her difficulties in a new light. All the help I had received in order to connect to myself, my loved ones and my work—none of it had been available to her. Maybe she didn't seek it out or know how to talk about it. I don't know. She managed with closed doors and as if her life were insignificant.

I wanted all my doors open. Every day mattered.

Sunday dinner remains a family tradition. We sit at the table and share a meal together. Friends, the stranger at the door, even our demons, are welcome. I often make my father's favourite: lemon pudding. If it's summer and my sister visits from Ottawa, she brings rhubarb or raspberries from her garden, and we might make a crisp or a pie.

My mother is delighted and surprised by everything. "Where did you learn to cook like that? Can I have the recipe?"

I put my arm around her. Every year she seems smaller, her smile sweeter. "I learned it from you, Mom. It's from your box of old favourites. You may have forgotten, but you were a fabulous cook."

When I take my parents back to the residence, I kiss them both. I make a point of saying "I love you." It's one of those things you just can't hear or say enough. Conditions only weigh you down. For a few seconds I feel the lightness of being I experienced wearing my wedding dress. Then I drive home.

Ray remarried soon after the divorce. They lived within a few kilometres of each other in Toronto but never saw or spoke to each other for twenty-five years until they reconnected with this memoir.

While writing the first draft, ANNE LAUREL CARTER impulsively decided to feng-shui the closet where her wedding dress hung squished at the back. Storing ill-fitting clothes and unused objects from the past (so the book advised) was sapping her energy. Did she want to live every moment in the present? YES. PLEASE. YES.

Eager, hopeful, she took half her belongings to Goodwill.

Sentimental, romantic, her husband stared in horror at her tidy, spacious closet and noticed one thing.

"Where's your wedding dress?"

If anyone locates the beautiful dress in the photo, please contact Craig Carter.

ILANA STANGER-ROSS

My Mother, My Wedding Dress

My partner, Jordan, and I had been together five years by the time I proposed in our neighbourhood park on a sunny autumn day, surprising him if not with the proposal then at least with the fancy watch I'd procured for the event.

Proposing hadn't been a simple decision for me. I had many reservations about marriage, and about what one contemporary journalist dubbed the Great White Wedding in particular. My argument against weddings went something like this: they were an expensive, discriminatory and dated artifice. My argument for marriage was harder to summarize but stemmed from the joy I felt while dancing at other people's weddings, coupled with the sense that, for someone rather young, I'd been to too many funerals.

As long as we live and love, I began to realize, we will lose people we care about. We will visit friends in hospitals; we will walk behind caskets at cemeteries. These events are inevitable.

But weddings, births, birthday blowouts—these things are not inevitable. We have to make the choice to celebrate and be cele- brated. Maybe, I came to feel, it's even incumbent upon us to do so. As a Jew, I knew that a wedding was considered not just a major simcha, celebration, but also an important mitzvah, commandment. Not everyone can make the choice to celebrate their relationship—families, money, and the government can all interfere. But I knew we could, and felt we should.

And so I proposed to Jordan. We'd talked it over so thoroughly that there wasn't really a need, but being a writer, I wanted a scene: one specific moment I could prepare for, and then reflect on, in the larger narrative of our relationship. I plotted and planned, strengthening my resolve as I paced the streets of Philadelphia's diamond district in search of the perfect watch. It involved some compromise. "The watch you're looking for does not exist," a kind jeweller told me when I said I wanted something similar to the Cartier 21, but for about two hundred dollars—we were both graduate students, after all (I earned a master's in creative writing, Jordan a doctorate in history). But I found what I sought, more or less, in a wonderfully cluttered shop that clearly didn't do much engagement business. In the end, I'd prepared everything but the asking, finally stammering out a long and muddled speech about love and commitment while Amish women hawked shoofly pie from a nearby farm stand. Although the question itself was lost in a sea of confused syntax, Jordan nevertheless said yes.

We rushed home to tell our cats, and then called our parents: his in Waterloo and mine in Brooklyn. "Yes!" my father cheered. "Oh my god, I don't believe it!" my mother cried, as if she hadn't been hounding us for years.

Pause. Two beats.

"Now," she asked, already getting down to business, "what about the dress?"

I knew that the dress would be an issue. Although I'd gotten my mind around marriage, I still wasn't comfortable with the bride-as-showcase aspect of a wedding that the dress epitomized. The white dress is a costume, one of the few left in modern Western culture that isn't linked to an occupation. Or maybe it is: the bride becomes a wife becomes a mother becomes a homemaker, so the old story goes. I worried that the dress was reactionary, and also that I would balk beneath all that attention. And then there was the cost—wasn't there something indecent about paying so much for something you'd wear for one day?

"You're thinking about this way too much," my mother told me. We were out for dinner, celebrating the big announcement. Though we were planning a wedding for the following summer—nine months away—she was already impatient with my ruminations. The way she figured it, I had less than six weeks to buy a dress.

"The alterations . . ." my mother explained, waving vaguely.

"The alterations take nine months?"

My mother shrugged. "Well, you're short."

It wasn't exactly the enthusiasm I'd expected. But my mother was right: there were things to be done. While swearing I wouldn't turn into either Bridezilla or the baby's breath bride—one viewing a wedding as a personal showcase, the other actually buying all that "holy matrimony" stuff—I set about making lists.

Weeks passed, then months. We made calls, listened to music samples, tasted hors d'oeuvres. But despite a few guilty peeks at *Martha Stewart Weddings* on trips to the supermarket, I still hadn't figured out the dress.

The summer before, I'd attended the wedding of a close friend, who wore her grandmother's dress down the aisle. It was a lovely dress that made for a touching tradition, though she later admitted to me that she committed to wearing it only after taking it for a test drive on her fiancé's lap. ("It got the right reaction," she explained.)

When I told my mother about the heirloom dress—leaving out the lap dance, of course—we both laughed about it. Only certain kinds of families, we felt, had ancestral wedding dresses in stock. "Our wedding dresses were burned during the pogroms," my mother said, a statement that was almost definitely technically untrue, but which nonetheless conjured some kind of truthfulness. My grandparents had emigrated from Poland and Russia in the decades before the Second World War. They never returned; they had nothing to return for. My mother remembers how her father would literally spit on the ground whenever mentioning the old country; my father recalls his mother's desperate, failed attempts to contact her parents and brothers after Hitler's invasion of Poland. As a child, I felt as though we'd been severed from our past—the very languages our grandparents spoke as irretrievable as the homes they had been born in.

Grandmothers' wedding dresses were up there with quilts and candlesticks and all the little luxuries of life that demanded not just a home but a mantel, a cedar chest, a mahogany breakfront where cherished objects rested through the decades, safe. Whether or not my grandmother's wedding dress was maliciously destroyed during a pogrom was not the point. The point was chaos, fear, poverty. The point was a boat on the water, a family leaving home, everything packed into a few trunks and no turning back.

My father, the youngest of three brothers, came from a family that always seemed to me to embody the American dream: raised in a Lower East Side tenement, he became a doctor; one older brother became a lawyer, the other a judge. My mother represented the other side of that dream. Both her parents worked in factories: her mother stitched artificial flowers; her father pasted together ladies' hats. But unlike my father, she was expected to achieve success not through her career but through her marriage.

My mother's older sister, Bernice, married when she was nineteen; my mother might have done the same had Bernice not given her that classic piece of older-sister advice: don't do what I have done. Instead, my mother was twenty-two when she walked down the aisle, an old maid for her time and place.

My mother's wedding dress was borrowed and ill-fitting and, worst of all, stained. This last point was repeated enough that, even as a child, I understood that it was a symbol for all that had disappointed her: her father distant, her mother depressed, her own marriage not the rescue of which she'd once dreamed. And so, for my wedding dress, my mother wanted white, she wanted designer, she wanted a woman to kneel down on plush carpet and place pins through silk fabric while I preened before the mirror, a few thousand dollars draped around my body.

My wedding was my mother's chance to give me what she hadn't had, what her mother hadn't even known to dream of. I was slowly becoming comfortable with this. Jordan and I both wanted our wedding to be an event that welcomed our friends and family into our relationship, allowing them to celebrate what they had supported and enriched for years. After attending the wedding of a relative whose look of detached irony—and refusal to get down on the dance floor—discouraged any festivity, I'd embraced a "give the people what they want" attitude. I'd pose for the family formals, slice a petal-splashed cake and slow dance to "our" song.

But the white wedding dress, and all it so obviously symbolized, still appalled me.

"When are we going dress shopping?" my mother would ask.

I stalled.

82

And then I got lucky.

"I found it!" my mother said, calling one winter afternoon. She'd read an article about the Bridal Garden, a store in midtown Manhattan that sold once-worn and designer-donated wedding dresses. Not only were they sold at a significant discount, but all the proceeds went to a children's charity. I felt my objections dwindling. The outrageous expense would go to a good cause, and I'd begun to realize I could handle the attention. As for the costume aspect, knowing that Jordan was the one who literally wore the apron in our home, made the gown seem more like dress-up than social commentary.

So, we were off.

I arrived with an entourage, like a good bride: my mother, my oldest friend and my father, dragged along to provide a dose of welcome realism. The one cramped room was ringed with dresses of every shape and size, model and make. It was terrific fun for the first two dresses, and then it wasn't: "You're lost in that"; "It makes you look like Cruella DeVille"; "No, no. Absolutely no."

But then there was a dress that, if it didn't make me weep and say things like, "This is the one!" was just about right for someone who cringed at the thought of such an exclamation. A simple silk A-line with just a hint of embroidery and crystal splashed across the bodice, it was the only dress to which my father gave a firm nod of approval.

My ego somewhat mended, we went to lunch. We would both get what we wished for: my mother would get to kvell as I walked down the aisle in what was originally a four-thousand-dollar Ulla-Maija cream concoction, and I could rest easy, knowing that, if my wedding wasn't actually making the world a better place, well, at least I was giving something back.

But then came the trials of a non-profit dress shop.

The dress was too big: my mom was right about that. We'd need three fittings, we were told; three turned into five. I made several appointments that were cancelled by the shop at the last minute; when I tried it on, the dress sometimes seemed to have been more undone than done since the last time I'd been there. Once, another bride-to-be showed up in the middle of a fitting. "Oh," the seamstress said, not trying to hide her confusion, "I didn't have you down for today. But whatever, it's no big deal, you might as well come in if you're here . . ."

The woman bit her lower lip. "I flew in from California for this fitting," she hissed.

I hustled out as fast as I could.

I had hoped that buying the dress would bring an end to my mother's wedding anxiety. Since announcing our engagement— an event I knew she was thrilled about—she'd reduced much of the joy of a wedding to a litany of worries: the weather, the food, the music. Instead of anticipating "the big day" with increasing excitement, she sighed over my to-do lists. Anything I could compromise on I did, yet she still replied to questions about the wedding with an exhausted, under-seige attitude more befitting a student approaching finals than a mother looking forward to her daughter's wedding.

A few weeks before the big day, Jordan and I accompanied my mother on an unusual excursion: we went to the cemetery to invite my dead relatives to the wedding. I'd been anticipating the Jewish old-country custom with some amusement. I hadn't expected the awkwardness of standing before the graves of my grandparents—only one of whom had lived long enough for me to really know—silently thinking, because I suddenly couldn't speak, an invitation. We shuffled our feet, we made jokes. When I invited two second cousins whom my mother remembered as having had a wonderful marriage, she insisted that I also invite all the other relatives buried in their vicinity, lest I cause offence.

But my mother grew quiet when she reached her sister's grave. They'd been extraordinarily close, and Bernice's death, from ovarian cancer when she was forty-three, had devastated my mother. Bernice had been dead for twenty-five years, but my mother still cried when she bent to place rocks along the ledge of her tombstone.

I was two when Bernice died. Watching my mother watch her sister's grave, I wondered about that long-ago year. I don't remember Bernice, and I don't remember my mother's mourning. But I know that my life is tied up with my mother's loss: I was the baby she held when she needed something to hold, when she hurt too much to let go.

I invited the dead to my wedding. And understood, as I did so, what it meant for my mother to watch me walk away down the aisle. It's a journey, in my time and place, as purely symbolic as the white dress. And yet it carries meaning: a moment, as with the proposal, when the couple signals to each other and to those they've asked to bear witness that they are starting a life together, a life for one another.

There's a Jewish saying: "Every time a marriage takes place, a new world is created."

But with every new world created, two old worlds, however gently, are destroyed.

The wedding day arrived. The alterations never were quite right—a shoulder strap hung a little low on one side, making me look easy—but I did get a kick out of wearing the grandest dress of my life. After Jordan and I signed our *ketubah*, the Jewish wedding contract, we walked into the room where we'd wait for the signal to begin the ceremony. Our guests were seated outside, but a few friends who'd been chosen to hold up our wedding canopy stood ready by the door. As I entered the room, veiled and gowned, I saw them turn to me, taken, as we all inevitably are, by the transformation that the Great White Wedding Dress engenders.

I paused, savouring the moment.

My mother, never one for savouring, plowed on.

She must have been just inches behind me when I went for the dramatic pause. A pileup ensued. She stepped on the hem of my dress, and then pulled back, surprised.

Everyone in the room heard the rip.

I had a Bridezilla moment. I had a baby's breath moment. I was ruined; everything was ruined.

Then I looked at my mother. And laughed.

So the skirt of the dress wasn't as attached to the body as it might have been. If anyone noticed, no one said anything. It really was a wonderful wedding. My mother even kicked off her heels, donned sneakers and went to town on the dance floor.

As for my wedding dress: dry cleaned, restitched and stuffed with tissue paper, it has undergone the wedding dress equivalent of cryonics. There's a New Jersey company that specializes in this, and I don't need to tell you that my mother found them.

86

Maybe one day, decades from now, my daughter, now seventeen-months-old, will open the box, eyes welling at the perfect dress preserved within.

Maybe.

But I wouldn't bet on it.

I hope my daughter does find someone to create her own

world with. And when she does, I hope I'll be able to look beyond the to-do lists to truly celebrate the moment.

I think I will. My mother taught me that.

Having married a Canadian, ILANA STANGER-ROSS now lives in Victoria, British Columbia, and studies midwifery at the University of British Columbia. A recent recipient of Toronto and Ontario Arts Council grants, she is currently working on a novel that takes place in a bra shop.

A Simple Dress

The amber bellies of logs
reflecting light in a log house.
You I grew inside of.
                    —Jane Munro, "The Fine Minutiae of Moments"

I made my first wedding dress, a lace sheath with scallops at hem and elbow, on the family-room table in the log house my father designed and built.

That house seemed almost alive, changing as the family changed, going through all the stages from rustic cabin to gracious home. My parents continued to live in it—and my father kept working on it—after I'd left; it remained the family's hearth for another generation. And then it burned down. My mother died as a result of third-degree burns she suffered in that fire. My father was also injured, but he survived.

Father blamed himself for Mother's death: he'd made the house for her, not realizing its logs would act like a furnace, holding in and intensifying the heat. After the fire, he wouldn't build a thing.

Five years later, Bob, my second husband, and I decided to change our lives—leave the city and move to the country. We began building a house on the west coast of Vancouver Island that reminded me of my childhood home. My father, who was by then not well, followed every detail of our plans and even came out here once to check on the progress of construction. The weekend we moved in, he died—suddenly, unexpectedly—on the sixth anniversary, to the hour, of the house fire. A couple of weeks later, I turned fifty.

I am now sixty-two. This morning, I tried on that wedding dress—the one I made forty-two years ago, when I married Jock. The challenge was pulling the zipper all the way up between my shoulder blades. The dress fit surprisingly well. Someone told me pregnancy expands the rib cage, and that makes sense. After three kids, the dress felt snug around my floating ribs. I stepped into it naked, having stripped off jeans, sweater and cotton undergarments. No buffers. I wanted to feel it.

Once I got the zipper done up, I tried pacing back and forth across the room, barefoot, balancing a book on my head, the way my father schooled me to walk when I was going to be a flower girl. The book was B.K.S. Iyengar's *Light on Yoga*—a suitably brick-shaped paperback from which I'm following a practice this week. In yoga, we're asked to do things without attachment to outcome. Karma yoga. We usually think of "karma" as "fate," but for yogis, "karma yoga" simply means "action yoga." The goal is to do things for the sake of doing them, with care and attention, but without expectations. You can see how this discipline plays out when practising yoga asanas, something I do for an hour or two every day. Our teacher corrects us if we say, "I can't do that," and don't even try. She insists we make our best attempt, then let it go. Just like we are to let go what we could do. The mind's job is to stay present and get on with what comes next.

The satin lining of the dress felt cool on my skin. Slippery. A bit like water. The spring air also felt cool and oddly dense, as if its invisibility were the lining of a hidden body. Wearing the old dress made me feel fresh. Present and refreshed. Alert to the young woman who took such care when making it.

Outside the window, lacy boughs of cedar caught the morning sun. Forty-two years ago, those trees would have been saplings. Uphill from them, you can find mossy hummocks where the buried ties of a logging railroad are turning into humus. What's now our land was clear-cut in the first round of logging on the coast; these cedars, like the other trees around, are second-growth. Bob and I have lived here for thirteen of the eighteen years we've been together. Both our marriage and our home seem like another kind of second-growth. A second chance.

In a fifties Pontiac
kissing the man I'd marry—
wet December night
the privacy
of a rain-splattered windshield—
taking off
his glasses, his pupils huge
as a buffalo on a
prairie—the dark lens
of a species
we squandered—the past's long gaze
fixing us

—Jane Munro, "Our History"

Jock and I were married in 1964 on a Saturday afternoon in early June in the Anglican church where I'd gone to Sunday school. Luckily, it was a sunny day, because the reception was in our garden. My mother got the home economics classes at her school to make trays of fancy sandwiches. My father filled a wheel-barrow with ice and loaded it with bottles of pink champagne. My sister, Aubin, was a bridesmaid. The children's choir she usually sang with preceded us down the aisle.

On my father's arm, pacing slowly, I looked left and right, exclaiming and nodding, delighted to see all the people who'd come. The church was packed, not only with invited guests, but also with kids from school, mothers of friends, neighbours, even my former Brown Owl. The word had gotten out that everyone was welcome at the service. I carried a bouquet of white and yellow daisies. My cousin's daughter, our flower girl, had a wreath of daisies in her hair and wore a yellow and white gingham frock my mother had sewn for her. Aubin and my other two bridesmaids also wore homemade dresses, theirs of yellow silk shantung, and carried daisies.

My mother made the three-tier wedding cake from her mother's recipe—a dark fruitcake—and packed away the top layer, saving it for our first christening. My brother tied strings of tin cans onto the fender of Jock's pink Pontiac and decorated the hood with tissue rosettes. Jock had the car loaded with cartons of our books, winter clothes and wedding presents. My gift from Mother and Father was a set of white suitcases—one medium, one small and one, a boxy overnight case with a mirror in its lid. After the wedding, Jock carried them out and squeezed them into the back seat just before we left. Suddenly, I felt terrible pangs about leaving home. Hugging Father, I'd started to cry. I can still feel his muscular arms encircling me, and hear his voice. He took my hands and said, "The way to make a marriage work is to never imagine it might fail."

Jock was twenty-six. The United States customs officials made him unpack the car and fill out forms. As a Ford Foundation fellow, he had a student visa; I was admitted as his wife. I stood by the counter in my high heels and going-away suit and listened silently while the men in uniform and my husband negotiated the bureaucracy of moving to a new country. It was getting dark by the time we arrived at the hotel in Bellingham. Ahead of us stretched two weeks of wending our way two thousand miles southeast to Bloomington, Indiana, where Jock would start work on his doctorate and I would finish my undergraduate degree.

I was twenty. I woke up the next morning with a new name, given to me by a man I'd known for only seven months, heading for a small town in a new country where no one knew me and everyone would ask, "Where are you from?" because my accent sounded so strange.

The lace for the dress came from Elle Fabrics in downtown Vancouver. Mother hesitated at its cost, but the saleswoman unfurled the bolt on the cutting table and I showed them how I planned to lay out the pattern. They agreed I could get away with fewer yards than called for on the back of the package. The lining is ivory satin, which shows through as a warmer and lustrous background. The satin stops below the neckline, leaving a sheer circle at the top of the bodice. Similarly, the skirt ends with a see-through border of lace scallops.

Essentially, it's a simple dress. I'd practised all the sewing techniques in earlier projects. The first of these was a costume I made on a toy sewing machine. The machine really worked, but you had to drive it by turning the flywheel with your hand. I stitched red and blue and green rickrack in wandering waves around and around the circular skirt, then drove the needle through all the thicknesses of the waistband. Mother coached me, and then defended my right to wear the skirt in a dance performance. That was before we moved into the log house; I was five. When I was eleven, I made myself an orange jumper with a dropped waist

and little box-pleated skirt. I was inordinately proud of the bound buttonholes. Ten of them, front and centre: precisely squared-off mouths with neatly meeting lips. By the time I got to high school, I was sewing most of my own clothes. The next step was to make myself and Aubin matching winter coats. Father took me to visit his tailor so I could see how to stitch in interlinings and padding for the shoulders. And then I began to sew for Mother, a girls' counsellor at a high school, making dresses and jackets she wore to work.

While making my wedding dress, I fussed over the points where seams met. My biggest regret was that I couldn't get a perfect match at the raised waistline across the zipper at the back. It was close, but the seam jogged. Mother said, "No one will notice."

I remember patiently easing the fullness of the bodice onto the skirt along its curved empire waistline, distributing and steaming the gathers so there were no puckers or bulges, and going through the same process when setting in the sleeves. I overcast the edges of seams, finished each dart with three stitches on the vanishing edge of its fold, rolled and hemmed the lace at the neck, sewed on pearl buttons and made knotted thread loops to slip over them. By the morning of the wedding, my dress was hanging from a nail on the log wall, next to the flower girl's gingham frock and Aubin's bridesmaid dress.

When we moved to North Vancouver, we lived in the twenty-five-square-foot first section of the log house. Father had his skill saw set up in the middle of the family room. Mother and Father slept on a davenport, and Aubin had a crib at the end of the kitchen. I shared a bunk room with my brother, Doug. Once Father added on the second section (with living room, three bedrooms and bathroom), all of us but Doug moved into new bedrooms. He stayed on in the old bunk room, away from parents and sisters.

People often said our house was like a ski cabin. We were partway up Grouse Mountain, and there were big trees around. "I love this house!" visitors would exclaim. There wasn't another like it. Strangers would knock on the door and ask if they could come in and look around. Every year, we'd give parties at which the whole family helped out. When I graduated from high school, we invited everyone in my class for a breakfast of johnnycake and maple syrup.

Norah, Father's older sister, came from Santa Barbara for the wedding. That morning, she was wandering around in her slippers and robe, tasting sandwiches, pulling flowers out of buckets left by friends who'd raided their gardens for us and sticking them in our hair. "We're having a wedding!" She was six feet tall—a head above Mother—and an artist. She lived in a Craftsman cottage tucked into a ravine, with a poinsettia so big that it shaded her patio, and taught painting at a college. She'd also sung opera, and would correct us: "Don't squeak, dear. And don't raise your voice at the end of a sentence. You are not asking a question." She was the most exotic member of the family, and also the one with whom I felt an intuitive link. When I was little, I'd start to chant "Aunty Norah's coming! Aunty Norah's coming!" days before she'd call (with no previous discussion) to announce she had a train ticket and would be arriving at the station. Mother would say, "Don't get your hopes up," but I knew when Norah was heading our way.

Mother did not want either of her daughters to take Norah as a role model. "She always has to be the centre of attention," she'd complain, and point out the consequences: Norah had neither husband nor children. On the morning of the wedding, Mother gave Norah the task of icing the cake. This entailed kneading cold marzipan until it softened, patting an inch-thick layer onto each tier of fruitcake, mixing icing sugar with lemon juice and encasing

95

everything in a frosting that would harden to a bright white shell. Norah got it wrong. Perhaps thinking like a painter tempering pigment so it would spread, she thinned the marzipan with egg whites, then heaped the resulting gritty, dun-coloured goop on the three tiers of cake. They sat like toadstools on the kitchen counter.

I cried, wanting perfection. Father got in the car and drove to the Park Royal shopping centre. He came back and corseted each layer with two bands of white satin ribbon tied with tuxedo bows. He drove long pins, like turkey skewers, through the ribbons into the cake to hold everything in place. Late in the afternoon, when Jock and I cut it—by then the tiers were stacked on pillars and the cake was decorated with flowers—we first had to loosen the bindings and then negotiate Father's criss-crossed skewers.

I once asked Norah why she had never married. "But I am married, dear," she said, "though no one in the family knows." And then she told me she'd fallen in love with a pilot and married him before he went overseas during the war. He disappeared. To search for him, she became a war artist, and went from hospital to hospital, camp to camp, sketching portraits of injured men. "They could send them to their loved ones." Everywhere she went, she looked for his face. When I told my parents, Father said, "Well, anything is possible with Norah."

You have all the tools you need.
Now, for God's sake, use them!
Also carried with me, him
pounding the patio table with his shoe. *No*
daughter of mine will put herself
before her children.
But he spent weeks when my marriage ended
ripping out a wall in the front hall,
freeing archways,

opening up the old house we'd moved into
to better suit his stubborn damn fool of a daughter
who never could explain to him
what on God's green earth
justified her actions. *It's not that I doubt your intelligence,*
he'd say, *but you lack experience.*

                    —Jane Munro, "Moving to a Colder Climate"

Jock and I split up after sixteen years of life together. Perhaps just as unreasonably as Father blaming himself for building a log house that killed Mother, I blamed myself for a flawed marriage whose breakdown stabbed the hearts of those I loved most. Father's stoic prescription haunted me: "The way to make a marriage work is to never imagine it might fail."

A few months before his death, with all his body's systems collapsing, he sat at our kitchen table and chanted: "Time and his alias, dark disintegration. Capitulate? Not I!" At first I thought he was saying, "Thyme and azaleas," but there were no herbs and flowers in his vision at that point. What remained of his life looked like a battlefield. I never did find the source of the line he was chanting; it's possible he'd composed it himself. "Capitulate? Not I!" sounded like his spirit speaking.

The log house burned down in 1987. It was my parents' neighbour, Phillip, who phoned me in the middle of the night. He told me that Mother and Father had been taken to the hospital in an ambulance. He said Mother wasn't going to make it. His smoker's voice was so broken, and I was so shocked, that I had to make him repeat everything. He'd found my number in the phone book. I called Aubin, woke my children and drove to the hospital. The nurses in the burn unit set up an extra bed for us; we stayed with Mother around the clock. She died a month later, on Father's eightieth birthday.

Bob came and sat with me in the burn unit the day after the fire. That's where he first met Father. Throughout the month Mother was in the hospital, Bob made sure I ate and slept and took breaks. He'd pick me up and drive me to his house for an hour, feed me soup and bread and wine, put on some jazz, listen to the details of what was happening, then bring me back to the hospital. By the end of the month, when he asked me to marry him, I said yes. He'd been a friend for five of the eight years since Jock and I had separated. We'd met when we were both hired as course designers at the Open Learning Institute. Within a couple of months, he'd moved into my house. We got married a year later.

At that point, I was a doctoral student. A few weeks before our wedding, when I had yet to come up with something to wear and had no time to sew, a friend from the same program told me about a warehouse sale in Gastown. We went. Women carrying skirts, jackets, pants and sweaters pawed through overstuffed racks in a large, poorly lit room. I found a long wool skirt—creamy white—and a lacy white blouse and tried them on between the racks. No changing rooms. There was a tilted mirror off in one corner, but I relied on my friend's judgment. She said they looked good—went together—would be appropriate. Other shoppers agreed. We'd all been dressing and undressing, dropping raincoats and umbrellas at our feet.

Bob and I were married downtown in the Anglican cathedral by a woman priest whom we both liked, and had our reception at the Western Front—an artists' collective with which Bob had a long history. Aubin's husband, Daniel, made us an amazing French wedding "cake" of stacked puff pastries—a cone of balanced pastry balls filled with cream, drizzled with caramel. Friends played the piano. Friends brought taped music. We danced. And ate. It was a great party.

A couple of years ago, our six kids decided they wanted to celebrate fifteen years of being a family. So, they all came out here—
complete with spouses and children—from France, Connecticut,
California, Edmonton and Vancouver for our anniversary. They
also get together in pairs or small groups without us—at conferences, for dinner parties, picnics, concerts, plays. While Jock
and I didn't succeed in making our marriage last, we've remained
friends. Recently, Bob and I went to Jock and his wife's house for
dinner to celebrate a cluster of family birthdays. It makes me
happy that our family has developed such texture in its relationships, and that it keeps growing. Beneath this expansion and
complexity, I sense a keel of grief allowing us to steer a more
compassionate course.

> *Through my enchantment of grief, mother's sharp whistle: two*
> *fingers under her tongue—come home now, come home.*
> *There is no place like home. Come home, spirit, knocking on*
> *doors, out on the streets in your slip.*
> —Jane Munro, "In the Time of the Dying of Mothers"

Mother sometimes taught remedial math and remedial English.
Believing it was essential to build up the morale of her students,
she'd invite them to get dressed in their best clothes and come to
our house for a party. She would glaze a ham, make casseroles of
scalloped potatoes and bake a fancy cake. Her measure of success
was when one or two began to believe anything was possible—
when they'd open up to her and make fresh efforts.

As long as she could talk, during the month after the fire while
she was in the burn unit, she would quiz the nurses and doctors
caring for her. "Are you enjoying your life?"

They'd look at her, swathed in bandages, immobilized, hooked
up to machines, and say, "Yes."

She'd reply, "Good. It's very important that you enjoy your life."

She would have enjoyed more years. And now, I feel her urging: "Do not put off those things only you can do. Do not waste your time. Get cracking!"

She saw the business of enjoying life as a spiritual skill: our happiness was not to be dependent on external circumstances, or on other people. We were to count our blessings, do our best, practise friendliness and compassion and let go of what held us back. No wonder I feel like I've come home when I practise yoga!

Walking around the house in my first wedding dress, I feel grateful to the young woman who made it. We tend to think we get smarter as we get older, but that girl gives me something I'd like to live up to—I don't want to let her down. Looking back, my adult years seem a dense, rich mixture, ripening like Mother's fruitcake. But now, it's as if I've come to the icing: a layer of marzipan.

The child who stitched rickrack round and round a yellow gypsy skirt hangs in with me as I feel my way, word by word, into the swirl of a poem. The girl who loved dancing thrives on my yoga practice. The teenager who holed up with books, spent hours after school in the art room or disappeared into canyons and creek beds, understands when I get absorbed in things. The bride setting off across the Rockies, never contemplating the possibility that her marriage wouldn't last, points out that hope does regenerate, like a forest. Time also has a more childlike character these days. It's hard to see ahead, and off-putting to think of how my body will change in the future. But, moment by moment, the days open. Time inhales the present and holds its breath. I find something in me now akin to that girl's inability to imagine the cast of characters, situations and circumstances of her life changed in any way. I sometimes fuss over the points where seams meet—wanting perfection in my relationships—but Mother may be right: No one will notice when there's a bit of a jog.

I want to do my best for the girl who made this wedding dress. Like Father building the family's log house, she took great care as a seamstress. Despite her efforts, all the seams haven't met, and goopy icing slumped over the wedding cake. Father's skewers have helped to hold things together, but they're also a hazard. Still, here I am at sixty-two, poised like a bride on the threshold of my swiftly passing present.

JANE MUNRO is challenged and inspired by her seventy-five-year-old yoga teacher. Although Jane couldn't sit in full lotus as a child, after she'd turned sixty, she practiced daily (exclaiming "anything is possible!") and succeeded in tucking both feet up. Writing this memoir helped her to work through places in her heart that felt as stuck and stiff as her hips and knees. It's left her feeling freer—and lets her sit in a more balanced position.

Until at Last

When I was a girl, I tore my mother's wedding dress. Its skirt caught on the latch of the cedar chest I was stuffing it back into after playing dress-up. I'd been forbidden to so much as touch the carefully wrapped garment, but I could never help myself: it was an irresistible sensation, slipping my scrawny under-developed person into this fully bloomed embodiment of womanhood. It was summer and school was out. The basement of our bungalow, where the cedar chest was kept, was cool and dark, and the silk satin was smooth against my skin—which was grimy with sweat from trying to keep up with the neighbourhood kids playing on the cul-de-sac of our suburban street.

I heard my mother call from upstairs, and I squirmed out of the dress and shoved it back into the chest. The lid was heavy: it fell with a clunk and a grinding crunch of metal. The teeth of the latch gouged the satin through the three layers of its voluminous skirt. It was like an animal bite into tender flesh, only there was no blood.

I can't recall if my mother punished me or not, but I know she was heartbroken. I didn't play dress-up with her gown again for another thirty-some years.

My mother's wedding dress began its yet-to-be-formed life rippling off a bolt of pearl white silk satin in the textiles department of the old Simpson's department store on Toronto's Queen Street in the summer of 1952. It was in the basement of that same Simpson's that my mother would later take me as a child for delectably foamy orange julep and hot dogs. The fabric for her dress cost ninety dollars, a substantial sum given the era and her finances; not only was she saving for a new life about to begin, but she was also helping to support my aging grandparents and her younger siblings. The family had lost their Vancouver Island home when they were evacuated in 1942 along with the rest of the coastal Japanese-Canadian community. After almost four years in internment camps, they were permitted to come east and resettle once the war was over.

So my mother scrimped and saved from her job sewing other people's dresses in a factory on Spadina Avenue in downtown Toronto. Impoverished as she was, she always invested in quality that would stand the test of time, even if it meant great sacrifice, and even if the gown would only be worn once—or twice, at most, she imagined, pondering the possibility of a future daughter. My mother had preferred lace, since it was the fashion of the fifties: Elizabeth Taylor wore lace in *Father of the Bride* in 1950, and Grace Kelly would don lace when she became Princess Grace of Monaco in 1956. My father, though, preferred my mother draped in satin. From their first meeting at the home of a friend from internment camp days, he'd been struck by her resemblance to the elegant screen siren Joan Bennett, who wears satin in the film noir *Scarlet Street*.

In the early 1950s, my mother sewed for Paragon Dresses, Title Dresses and other companies; she was paid per dress that she sewed, earning an average of about twenty-five dollars per week. Once, she was relegated to a cramped dark basement with no fire exit; she hastily moved on but later heard that the workers had barely escaped a fire. Still, she knew she was lucky to have a job. Hiroshima and Nagasaki had been bombed in 1945, effectively ending the war; the internment camps had been disbanded in 1946. But Japanese people, including Canadian-born citizens of Japanese ancestry, like my mother, were still viewed as the enemy, albeit vanquished.

The experience of evacuation and internment as an enemy alien was a shabby legacy to pass on to your children, so nobody spoke of it. Everyone bore it quietly. But the dresses in which my mother clothed her nine sisters during the war and after were neither shabby nor quiet. The girls played their own game of dress-up in designs copied from magazines, crimping their poker-straight hair into Betty Grable and Rita Hayworth styles. In the camps, my mother cobbled together whatever fabrics she could find in the canteen to create dresses for her sisters to wear to prom-like dances held in the main mess hall. There, swirling in their elaborate dresses on the dirt floor, they could make believe it wasn't wartime, that they weren't enemies of the state, uncertain of their future; rather, they were footloose and fancy-free, just like the tap-dancing Ginger Rogers. These dresses lifted their spirits with their fluttery skirts, lending them girlish pride with their pert collars and cinched waistlines.

My mother designed her own wedding dress, as well as that of her best friend, Mitsuko, who sewed it. In addition to countless party dresses, my mother sewed bridal gowns for two of her sisters and one sister-in-law. In total, she would sew four wedding dresses in her lifetime, or four-and-a-half if you count mine.

My mother often lamented having married at the ripe old age of twenty-five, at least two years older than each of her sisters at the time of their nuptials. But her lament grew to a distant echo as I passed that same age without a prospect in sight and the years went on. One by one, then two by two by five by six, nearly all of my thirty cousins settled down to wholesome married life. With dutiful good cheer, my mother waved on a parade of bridal showers, weddings, then baby showers. That good cheer diminished through two decades during which the spectre of being son-in-law-less and grandchild-less began to loom ever larger before her. In recent years, she'd become resigned to that fate.

Until, at last, I met my man.

Our first brief encounter was over a plate of peanut butter and jelly sandwiches at his sister's baby shower. His niece was unexpectedly born five days later. A month after that, his sister and a friend conspired to bring us together, but the newborn infant was the tiny bud from which our love bloomed.

On Christmas Day of our third year together, he proposed. At noon, we drove downtown along empty streets to the restaurant of the Four Seasons Hotel, where holidaying guests were filling their plates at an opulent buffet. At a window-side table, he presented me with a small handcrafted notebook, a poetic chronicle of our love, authored in photographs and rhyming couplets. It culminates in a photo of him looking precisely as he did that day: the same shirt, the same jacket, seated before me at the same table in the same restaurant. In his hands is a small box. When I looked up, he was smiling at me with the same loving gaze as in the picture, with the same small box in his hands. (It was for the maitre d' of the restaurant that he'd posed so lovingly two days earlier.) I turned the page, and through blurred, brimming eyes, I glimpsed the letters puzzling together the question, "Marry Me?"

Later, we went to my parents' home for turkey dinner, anxious to give them the news. We were late and breathless; they were hungry and impatient. As we hastily sat down at the dining-room table, I wordlessly flashed my engagement ring at them. To which my father, with the barest hint of a grin that only my mother and I could ever perceive, said, "Pass the turkey, please." My mother sat still for a second and with a shy smile and raised clasped hands, murmured, "Oh, that's so nice."

I'd expected so much more: tears, laughter, hysterics, especially from my mother at having narrowly escaped what she considered her ignominious fate. But unbridled emotion was more the mode in which this scene might be played out among other families (as it later was with my beloved's parents), in someone else's photographs or in movies. I had to remind myself who my parents were, who I was. They weathered life with quiet equanimity, the ups and downs, the joys and sorrows. They knocked on wood at every chance, expecting no guarantees of health or happiness or even sameness. They were, I told myself, warily happy. I understood but wanted to shake them, to dislodge their restraint and carefulness. I viewed them anxiously through the eyes of my beloved, who was deflated and a little puzzled by their response.

It was not long after that I announced to my fiancé that I preferred our nuptials to be a low-key, even casual affair. We weren't twenty-year-olds, I heartlessly reminded him, and this was his second time around. His first had taken place when he was a mere twenty-four, an age when I still wasn't sure who I was, let alone who someone else was. The wedding had been a fairly traditional one, held at Casa Loma, a majestic twentieth-century castle in the middle of the city. In a dusty album consigned to a cardboard box stowed in our garage, I'd glimpsed a puff of white and a veil typical of an era still under the spell of Princess Diana. There was a bedecked procession of ushers and bridesmaids in matching full-length gowns clutching plump bouquets. Though the storyline of that picture book ended very far from where it first began, it haunted me with its seeming ideal of youthful wedded bliss in which my husband-to-be had already played his part. I was determined that our wedding be very different from the one in those pictures.

Enticed by a SALE—ONE DAY ONLY sign in the window of a shop whose name seemed to speak to my own inner princess, I made an impulse purchase. The Paper Bag Princess was brimming with dresses possessing past lives: glamorous, elegant, notorious even. But one dress with perhaps a more modest history charmed me. It may have been the pert daisies appliquéd on its bodice, or the resolutely pointed darts at the bust, or its full pink skirt. Maybe it was the sheen of the polyester, the novel fabric of the fifties, when my mother was in her sewing prime. This dress emanated an appealing freshness despite its vintage, and seemed homey at the same time, or familiar. The ever-so-slightly yellowed label read, "David B. Rea, Toronto." I couldn't help but wonder if, in addition to Paragon Dresses and Title Dresses, this was another of the companies my mother had worked for. If so, could she have sewn this very dress? Across the years, out of the racks and racks of dresses circulating through the city from factory to shop to closet and back again, amid the flux and flow of time and lives? Was it possible?

It was a fanciful notion. But as I considered it, I was reminded of how hard my mother and my father had worked to give me the privileges they'd been denied. That fleeting sense of homey comfort I'd felt turned to discomfort as I saw myself as the moneyed consumer of the product my mother, the worker, had produced. My parents were the first generation born of immigrants to whom the golden opportunities of Canadian citizenship were supposed to have accrued. Instead, they'd had to start over after leaving the camps, just as their parents had done arriving here at the turn of the last century: a kind of second generation of immigrants, once again struggling into citizenship.

My mother scoured her memory but couldn't recall sewing for David B. Rea. When she saw the dress, she gasped. "That's not a wedding dress," she cried accusingly, not the usual stoic mother I knew. "That's a bridesmaid's dress!"

It was true. In my defence I declared that I had had more practice being a bridesmaid (four times) than a bride (zero). So what did she expect?

My mother marched me down to Spadina Avenue, to the shmatte district, her old stomping grounds. I recalled the story she'd often repeated about how her knee had given way, sending her tumbling to the ground, when she was seven months pregnant with me. A handsome stranger had helped her to her feet and then lingered gallantly to make sure she was all right. The latter details were what she relished telling most, as if there were another story not told; a road not taken. The two of us rounded the corner of Spadina and Adelaide, the original spot, I'd always imagined, the spawning ground of this bit of family myth and a dose of Freudian guilt (mine, since her knee would never be the same). Of course, she'd never said where the event had actually occurred.

We went into the first shop we came to, Bridal Fantasy. There before us were racks of polyester that seemed to send my mother into a nostalgic reverie. These were not unlike the fabrics she had slid beneath her able fingers at the Singer sewing machines all those years ago. But now the dresses were made in China with prices to match—cheaper even than the redundant vintage bridesmaid dress I'd acquired.

I tried on gown after gown, each time stepping up and turning before a three-panel mirror on a circular platform that made me feel like I was riding a Lazy Susan at a Chinese banquet. None felt right: they were too white, too poufy, like ominous clouds; the pictures from my fiancé's first wedding rose like dust from their laden album into my head. But then my mother's austerely pursed lips parted; she smiled. "Yes, that's the one," she said, as I turned once again before the mirror. I could not object. The gown was lovely; its beaded halter bodice, minus the skirt, would've been perfect for a figure skater performing a short pro-gram choreographed to "The Wedding March."

After the alterations were made, we picked up the dress and brought it home. I put it on and stepped in front of a mirror in my stepson's room, stumbling over some errant Lego blocks. The curling hem seemed to smile a derisive smile at me. Beneath the flimsy polyester skirt, a crinoline of chicken wire showed through. It was so scratchy I feared that my betrothed, on our wedding night, might be warded off by a DANGER—KEEP OUT! sign that wouldn't seem at all out of place on it.

My mother and I stood there, our sad gazes meeting in the mirror. "It looked different in the store," she murmured.

That was when I returned to the scene of the crime, the cedar chest where my mother's wedding dress was stored. I took it out of its fifty-year-old plastic wrapping. It was no longer the same pearly satin of my memory. It had grown grey and smelled of mothballs. I struggled into it, and it was icy cold and heavy, as if weighted by the passage of time. I could hardly fit my wrists through the sleeves, could barely zip up the waist. I was straining against the slender-boned ghost of my mother's twenty-five-year-old self. I looked at myself in the mirror in my parents' basement and saw the teeth marks in the dress, in the back and front of the skirt, and the peplum—as fresh as yesterday, though the satin itself had aged.

Two years earlier, I'd been browsing in my favourite fabric store on Queen Street, just off Spadina. I hadn't been there in a long while and the owner, Susie, scrutinized me and said in her thick Guangdong-accented English, "You look different. You look good. Something happen?" I told her I'd bought a house with my boyfriend and moved out of the neighbourhood. "You find love. That why you look so good," she said.

I couldn't help smiling, because I was in love for the first time in my life. On that occasion, I treated myself to two yards of frivolous antique white silk tufted with frills, perfect for a funky minidress. As Susie unrolled the bolt, she smiled knowingly. "This will make beautiful wedding dress," she said.

I'd barely begun sewing when the demands of writing, looking after a then eight-year-old stepson and keeping romance alive rightfully intervened. The fabric sat for two years beside my dormant sewing machine. Just when my mother and I were about to resign ourselves to my skating down the aisle in chicken wire, I remembered it. We set to work immediately.

Whether or not I'd sensed it in some subliminal region of my heart two years earlier, I now knew this was to be my wedding dress. I felt like Cinderella, with the Disney kingdom rallying to help me: singing birds, squirrels, rabbits. But that kingdom was my mother. We improvised, stitched and restitched until it was right. We went back to Susie for more fabric, but after two years there was none left. She found us a matching silk crepe for the skirt and sleeves.

By then, the casual venue I'd first chosen, a party room in an apartment building, no longer seemed right. My mother confessed that she and my father wanted something more elegant, more grand. This was the "more" I'd hoped for weeks earlier when we had first told them the news. We acquiesced.

The two weeks before the wedding were spent before a mirror with my mother pinning and snipping, and at my sewing machine. When my mother pinned the sleeves into place, it felt to me like birds fluttering to my shoulders and securing them just so: like the most natural thing in the world. Just as I felt walking down the aisle with my father on one side and my mother on the other, as the silk of my custom-made wedding dress swished around my ankles and my beloved awaited me.

KERRI SAKAMOTO is a Toronto-based writer of novels, screenplays and essays on art. Her first novel, *The Electrical Field,* received the overall Commonwealth Writers Prize for Best First Book and the Canada-Japan Literary Award. Her most recent book is *One Hundred Million Hearts,* published by Knopf Canada. She was married at the Royal Ontario Museum in Toronto in April 2006. She lives in relative bliss with her husband and stepson, with three wedding dresses in her closet.

REBECCA CUNNINGHAM

With Patience She Stands Waiting

If wedding dresses had names, the way ships and other vehicles of journey do, the name of my wedding dress would have to be Patience. A close runner-up would be Faith. For I had bargained with faith, and on this dress, long before I graced the aisle of a church as a bride. But Patience is what names her best.

The dress was the creation of a tailor who was wise enough to thread patience into the seams of her soul, for the dress endured a long courtship before she danced in the arms of a groom. For months she stood in the elegant arch of a dressmaker's first-floor window, just around the corner from my favourite movie theatre. I should say *our* favourite movie theatre, because I enjoyed many a double feature there with my boyfriend, John, during our first years together. After a night at the movies we would wind our way home, deep in conversation. Truthfully I think we often enjoyed the walk home more than most of the second-run films themselves.

We always took the same route. As we turned south under the glare of the Honest Ed's sign at the corner of Markham and Bloor, the softer hues of an eclectic group of shops beckoned us onto Markham Street. Soon we would head over to Palmerston Avenue, where a magical string of globed lights welcomed us into indigo evenings. Deep in conversation, we would barely notice the window displays—least of all the wedding gown in the dressmaker's window.

I first noticed her one evening when I was on my way to the movies to meet John. I was late, as usual, and in a hurry, and the warm glow of the dress in the window caught my attention. I crossed the street for a quick look.

She was lovely yet unassuming. At first glance you wouldn't necessarily know she was a wedding dress. Slightly off-white, her antique lace bodice embraced an anonymous bust without head or hands. At her waist, a champagne silk sash gently gathered itself into a knotted flower that perched delicately on the right hip. Arms: three-quarter length, hung without gesture at her sides. The neckline: a simple scoop, echoed by the gentle curve of a hem that would hover sensibly just below the knee. The back (slightly more daring) came to an open V just above a mother-of-pearl button that would hold a modest hint of a train when invited to dance.

My tentative but noncommittal courtship with the dress lasted well into that season of humid summer nights. I exchanged secret glances with her during evening walks home after the movies. It never occurred to me to pass by during the day and enter the shop to inquire about her. After all, there was no proposal. What was I doing looking at a wedding dress?

Certainly John and I had been together for a few years. We loved each other and loved being together. But marriage was a long way off for me. I was twenty-three. I wanted to travel and to live abroad on my own. In fact, when I first met John, I had just handed in my application to work overseas. He had just returned from two and a half years of teaching as a volunteer in Botswana. When I asked him out for a coffee so that we could talk about his experiences in Africa, I had not planned on falling in love. Weeks after we started seeing each other, I was offered a contract to teach in Malawi. I decided to defer. I knew the dream of living overseas would wait while I figured out where my heart stood with John.

We moved through the first months of our relationship with the understanding that at some point I would be going away on my own. Months turned into two years. I loved John but knew I would resent him if I never went overseas to follow my dream. We both knew it. That summer the only date circled on the calendar was my impending departure for a year-long internship in Peru. If it was meant to be, our relationship would survive the time apart.

I left for Peru on Canada Day, exchanging Toronto's bright summer days for the grey dampness of Lima's winter season. Despite the distance, John and I grew closer. In those days before email, I anxiously awaited his double-sided, eight-page single-spaced letters. I sent my own postage-laden letters back. We did talk about marriage but agreed to wait for any serious discussion until I came home.

I returned a year later. John and I were committed to continu-ing our relationship. Marriage, however, still seemed a long way off. I needed to adjust to being back in Toronto. I wasn't pre-pared for how difficult this would be. Without a job or a place to call my own, I felt unsettled. I didn't want to get married because it was expected (yes, the relatives were asking). I was determined to marry when my heart felt right.

A few weeks after my return, I decided to take a stroll past the dressmaker's shop. I figured if the dress was meant to be mine she would still be there. Up to this point I had seen her only in the romantic evening light after our late-night strolls home from the movies. This was the first time I would see the dress during the day. I wondered if her magic would be lost.

As I made my way up to the dressmaker's shop that hot July afternoon, I found the window papered over, the door locked, the word CLOSED smirking through the glass. Surely there must be some mistake. John had waited. Where was the dress? I left the shop wondering if the universe was trying to tell me something. Had I waited too long?

Thankfully, virtues like patience have sisters like forgiveness. A few days later I passed by the shop again, hoping against hope that I would be given a second chance. In the electric heat of mid-afternoon, my heart skipped a beat to find the dressmaker's door propped open with a broom. As I enter into the memory of that day I still feel hope rising in my chest.

I knock and enter without waiting for a reply. Inside, the shop is still and almost dark. The afternoon light filters in through the doorway and catches the dust fairies lazily waltzing through the air. From the shadows in the back a young woman appears. She is packing up bolts of material and rushing to clean up before a hot July weekend.

"Excuse me," I begin, "I guess . . . the store is . . . ummm . . . closing . . . closed?"

The young woman acknowledges my profound sense of the obvious with a sweeping gesture around the room. "Looks like it." There are a few boxes, a phone on the floor and anonymous clothing draped over scattered chairs. "Can I help you?"

We exchange pleasantries. No, she is not the owner but is just helping to clean up. The dressmaker is returning to costume-making at Stratford and plans to finish moving things out there by the end of the week. The velvety drapes of the change room encourage me to try for one more curtain call.

"There was a dress . . . in the window," I begin. "A wedding dress. It was there for ages—well, months, I guess. Might you know where it is?" I fumble for words that will do the dress justice. "It is sort of . . . elegant looking . . ." Nothing registers on the face of the young woman. I continue. "Off-white with a sort of sash thing . . ." Something twigs and her expression changes.

"Hold on a second. There's some stuff packed up in the back." She disappears. I wait. The air is still. I hear the sound of rustling bags and a few boxes being moved. The woman reappears framed by the back doorway. She unties a garbage bag. "Is this what you are looking for?"

A creamy pool of fabric spills itself out into the afternoon. Despite the heat, the dust and the dishevelled look of the room, it does not take long for Patience to regain her dignity. The dress falls into a graceful arc, cradled in the young woman's arms. I exhale. She carries it over the threshold towards me. "Is this it?"

She was as beautiful as ever. Magic. Almost giddy, I tried the dress on. It was a tad too big, but I figured I'd either grow into it or could get it altered. The young woman assured me that alterations would not be difficult. She made a long-distance phone call to the dressmaker, who was more than surprised that anyone remembered the gown and was interested in it. Of course she would sell it. Did I want to buy it today?

That afternoon I had no engagement ring, no wedding proposal, no job and little savings. However, I did have a wonderful, faithful partner, a sense of destiny and enough in my account to buy the dress for a song.

I did not tell anyone I had bought the dress. Superstition, I guess. I didn't want to tempt fate or bad luck. I did not want to join the list of brides-never-to-be (or brides-who-wish-they-never-did) who put more energy into finding the right dress than into finding the right man. Or perhaps it was my pride. What was I doing buying a dress when we hadn't made the big announcement? What if things didn't work out with John? Why weren't we married yet? What were we waiting for?

Funnily enough, carrying the dress home I felt a sense of calm. Whether or not the universe was trying to tell me something, I just loved that dress so much. She reminded me of those early days in our relationship, when things were so romantic and easy and we just loved being together and going to the movies. There was no one pressuring us with, "So, are you two getting married or what?" It was almost as if the dress were a witness to those moments and had faith that we would work it all out somehow. She had seen us at our best. She was rooting for us.

That afternoon I gingerly packed the dress into a cardboard box marked JOHN—DO NOT OPEN UNDER ANY CIRCUMSTANCES! (*Please*). I stored the box on the top shelf of the bedroom closet. And so Patience began her long, faithful wait.

Five years later, after several moves and various closet shelves, I opened the box again. Five years! It had taken a long time for us to settle into making a commitment. What took so long? Looking back, it is hard to say exactly what it was. There were issues that both of us needed to work out. It was hard work, but we were committed to resolving those issues, no matter where that led. Thankfully, John and I travelled the journey from not being sure to happily making a lifelong commitment to each other. I don't regret taking that time. Neither of us do.

We were married at five o'clock on a September afternoon. On the day of our wedding, Patience sighed her way over my shoulders and fell easily across my hips. Surprisingly few alterations had been needed after all. I felt comfortable and happy. We broke tradition by walking down the aisle together. After all, we had been walking side by side for so long. That day we walked into our marriage hand in hand.

One of my favourite pictures captures the two of us heading down the aisle together after the ceremony. With gratitude I strode, knowing that John was the one for me. Patience had been right all along.

Today the dress hangs, carefully stored, at the back of my cedar-lined closet. No warning sign this time. I try to remember to take her out every year on our wedding anniversary. It will be eleven years this summer. My daughters (now eight and six and planning for the future) gently finger the lace and ask if they might wear the dress when they become brides. "Someday, my dears. If that's what you choose. You'll just have to be patient." I know the dress will wait.

REBECCA CUNNINGHAM lives in Toronto with her husband, John, and two daughters, Stella and Sophie. She continues to buy clothing on a whim but wears these purchases immediately. Any clothing not worn in a year is given away (except for the wedding dress, of course). There is, however, one dress from Peru (a deep royal blue with a fabulous hand-embroidered trim—a gift from John) that is waiting for the perfect occasion—mother of the bride?

SUSAN WHELEHAN

The Past, the Pearls, the Politics

My wedding dress? I know exactly where it is: in the back of my closet, on the right, in a box, on the floor, past those tops on the low rod that are on the end because I haven't worn them in years because they haven't fit me in years, but I'm sure they will soon because I started a diet and exercise program recently. Okay, this morning. It's just so hard losing those last few—okay, forty—post-partum pounds. But I'm determined this time, and with the support of my husband and teenage sons, I'm sure I'll do it.

My fabulous frock is just lovely. I stood tall in it. Not too plain. (This was a very special occasion, after all.) Not too pouffy. (I was thirty-four, after all.) Just right. Perfect.

I kept meaning to have it "preserved." I'm not sure what that entails, but I think they clean it and put it in a bag and suck all the air out and say magic words and you can look at it through the clear covering forever and it will not disintegrate. Kind of like St. Bernadette, whose body is still on display in France, more than a century after her death. But I never got around to it. It's been twenty years. I never got around to France either. Oh well.

I had been living in Toronto for many years before I met Francis. And I met Francis through my fabulous friend, Elaine. Elaine and I had a lot in common: we met as members of Teachers for Social Justice, we were feminists, we studied dance together, we loved Bruce Springsteen and we laughed out loud. Elaine and Francis had been "an item" a few years before and had remained friends after breaking up. I had heard about him, but we had never met. When Elaine went over to Africa to teach, Francis went to visit. She bought beautiful fabric for me and sent it back with him. We met when he came over to bring me the fabric. He was wearing pink high-top running shoes. The rest is history.

Francis and I had a lot in common. We realized we had both attended the same series of lectures sponsored by a Social Justice group in the diocese. He was a feminist, a wonderful dancer, liked Bruce Springsteen and enjoyed women who laughed out loud. Six months later we were engaged. He bought me a beautiful strand of pearls for our engagement. As both families lived out of town, we were on our own planning the wedding. And I was on my own choosing a dress. Neither of my mother's wedding dresses would do.

My mother, Betty, had been married twice. She was first married during the Second World War. She was supposed to have a fabulous wedding in Rochester, New York, amidst all her family and friends. However, her fiancé's new orders dashed those plans, and he was informed that he was heading overseas very soon. So she boarded a train with her parents and sister and dress and headed across the country to his base in Denver to be married at the chapel there. She wore a gorgeous gown of ice blue satin, with a train and tiny covered buttons all down the back. I've seen the pictures of her in that dress. She looks very happy.

Her husband was declared missing in action a few months later. I can't even imagine.

Aunt Dorothy, my mother's youngest sister, wore the ice blue gown for her own wedding seven years later. I never sought it out from my beloved aunt. Both she and my mother were six inches shorter than I, so it would never have worked on me. But her daughter, my cousin Joanne, wore it for her wedding ten years ago. It is still in the family.

When my mother married my father, Bill, she wore a dark belted dress (very appropriate for a second marriage at the time) and a hat with Ostrich Feathers of the Universe. How I wish I had that hat. My mother died when I was fourteen, so there is no way to find out what became of it. I don't remember seeing it as a child. But I have a picture of her on her wedding day, with all that plumage. She looks very happy.

My mother died of breast cancer back when it seemed no one else had it. There were no magazine articles on it or movies of the week. It was never spoken about in polite company. She had one breast removed in 1961. Her eighth child died on the delivery table in 1962. Her second breast was removed in 1965, and Mom died a year later at the age of forty-seven. She never told me she was dying.

I remember Mom and Dad having an argument in the den one night. He said she had to go into the hospital the next day. She was angry because she wanted to take me the next night to the Mother–Daughter Charity Fashion Show for the hospital where she volunteered. I knew she hadn't been feeling well. I knew she had gained weight and looked pregnant, and that she couldn't possibly be since she had had a hysterectomy. I knew that she was tired all the time, but . . . She arranged for a friend's mother to take me. It wasn't the same.

Mom went into the hospital that day. I visited her every day, hoping she would be home by the next weekend to come and see me perform in *A Midsummer Night's Dream.* But she got weaker and weaker and didn't come to the show. That Sunday night, right after the Cartwright boys rode into the sunset on *Bonanza,* my father told my older brother and me that she wouldn't be coming home. We weren't to tell the little kids. I never told a soul. I visited her after school on Monday, and we didn't say a word about it. We both just smiled and talked about the play and the little kids and how the ribbons on her nightgown were lovely. She died the next day.

I'm sure she thought it was best that way. I'm not so sure it was.

I got to choose the dress she was buried in. I remember being glad I could do that. And now I don't remember a thing about that dress.

My mother loved clothes and had her own sense of style. She always had a hat made to match a special outfit. She could look so glamorous dressed in a gown to go to a charity ball with my dad. I loved opening the corsage he always bought for her, lifting the white lid off the box, peeling back the layers of green tissue and lifting out an orchid or a gardenia. She would let me pin it on her with a pearl-tipped pin.

I remember when I was around six we had matching sleeve-less seersucker dresses with patch pockets. I loved those dresses. I wonder what became of them. Mind you, I could also be embar-rassed by her choices at times, as any teenaged daughter could. Oh that green fuzzy sweater with gigantic buttons! I mean, really! Out in public? She would just laugh and wear it anyway.

I'd love to have some of her clothes today. Just to have them. A brown hat with pheasant feathers. A blue shawl from Ireland. Even that green fuzzy sweater with gigantic buttons. I'd happily wear it out in public. But a few months after she died (okay, maybe it was a year), friends of hers came while I was at school one day and cleaned out her closet and dresser. They took it all. Her clothes. Hats. Purses. Jewellery. Everything. Gone. All gone.

I'm sure they thought it was best that way. I'm not so sure it was.

As there was no family dress for me to wear, I started looking around by myself. When I walked into my first bridal store, I was haughtily reproved for not having made an appointment. Excuse me? Is everyone supposed to just *know* this? I knew I was out of my league.

Enter Kath, my lovely friend since high school. She also had chosen Toronto over Rochester after studying here, and she offered to make my dress. Her first making of a wedding dress. My first wearing of a wedding dress. When she presented it to me, she hung it on one of those fancy hangers that I would never buy for myself: blue satiny material covering cushy padding, with little flowers and ribbons at the hook part. So thoughtful. Thank you, Kath. And didn't she do a beautiful job? I should say so.

Rounded neckline. Sleeveless ivory sheath. (Try saying that five times really fast.) Over the satin sheath is lace. Chantilly, I believe. And so, of course, that song starts in my head. And now, perhaps, in yours. Sorry.

But, to be honest, menopause has taken away so many details, and entire periods of history, that I really can't be sure if it is Chantilly lace or not. Long lace sleeves. There is a wide band of ivory satin forming a sash below my waist, flapper style, and then a very full skirt of satin with lace over it to mid-calf. Great for twirling and swirling. Which I am wont to do. Even when I am not getting married.

All of this beauty was accented by a pair of earrings, each bearing five gold arms in a fan shape with a pearl on the end of each, and a double strand of pearls around my head, knotted at the side. This headpiece was inspired by two beacons of fashion. In my grandmother's wedding picture, circa 1917, which hangs to this day on the wall going up our front stairs, she is wearing a single strand of pearls around her head, with a veil attached to the back. In Bruce Springsteen's *Born in the USA* poster, which hangs to this day on the wall in my office, he is wearing a bandana around his head. Oh, how I wanted him. He never knew. (Deep sigh.)

Around my neck I wore my mother's engagement diamond, which my father and stepmother, Esther Mary, had set on a gold chain, and the string of pearls from my beloved, Francis. Once we got to the reception, I added a commemorative pin to my chest.

Well, a commemorative button, really. Francis and I decided not to have matches printed for the guests. (Can you believe that was common back then? Matches! And now I can never find a match when I need one.) Instead, given my predilection for collecting political buttons over many years of demonstrating, we had buttons printed to commemorate the happy day and put one at each place setting. My sister-in-law, Jane, designed it: a simple white circle with red hearts and doves, and the words "Susie & Francis, July 12, 1986" around the edge. In the centre it read, "A Nuclear Weapon–Free Wedding." And it worked. After Peter, our emcee, welcomed everyone, he assured us that there was not one single nuclear weapon in the church hall that night. Everyone was very happy.

126

Now for the feet. Hmmmm. Seeing as how I had lived in Birkenstocks for the previous few years (yes, okay, okay, I wore them with socks!), I wasn't sure how I was going to squeeze my feet into anything resembling shoes for a bride. I remembered that for my junior prom in high school I wore ribbon on my feet. The theme that year was "Barefoot in the Park," so I made my dress with ribbon on the bodice (a word I seldom get to work into a conversation) and wrapped matching ribbon around my big toes and across my feet and around my ankles and tied it in a bow. Voila! Barefoot in the Park! But, being a grown-up now, I bought a pair of ivory heels and practised walking in them for the week before to break them in. After all, it was my *wedding!* So, heels and cut-offs. Heels and nightgown. Heels and bathrobe. I was a definite fashion "don't," but it was in the privacy of my own home, so, too bad. It didn't work in the end. I got blisters anyway. Francis, however, was comfy as could be in his pink high-top running shoes. He changed into them at the reception and supplied all the groomsmen with red ones. He still has his.

I gave my shoes away and kept the dress. I planned to pass the dress on to my daughter. You know what they say about the best lace plans—I had two sons. My sons are now fifteen and eighteen, and neither appears to be interested in cross-dressing. Besides, they are both much taller than I am. The whole mid-calf thing would be lost on them.

I planned to use some of the lace for a baptismal gown. Instead, they both wore the family heirloom baptismal gown made by their great-grandmother in 1890. That, too, is in my closet, right beside my wedding dress.

So, what am I saving my wedding dress for? What to do? What to do? Is it time for the Salvation Army? Maybe. However, would the next bride to wear it have as much fun in it as I did?

Would she walk as confidently, wave as happily, hug as tightly and twirl as gracefully? No way.

But at least it would get used. It would have a life. Yes, take it out and donate it.

Oh, I don't know. Could I stand to drive down Roncesvalles and see it in the window on a mannequin—blank stare, blonde wig askew, plaster arms and fingers with chipped blood-red nail polish reaching out of those lovely lace sleeves? Oh my God! And never mind! What if its fate rested in being bought as a Halloween costume? What if some teenager (with excellent taste, mind you) bought it, and it ended up stained with chocolate and beer and salsa and wine and . . . and . . . Never! No. I'll leave it where it is. Just a while longer. I'm only fifty-four. In this day and age, I could still have a daughter. And as for my sons, well, if they decide to get married, and get really sentimental and mushy and want to include some meaningful heirloom or family tradition, they can always wear their father's pink high-top running shoes and I will design their wedding buttons.

SUSIE WHELEHAN teaches and writes in Toronto, where she lives with her husband, Francis Corrigan, and their sons, Ben and Jesse. Her pearl wedding earrings still fit, and she still wants Bruce Springsteen. It's okay. Francis knows. If only Bruce did.

JENNY MANZER

The Wedding Promise

"Mum, I went for my dress fitting today."

It was only four days before the wedding. My dress—a tank-style, ivory satin with a sparkly bodice—had needed no alterations, so I sailed out of the shop into the October sunlight. Then I went to give my mother a full report.

"And?" she asked from her hospital bed. At age sixty-six, her hair was still a natural chestnut brown, glossy and thick, despite the round of chemotherapy.

"It fit perfectly," I said.

She was lying in the cancer ward of Toronto's Sunnybrook and Women's Health Sciences Centre. Her forearms were a topographical map of bruises—a side effect of medication. There was the steady drip of an IV. Minutes later, she began writhing under her bedsheets and moaning softly. My father buzzed for a nurse, who bustled in and gave my mother an injection.

"The pain will go away in a few minutes, Mum," I said.

"Promise?" she asked.

"I promise. They just injected you with a gin and tonic."

She laughed at the thought of her preferred cocktail. A few minutes later, she settled. Some promises are easier to keep than others.

My mother was always active and industrious. In March of 2004, she was still scampering around tennis courts. That spring she even single-handedly retiled my bathroom floor to help sell my Toronto home. My fiancé, David, and I were in the midst of moving to Victoria, British Columbia, and changing jobs. We had also become engaged in May and needed to confirm a wedding date. Our lives were so stressful, we thought. In late spring, my mother began to feel pain in her legs and back. By the summer, she needed a walker even to take a few steps. The change was shocking, as if her hair had turned white overnight. One day in early July, I was sitting with my mother on my parents' cedar deck in suburban Toronto. The deck overlooked a decades-old apple tree and my mother's thriving flowerbeds. It had always been a favourite place of hers. My mother took my hand. The cause of the pain in her limbs and back was not, as previously suspected, arthritis. It was cancer. I felt like the deck was collapsing beneath me. Even though she did not give details about her prognosis, she was insistent about one thing. "I knew within twenty minutes of meeting David that I wanted you to marry him," she told me that day. "Whatever happens," she said fervently, "promise me you'll marry David."

In August, David and I learned about a last-minute cancellation at the McMichael Canadian Art Collection in Kleinburg, a town about forty minutes from Toronto. The available day was on the Thanksgiving weekend, just two months away. Our newly married friends warned us that two months was not enough time.

"That's crazy," people said. "You'll never get a dress." *Cancer is crazy,* I thought. My mother was doing well, but waiting almost a year seemed risky. We took the date.

David and I moved out of our Toronto house, and he flew to Victoria to settle into our new place and prepare to start his new job. I stayed on at my parents' house, trying to cram a year's worth of wedding planning into two weeks. I kept waking in the middle of the night, rigid as a diving board, thinking about another detail left unsettled. Many mornings, my parents would find me at the computer, an empty coffee pot sitting on the stove.

While my mother recovered from hip surgery to repair damage from the cancer, I criss-crossed the city, dropping subway tokens like bread crumbs, meeting with caterers, photographers and our minister. My sister, Patricia, the maid of honour, combed the city for the perfect cake. I checked off the wedding licence, music, bridal shoes and hotel rooms from the to-do list.

Remembering the dire warnings, I headed downtown on a solo dress-shopping mission. I found the dress in less than an hour. It was the first one I plucked from the rack, and it fit as if it were made for me. It was simple, but with fine details: a floral lace bodice and tiny buttons running down the back. It was lovely and light. I am tall, but I slouch. In the dress, I stood straight.

Most dresses in the boutique needed to be ordered three months in advance, but mine happened to be a sample size, so I could take it right away and even get a discount. "It's as if it was meant to be," my sister said later.

When I returned to pay for the dress, my dad came with me, lumbering around the boutique taking digital photos to show my mother in the hospital. She approved of my choice and was amused at the new family tradition. Her own wedding dress had been a sample size, too.

My mother was released from the hospital, in pain, shaky and reliant on her walker. She gradually became more mobile, climbing stairs with some help, and poured herself into the wedding preparations. I found her sitting at the dining-room table, addressing one hundred invitations with a sure hand, despite the abundance of painkillers she was taking. "Ronald and Kathryn Manzer request the pleasure of your company . . ." At the other end of the table, my father stuffed the envelopes.

Not long after, my mother started radiation therapy, and my upcoming wedding became well known among the hospital staff. In between medical appointments, my mother helped choose the catering menu and even coaxed her walker into the flower shop. Though I drank up her help greedily, I wondered if the stress was good for her recovery. "Who's going to stop her?" my father asked.

By summer's end, I was ready to join my fiancé in Victoria. It was hard to leave my mother, but my parents, who never liked to be apart themselves, encouraged me to be with David. And my mother was holding steady. Before I left for the airport, I sat at the kitchen table with my mother. We were speaking about something else when she said, "Remember, whatever happens, I want you to marry David."

I wasn't sure if she meant on October 9, or in general, but I was alarmed. Had the prognosis changed? No, everything was still fine, she assured me. My father and I loaded up the car for the airport. My mother stood in the doorway, her arm slowly waving in a windshield motion as we pulled away.

David and I distracted ourselves by settling into life in Victoria. I busied myself with work and met my new neighbours, enjoying a blissful break from wedding decisions. Suddenly, as if I'd slept through a plane ride, the wedding was just two weeks away. "We have no ushers!" I wailed. "We have no programs!"

Just as abruptly, David and I received an unsettling phone call. My dad had taken my mother to the hospital, where she was diagnosed with pneumonia. Weak and confused, she was treated for dehydration and given intravenous antibiotics. The doctors thought she would be home in a couple of days.

The pneumonia started to clear, but she remained confused. "Oh, is Jenny getting married?" my mother asked my father. The doctors did not know why she was confused, so they did a CT scan of her brain. While we waited anxiously for the test results, David and I got through the last of the wedding plans. We ordered tiny boxes of chocolates, tied with gold ribbon, as favours for our guests. We studied the DJ's catalogue, negotiating the music playlist as if the future of an oil-rich republic were at stake.

We felt some relief. The scan did not show cancer in my mother's brain. But the tests continued. Then, just one week before the wedding, my father called, his voice leaden with exhaustion. New test results had shown that cancer had invaded the fluid around my mother's brain. Still, he spoke about taking her to the wedding in a wheelchair. I dug my nails into my palm to keep from sobbing into the receiver. "Knowing what she is like as a person," I said, "I don't think she will want to be there if she isn't herself."

We had all been running, I thought, but the cancer was faster. When it reached her brain, I knew she would never be the same. My mother would not be at my wedding. I believe I started grieving for her then. My mother's illness was so swift, and she was so private about it, that only a handful of people knew she had cancer. She hadn't wanted us to tell people how sick she was. I finally told David's parents over the phone on Sunday, six days before the wedding, struggling to steady my voice. David sat next to me, his tall body slumped, tears streaming down his face. My future mother-in-law cried into the phone and said she would pray for a miracle.

On Monday, I flew to Toronto. I visited my mother in the cancer ward that evening. Her eyes brightened when I walked in. "Hi, honey," she said, her voice as strong and clear as ever.

I presented my engagement ring, recently purchased in Victoria, for inspection. I held her hand. "You've still got a good grip," I remarked, as the machines by her bedside squawked and hummed.

"That's nothing, kid," she said. It was a flicker, for a moment, of her familiar spirit.

When I leaned towards her she gently placed a hand on either side of my face, holding me there, her brown eyes taking me in.

Three days before the wedding, my mother was moved to palliative care, a quiet room overlooking a tree-lined garden. As part of the intake interview, a nurse asked her, "Kathryn, what is important to you?" The cancer had knotted her thoughts, and she couldn't think of what to say. My father eventually answered for her: the wedding.

I made final arrangements with the caterer, the cellist and the florist. Three days before the wedding, my father called from the hospital to say he was on his way home after his evening visit. On a whim, he handed the phone to my mother. "Hello, Jenny, Jen, Jenny," she said. Her chatter rolled and ebbed cheerfully, if not always coherently.

The next morning, two days before the wedding, the phone rang at 6:30 a.m. I could hear my father talking softly in his bedroom and knew immediately what it meant. "It's harder for us," I said after the call, embracing him. "But better for her." My mother had died in her sleep, just minutes earlier. I felt a shock, as if thrown into the ocean. Then I went numb.

We made many phone calls. Absurdly, the first was to a beauty salon. I cancelled pedicures and manicures for my sister and me. My father went to the funeral home. There would be a private viewing, family only, but no funeral, since we aren't churchgoers. A memorial service would be held in a few weeks.

In between answering phone calls from neighbours, the hospital and the estate lawyer, I sat at the dining-room table, making place cards for the reception. I wandered out on the deck. I looked at my mother's empty chair, still facing her garden, and cried.

Then a young woman called from the hospital. My mother's wedding ring had been set aside for safekeeping, she told me in a quavering voice. We could go and pick it up. I thanked her and quickly hung up before one of us burst into tears. I sat back down at the table, my breath coming in gasps.

It never occurred to us to cancel. We were all used to doing what my mother told us to, and weren't going to stop now. Besides, we all wanted the wedding to happen. Cancer had taken enough from us.

David flew in from Victoria the morning before our wedding. At 1:00 a.m., he appeared at my parents' doorstep. His face ashen, he wrapped his arms around me. We sat at the kitchen table, talking and drinking beer until 3:00 a.m., surrounded by a strange mix of get-well cards, sympathy cards and wedding gifts. I tried not to think. Mercifully, I managed to sleep.

For the viewing that afternoon—the day before the ceremony— my mother was wearing her wedding attire. It was a beautiful outfit, the suede jacket the colour of coffee and cream. "Too much lipstick," observed my sister, looking at my mother's bright apricot lips. We placed a copy of the wedding program in the casket. It had been her last big project. I touched her hand. "Goodbye, Mum."

My wedding day dawned overcast and windy, and the air pressure threatened to wedge a migraine into the side of my head. My sister and I met at a salon, where my hair was twisted and pinned to resemble a shining blonde loaf of Easter bread, crowned with a single coral orchid. I surveyed my salon-perfect makeup. "Too much lipstick," I thought. My nerves jangled like a charm bracelet.

Once at the gallery grounds, my sister and I scurried to a small cottage to relax before the ceremony. My best girlfriends were there, filling the space with chatter. Finally, my dad came to collect me, and we started our trek to the ceremony. I took my father's arm, straightened my back and remembered to smile. The cellist began to play, and my dad and I headed down the aisle. "Yea-ahh!" yelled my cousin's toddler, and laughter rippled around the room. Then I was at David's side.

My wedding dress seemed like a kind of sail, and I drifted through the evening, trying to focus on who was there rather than who was not. There were cocktails on the terrace and salmon and lamb shared at candlelit tables strewn with yellow petals.

I stepped up to the podium to give the first speech, a break in tradition. "Right now, I'm thinking what all brides do at this point," I began. "Would I do this all again if I knew how much work it was?" There was a collective release of breath, then laughter. "This is a mixed time for my family," I continued. I mentioned my mother's feelings about my marriage to David and the promise I had made to her.

"My mother worked very hard to make this wedding happen," I said, my voice steady and clear. I looked at the familiar faces in front of me and thought about how many of their lives had been changed by cancer. Still, there were no tears or long faces. We were there to celebrate the beginning of something. My father and I danced to "Trouble in the Fields," a country ballad about sticking together in tough times. Then everyone piled onto the dance floor. It was, I am told, a fantastic night.

The next few days were quieter. We opened wedding presents and wrote my mother's obituary. I thrashed through nights of bad dreams, grief seeping through my exhaustion and elation. Going ahead with the wedding wasn't something we did for my mother, I reflected. It was something we did for ourselves. Thinking of her just gave us the drive to see it through.

When it was time for David and me to fly back to Victoria, my dad and I realized only ten days had passed since my arrival. In those ten days my father had said goodbye to the love of his life and I was married to mine.

My father stood in the driveway waving goodbye, alone, and I turned my head so he wouldn't see my tears. Just six weeks earlier, I had set off to make the same trip. My mother had stood in the doorway, waving, her face filled with fierce love. She always hated to see me go.

JENNY MANZER was on a flight home to Victoria after a visit to Toronto, where she'd grown up. Over the previous ten days, she'd become both a grieving daughter and a newlywed wife. Her body buzzed with fatigue.

Instead of sleeping, she pulled out one of her reporter's notebooks and scrawled down the story of her wedding. If she didn't do it then, she never would.

She now knows that having the wedding without her mother was the easy part. The struggle is facing the everyday ache of just wanting to hear her mother's voice or to tell her all about her new grandson.

KATHLEEN BOYLE HATCHER

Shop/Talk

It was my aunt who took me shopping for my wedding dress. I grew up in New York City, and Auntie had been tutoring me in the fine points of bargain hunting since I was still young enough to duck under subway turnstiles.

You always start shopping at the back of the store, that's where the markdowns are. Don't just look in your size. Someone may have put something back in the wrong place. More likely, someone your size may have tried to hide something while she thought about whether to make the purchase. Only someone poorly instructed in the art of shopping could fail to realize that you never put anything you are remotely interested in down. Auntie would be there to pounce.

She knew the strengths of all the department stores, which big-name manufacturers were behind which store labels and where to buy the best knock-offs.

We usually started our forays into the heart of the city with the earliest commuters. If we were hitting the garment district, we would need to be early. It didn't faze Auntie that we were retail customers. She would knock on the glass door or ring the buzzer and wait smiling and wide-eyed for the door to be unlocked. If she was waved away by someone who pointed to the sign reading WHOLESALE ONLY, she would ratchet up her Irish charm, bat her eyes and put on her coy "Surely that sign doesn't mean me" face. If that wasn't enough, she would point to something in the window or on a rolling rack, clasp her hands in supplication and hold her heart as if to go into a swoon. We'd usually get buzzed in.

Once inside, we would fan out, flipping through the racks for colour and size. There was no trying on. No returns. Prices were revealed on a "need to know" basis. Auntie always made sure to remark on the lovely colour or the interesting collar, but then would turn and say something vague like, "Now that I see it up close, it's not exactly what I was looking for." The wholesaler would answer her opening volley with some comment about it being the latest style, how he wished he could reveal which upscale store had placed an order for this very dress, how nicely finished it was on the inside. Auntie would nod and agree that the garment in question was obviously top quality, but she was really looking for something almost exactly like this, except with pockets. Or without them.

Auntie knew she had the advantage. If the first customer of the morning walked out, it was not an auspicious start to the business day. Perhaps if there was some movement on the price, the vendor suggested, Auntie might be able to overlook the pockets, or the lack of them. Maybe, Auntie would say. It all depends.

A few minutes later, negotiations would be complete. The dress would be folded up and put into a shopping bag Auntie always remembered to bring from home.

In the summer of 1975, I made the big jump from being the girl with the arrogant, unpopular boyfriend to the young woman with the fiancé everyone tried to like. I arrived home from a visit to Ontario with a diamond chip on my finger. It was the middle of July. I told the family that we planned to get married in August.

"Oh, good," my mother said. "That gives us a year to prepare."

"No, Mom. This August. Next month."

My parents put on a good front and never tried to dissuade me from the hasty wedding. I'm sure the family thought there was a biological imperative.

Our motives were more mundane. That summer I had been "restructured" out of a junior-level corporate position and was job-hunting. My fiancé was a graduate student and needed to find a new roommate by September. It seemed like the perfect time to marry. Our wedding date was selected to jibe with the start of the new school year.

My mother described my engagement ring as "cute." Auntie held my hand and pretended to squint. She smiled and patted my cheek. "This is just about the size of the first ring Uncle Pete bought me. It was right after the war. I remember telling my father that Petey sold his car to buy it. Your grandfather asked if the car he sold had a motor or just push pedals."

My mother put her hand over her mouth to stifle a giggle; Uncle Pete rolled his eyes and was a good sport. It was an old story. My father sat grim-faced and silent. Auntie turned to my mother and said, "She needs a wedding dress, Anna, and we don't have much time." At that, my mother's face clouded. I was getting married, leaving home. It was going to happen all too soon.

It was no secret that my mother lacked the shopping moxie of her sister. She had a hard time with the snap decisions required of a truly talented bargain hunter. With the wedding deadline my intended and I had imposed, snap decisions had to be the order of the day. I could imagine my mother cracking under the stress, immobilized by racks of white dresses, sobbing into pools of organza. Instead, she said, "Catherine? Would you mind taking her? I think you'd be the better one."

I was an unusual bride in that I wasn't overly focused on what I was going to wear. An actual wedding in white with flowers and attendants seemed like something other people did. Older people. My main concern was to get through it without looking ridiculous.

Auntie wanted me to look terrific and not to pay a dollar more than necessary. We decided we would go into Manhattan and visit the bridal wholesalers, which were clustered along the same city block. As usual, we set out early. We picked a likely building, then followed someone pushing a rolling rack of wedding gowns into a freight elevator. We got off when he did and trailed him into a showroom.

"Excuse me! Excuse me! What are you people doing here? Who are you with? This is a wholesale business only. Out! Out!"

He was a small, stoop-shouldered man who didn't wait for answers. He took me by the elbow and propelled me towards the door. It happened so quickly even Auntie was flummoxed.

"This building is trade only! No retail! Here's the elevator." He pushed the button and barked once last time, "Out!"

We waited for the elevator until he was gone. Then we headed for the stairs.

We walked up a flight and Auntie opened the door to another floor of showrooms. The hallway was identical to the one below us—scuffed walls, dingy linoleum floors, exposed tubes of fluorescent lighting. The doors were all closed. Auntie shrugged and pressed the nearest buzzer.

Seconds later, a woman with painted eyebrows, jet black hair and too much face powder stood in the doorway. She sized us up immediately. "Sorry. Wholesale only." She started to close the door.

"Please," Auntie said. "My niece needs a wedding dress. She's getting married next month and ordering retail takes too much time. You know how long somebody has to wait. She doesn't have time to place an order through a store."

The woman at the door passed an appraising eye over my figure.

Auntie pressed on. "She's going ahead with a church wedding, but getting a dress on such short notice, that's a big problem. Don't you have anything we could look at?"

I looked up from my feet to glance at the woman's face. She was wavering.

"She's a model size," my aunt appealed. "An easy fit."

The woman hesitated, then waved us in. "Forget fit! It's right off the rack. Have a look at the samples. And it's cash only!"

Auntie nudged me and gave me a thumbs-up.

"I am *not* pregnant!" I hissed. "This is not a 'shotgun' wedding!"

"I know that," she said. "But she doesn't have to."

I stepped behind the rolling rack to try on dresses. I started with the plainest one in the selection. A single layer of organza floated over a plain taffeta-like skirt. A soft ruffle framed my face. There was no train, but the outer layer could be hooked up to the waistband to form a sort of bustle. A wisp of translucent organza was fashioned into a short jacket, which made the halter top almost demure. It was simple and, I thought, elegant. I tried on other dresses from the sample rack, but they all had lacy bits or pearls or sequins or balloon-like sleeves.

I bought the first dress. It was eighty dollars.

With that accomplished, we headed to a luncheonette for an early lunch. We slid into a red leatherette booth, immediately ordered tea with tuna sandwiches on toasted rye, extra mayo, pickles on the side. The white gown billowed in its plastic wrap on the seat beside me, the silent guest of honour.

Auntie beamed. Her mission was accomplished. I would look great on my wedding day, much better than if I had paid retail. I patted my dress, thinking that my high-speed performance in the bridal gown selection category must have earned me a notable achievement award.

"I bet it took you longer to shop for the perfect wedding dress," I gloated.

"Not exactly," she answered. "I never bought a wedding dress."

"What!"

"I borrowed the dress. My friend offered it. It was beautiful, and she was never going to wear it again. I would have been a fool to pass it up."

"And what about the bridesmaids' dresses?" My mother had been maid of honour.

"Saks Fifth Avenue. You know your mother. She likes the nice department stores. My dress was taken care of, and your mother and the other girls were thrilled with the dresses at Saks. They really were gorgeous."

She must have read my mind.

"We had an aunt who worked at Saks. She was an alterationist. We got a pretty good discount."

She nodded at my dress. "I remember my wedding day so clearly."

I stirred my tea. I had seen her wedding pictures. I hoped I would be as confident and radiant a bride as Auntie had been.

"I remember standing at the back of the church, listening to the organ play. My heart was pounding. The priest was standing at the altar rail and gave us the signal. I turned to my father and said, 'I've changed my mind. I'm not doing this.'

"Your grandfather said, 'Too late. We've paid for the hall, and I'll not be embarrassed in front of all these people.' Then he took my arm and said, 'You look so beautiful in that dress, how could it not turn out right?'"

I squirmed. I looked at the dress that had taken me a half-hour to decide on and wondered about the brief six-week engagement I had allowed myself. Everything seemed to be rolling along. Maybe I should be having doubts, or at least deep thoughts.

"I could never tell my mother that I almost got cold feet at the back of the church. It felt like it would be admitting to something shameful. It was just a moment when it all felt too much."

We sat for a minute, drinking our tea and watching the dress, as if it would comment.

"Your grandmother was lovely, but she got embarrassed so easily. She could never bring herself to talk about, uh, you know, sex. When I was about twelve, I started growing pointy little boobs. I hadn't started my period yet, so my mother decided she had to prepare me.

"'Catherine,' she said. 'Something will happen to you soon. Something that also happened to the Blessed Virgin Mary.'

"I didn't know what to think. Was I going to have a baby? Was I going to be assumed body and soul into heaven? Would I be able to touch wood and have roses appear? Your grandmother was so serious I thought I might be receiving some ability I could be canonized for. But instead she said, 'Every month you are going to bleed, and it's what you'll hear called "the Curse." But it even happened to the Blessed Mother, so how can it be a curse? There, now you know!'"

Auntie said, "Well, I knew at least as much about the monthly bleeding as she had just told me, but the connection to the

Blessed Virgin Mary, that was new. My head was spinning because, for a minute, I thought I was going to be able to perform miracles and, well, the Curse was a bit of a disappointment. I didn't know whether to laugh or cry. I could feel a sound coming up out of my throat, and I thought it might be a laugh, but with my mother you were *always* better off crying. So I cried.

"My mother patted my arm and said, 'There's a good girl. Now go tell your sister.'

"And I cried louder and said, 'No!'

"She held on to my arm and yelled, 'Anna! Come here! Catherine wants to speak with you!'

"'I do not!'

"'Get in there!' said your grandmother, and she pushed us into our bedroom and closed the door.

"I tried to get out, but she must have been holding the knob on the other side. I was throwing myself against the door and crying, and your mother didn't know what was going on. I figured Momma wouldn't let us out until I passed the story on to my sister, so I said, 'The Blessed Virgin Mary bleeds every month, and they talk about it as the Curse, but how can it be? This is going to happen to us; I don't know when. The end. That's all I know.'

"Your mother burst out laughing. She had heard some story going around about the Curse, but the version she heard didn't have the Blessed Virgin Mary in it. I was still crying and your mother was giggling, and when Momma heard laughing she let go of the doorknob, came in and swatted the two of us."

"No wonder you couldn't tell Grandma you were nervous at the back of the church!" I said.

She smiled. "You nervous?"

"Me? No. Remember, everyone thinks I'm pregnant anyway. It'll all be fine."

"Of course it will. How could it not be?"

I nodded. I could almost hear the echo of my grandfather's voice.

"You know how you were with this dress today? As soon as you found it, you could tell it was the right one. We could have looked at dresses all day, and you still would have liked that one. It was the same with Uncle Pete. He was the right man for me. I wasn't nervous about that part. It was just the spectacle of it all. It was that long walk down the aisle in a wedding gown."

We sat back and stared at the dress.

"You know what else your grandmother told me? When a woman whistles, it makes the Blessed Virgin Mary's nose bleed. It's probably not true, but never in a million years would I ever whistle."

"Auntie. It's not true."

She smiled, unconvinced, and rapped on the table. "Drink your tea. I want to have your veil bought before rush hour . . ."

KATHLEEN BOYLE HATCHER is an adult literacy worker, writer and quiltmaker who lives in Toronto. After twenty-eight years of marriage and three children, she is separated, happy and no longer concerned about whether she looks ridiculous. The dress looked great on her wedding day and now lives with her intended ex-husband in a box at the back of a closet. Auntie passed away after fifty-six years of marriage to Uncle Pete, who was indeed the right man.

PART THREE

Something Borrowed

Edeet Ravel

Waiting-Room Wedding with Veil

I never did understand the concept of marriage, let alone a public celebration of marriage. Someone might need to marry for technical reasons, but why would anyone impose a wedding party upon themselves? The idea has always seemed slightly embarrassing to me; after all, one is essentially announcing to the world that one is in love and having sex (or, in more restrictive circumstances, about to have sex) with a particular person. Why would I want anyone else to be part of so intimate and private an event? I imagine a Felliniesque scene: a troop of semi-strangers, decked out in lavish dresses and heavy makeup, crowding at the bedroom door, peering in.

And so, when I fell in love in what I considered to be a permanent and final way, I had no intention of marrying my true love. Yaron didn't care one way or another, but he agreed with me that marriage had nothing to do with the immutable fact that we would live together, bound by utter devotion, until death did us part. As a romantic gesture, however, Yaron did buy me an 18-karat gold ring.

It was a beautiful ring—not the standard gold band, but a thin, delicate polygon with thirty or so tiny sides. And it was, of course, a perfect fit: Yaron had memorized the shape of my fingers, along with the rest of me, and could have written a thesis on my various dimensions, all of which (being a somewhat visually impaired albino) he considered to be perfect.

An odd thing happened the night he gave me the ring. I was deliriously happy at the time, and continually amazed, for this was all very new for me. I'd had the usual school pals over the years, but what I'd always longed for was to be as close to some-one as it was possible to be. Now my dream had come true: no one could wish for a better or closer friend. I happily slid the ring on my finger; we went to see an Ingmar Bergman film at the Tel Aviv

Cinematheque; we ate at Mandy's; we fought about how rude Yaron was to the rude waiter; we made up; we did the things lovers do; we went to sleep. I woke up early the next morning and left in the usual mad rush for either my child-care job or classes in Jerusalem—I forget which. Once seated on the bus, I looked down at my hand to admire my beautiful ring—and it was gone! It could not have slipped off, for it was a snug fit. Nor had I taken it off.

I was distressed and mystified. But that evening I found the ring neatly stored under my pillow. Apparently I had removed the ring from my finger while I was sleeping and placed it there. This unconscious move was unusual for me. I had been told more than once that I was the sort of person who was half-awake when asleep and half-asleep when awake. During the night I usually woke to turn, woke when Yaron turned, fumbled with a pen in the dark to write down dreams I'd had, decided to put less parsley and more onions in the soup, and was generally at my most lucid. A few nights earlier, I'd sat up and said triumphantly, from within a dream, "I don't know who I am and where I am." Yaron, who was reading in bed, had offered to bring me my ID, and I'd smiled, aware that I was both dreaming and awake.

But I'd pulled the ring off my finger without knowing it.

At first I was worried: did this mean that on some level I didn't want to be with Yaron? Perhaps I associated the ring, an ancient symbol of bondage, with the loss of freedom, and I wanted to maintain a distinct identity. This seemed impossible, given the depths of my undying love; I identified with the legendary woman who disguises herself as her condemned husband so she can die in his stead. When I returned home from work or school, our reunion resembled an audition for the Bolshoi's *Romeo and Juliet*.

Almost at once a more benign interpretation came to me: I wanted to keep our marriage secure, take good care of what we had together, protect our passion. For a year or two, when I was in elementary school, I had slept with a little bible scroll under my pillow. We'd been given the miniature scrolls at the Jewish school I attended in Montreal, and I loved the crinkly gold paper wrapping, the ancient Hebrew letters, the mysterious, poetic text. Hiding the ring was no doubt a similar gesture: I'd transformed it into an amulet or lucky charm, intended to ward off danger and sorrow.

I did not in those days think very much beyond the due date of my next term paper. The future, I blithely assumed, would look after itself. This approach meant that I did not give much thought to the army. I was an Israeli citizen, even though I had grown up in Canada. Theoretically, I was obliged to enter the army as soon as I stepped on Israeli soil, but I'd been given a deferral so that I could study first. Had I been required to go straight to the army, I would have stayed in Canada. The immigration board knew this, and they wanted me back.

I'd been called to the induction centre twice since I'd arrived in Israel, but I remained in denial. Perhaps I imagined that the army wouldn't really want me, that they would be deterred by my many deficiencies. I had failed the psychometric exam (short version): I had no idea what shape came next, the black half-circle, the white triangle or the grey square. By the time the buzzer sounded, I had answered six of the fifty questions, thereby exhibiting an IQ of about 40. I had also scored poorly in my Hebrew exam. I was able to say, in Hebrew, "The shower's broken again, but there's no water on Thursdays in any case" but was at a complete loss when it came to "Launch missiles in order to strike military and security targets." Without my contact lenses I could more or less tell that I was inside a building rather than in the middle of a forest, but the uniformed person facing me could have been a large stuffed elephant and I'd be none the wiser. When I placed my wet foot on a piece of cardboard, I was found to have only the barest of arches, and my attempts to make a small metal ball rise by blowing into a tube led to much mirth in the room. The soldier administering the test kept asking me whether I had understood the instructions: I had to exhale hard, as hard as I could. "I *am* exhaling as hard as I can," I insisted. "Try again," she said. I huffed and puffed, but the little metal ball remained decidedly inert.

There were less tangible drawbacks as well. I had attended protest demonstrations, and when the university had held open-ballot elections (our ID numbers were recorded on the envelopes), I'd voted for the most radical party on the list— the one in favour of an end to the Occupation and the creation of a Palestinian state.

None of this made any impression on the army. I was deemed fit to serve. It didn't matter if I was slow or weak or reluctant; there were plenty of jobs that required only minimal skills. I could stare at a dot on a screen, make coffee for the officers, maybe even type documents in English. This was only a few years after the October War of 1973; over 2,500 Israeli soldiers had been killed in that pointless war, and thousands more were wounded. The army was desperate, and even men with the lowest profile, "21," which indicated severe mental or physical handicaps, were called back for reassessment, to see whether there was any way to raise their profile to "34" and give them some sort of job. We knew this reassessment was going on because Yaron had a "21" profile: albinos were automatically excluded from conscription. Now even he was called up, and it was only because the examining doctor was a music lover that he didn't raise Yaron's profile to "34." He wanted to attend Yaron's next performance of Bach's D Minor Piano Concerto.

Had I grown up in Israel, I would probably have gone to the army, though I doubt I would have lasted long. I was sensitive; if people yelled at me, I cried. I was also stubborn and independent, and couldn't handle being bullied. With the passion of youth, I rejected all authoritarian structures and was convinced that the seeds of fascism were everywhere, even in the insulting comments that Professor D. scribbled on student essays—in red ink. As for the rigours of boot camp, I was so clumsy and unathletic that most sports terrified me, and I ducked if someone threw a beach ball my way. I would have had a nervous breakdown within days.

Additional obstacles now presented themselves: I was an outsider who had grown up in Montreal; I would be three years older than the other conscripts; my Hebrew was far from fluent; and I had not had the ongoing psychological indoctrination and physical training that begins at nursery school in Israel and that would have prepared the other girls for the duress of army life. I wanted to continue my studies and do an M.A. And finally, I lacked faith in the army, or rather, in the government. I was, like most Israelis in the seventies, remarkably unaware of what was going on in the Occupied Territories. But I was part of a subculture that religiously read and passed on the book *Peace, Peace, and There Is No Peace.* We distrusted basic government policies, we were uncomfortable in principle with nationalistic fervour, and we were, in a sense, conscientious objectors, for we were certain that the Occupation spelled disaster for everyone.

And so, when the call to join the Israeli army arrived in our mailbox just before exams, I did not consider accepting. "I can say I'm mentally unfit," I suggested, but Yaron said I didn't have a chance against a team of psychologists: I was far too sane and far too easily intimidated. The situation has changed, but in those days very few people succeeded in avoiding conscription on grounds of emotional instability; you had to begin training and then visibly and convincingly break down before you were deemed unfit—and back then, even threats of suicide could go unheeded, sometimes with dire consequences. Nor would I be able to claim that I was religious—they checked up. There was only one way to avoid the army: we would have to marry, for married women were exempt from service. This solution was fine with me. It would be as meaningless to have a piece of paper saying we were joined together in the eyes of the world as it would be not to have it.

I am often asked whether *Ten Thousand Lovers* is autobiographical. This is usually an indirect way of asking me whether there really was such a person as Ami and is it possible to see a photo? One student from Berkeley wanted to visit his grave.

Ami is fictional, but many of the events in *Ten Thousand Lovers* really did take place as I describe them, and the wedding, apart from the fact that I wasn't pregnant, is one of them. There are no civil marriages in Israel, and the only way Jews can marry is through the rabbinate. Yaron was not at all happy about being forced to undergo a religious wedding, but I didn't mind. I was accustomed to a religious environment, since the school I'd attended in Montreal had crept ideologically over the years from Vague to Conservative to Orthodox. The ritual was so random in my eyes that it could have been a Buddhist ceremony for all I cared. But most secular Jewish Israelis had a less tolerant outlook, for the religious parties controlled other aspects of daily life, such as transportation on Saturdays, and their power was resented. I was always amused, the day before Passover, to see Israelis defiantly loading their wagons with bread for their freezers, as none could be legally sold during the holiday.

In order to discourage people from opting for a free ceremony, the rabbinate conducted its freebies in the waiting room, in the presence of other couples who had arrived for their appointments. The service, when stripped of extraneous tradition, lasts 120 seconds from beginning to end. In the presence of ten (male) witnesses, and under a small canopy, Yaron would tell the rabbi how much money he'd give me if we divorced, he'd repeat nine words, he'd put a ring on my finger and—God willing—we'd be husband and wife.

The pre-marriage requirements were a little more demanding. I had to find a male friend of good standing (read: indisputably Jewish) who was willing to testify to my character (read: virginity) and confirm that I was single. There was a small snag, since Yaron and I had the same address, but the rabbis quietly solved the problem by inventing a different apartment number for me. I also needed a letter from an Orthodox rabbi in Montreal who could verify that I was Jewish, and I had to pass an interview on the same subject. The rabbis were disconcerted when I informed them that my mother's father was called Julius—not a Jewish name. I knew he also had a Hebrew name, but I was feeling a little rebellious and insisted on Julius. However, my grandmother's name, Shifra, reassured them, and I got through, since it's the status of the mother, not the father, that determines whether a child is Jewish.

I then had to book a date for the wedding, which would be based on when I was expecting my next period. According to Jewish law, I could not be married while in a state of impurity, but as it turned out, this was only a formality—I suppose because wedding halls have to be booked way in advance, as do caterers and musicians. In my case, I needed to get married on June 20 because of my exam schedule. I told the tiny, nervous woman who was in charge of bookings that I was due in a week and that I had a twenty-eight day cycle, but math was never my strong suit, and the calculation didn't work out. The woman told me to go out to the waiting room and "reconsider." I went out, watched the sad wedding I describe in *Ten Thousand Lovers*, and returned with another unsatisfactory answer. The woman gave up and said, "Do you think you're due in ten days?" "Yes, yes, that's right," I replied quickly. Unlike my character Lily, I was polite and well behaved.

The woman passed me a worn newspaper article sheathed in plastic, which informed readers that according to recent studies, having sex when you had your period could lead to cervical cancer. I gave a noncommittal nod. The seculars were a hard sell, and the woman knew it, but at least she'd tried. I felt bad for her. I know how frustrating it is to be convinced that something is unadvisable, and know that people will go ahead and do it anyhow—like my attitude to fast food.

The last hurdle was the mikvah, or ritual immersion. If you married on a kibbutz, or had a large wedding, the absence of the blue ticket given to the bride-to-be as proof that she'd been to the mikvah could be overlooked. But it was made very clear to me that this would not be the case here. "No blue ticket, no wedding," I was told severely on more than one occasion. I assume they were insistent on this point because other secular couples had shown up for their weddings without the ticket.

I was squeamish about dunking in water that other women had been in, but Lutzi, Yaron's father's wife, told me there was a very clean mikvah in what was known as "the German synagogue." I also found out that if I wanted to be the first woman in the water, I had to arrive an hour early.

A round, cheerful woman in a stiff blonde wig was in charge of my mikvah. She was extremely pleasant; maybe she was hoping that if I had a good experience, I'd undergo a religious conversion and return voluntarily to purify myself each month. Or maybe she was just a cheerful, pleasant sort of person. The room she ushered me into was large and luxurious and, aside from the little pool in the corner, could have been an oversized bathroom at the Hilton hotel. I had imagined a large communal bath that was meant to be shared by several women, but this synagogue had small individual pools in separate rooms. The jovial woman (she reminded me a little of Mrs. Jennings in *Sense and Sensibility*) left, promising to return after I'd showered and combed my hair. In *Ten Thousand Lovers*, Lily blushes when the mikvah lady tells her to comb *all* her hair, *everywhere*, but I wasn't at all embarrassed. I found the injunction amusing and also intriguing—after all, this was an ancient custom, and though it may have had something to do with lice back in the first century, it also suggested a pragmatic attitude towards one's body that I had probably inherited. Of course, the woman knew I wasn't going to follow her instructions (seeing as I didn't have a comb), but she'd done her part. I had a lovely long shower—a luxury for me, because hot water was so expensive.

When the blonde woman returned, allowances were again made for the *apikorus*—the Jewish atheist or heretic—and the woman overlooked my inability to repeat the complicated prayer, which I mumbled unintelligibly. The dunking turned out to be more difficult than expected. I had to try again and again, since, apart from being unathletic, I'm water-phobic, and each time I came up for air I was informed that I had not dunked deep enough. But my problems were negligible next to those of the woman in the next room. She was a Holocaust survivor, and she was screaming hysterically in Yiddish, Hebrew and a language that may have been Polish, "Nazis, Nazis!" Several people were trying to calm her down. Being naked in front of strangers while dunking in water was deeply traumatic for her. I hope even more allowances were made for her.

The day before the wedding, Yaron's father appeared at our

door with two head coverings: Yaron's creased but still shiny bar mitzvah kippah, and a white veil for me, on loan from Lutzi. I needed something to cover my head, and like many secular women who were having only a waiting-room ceremony, I was planning to grab any old shmatte—handkerchief, table mat—that was lying around. Lutzi was scandalized, and though she did not usually like to share her things, she made an exception and generously lent me an authentic teichel made of delicate lace. I graciously accepted. Apart from the veil, I had to wear either a skirt or dress. I owned three summer skirts and an all-red dress my mother had unexpectedly sent me in the mail because it had stirred a childhood memory—there had been a talent show on Mount Royal in 1942, and beautiful fifteen-year-old Lillian Abramowitz had stood in the gazebo in a red hat, red dress and red shoes and sung "The Lady in Red." Her performance earned her first prize, and roused in my mother dreams of similar glory. I was, however, too fair to wear bright red, and my style was too low-key. I would have to go with a skirt.

I decided to wear the prettiest one. Why not? If I couldn't wear jeans, I might as well dress up, I might as well wear my favourite clothes. My best skirt was a silky forest green with tiny flowers and leaves. Even though I'm twenty pounds heavier now and would not be able to wear it, I wish I still had that skirt, for it was exceptionally beautiful. My prettiest top was a pink silk blouse that my friend Daniella, a wonderful artist, had made for me. She had cut and sewn the silk fabric and then painted Japanese-style branches and flowers on it. I still have this work of art, but the fabric was ruined shortly after the wedding by deodorant stains, and can no longer be worn.

We didn't invite anyone to the wedding. Two attending rabbis were available to act as witnesses/canopy holders, but we needed ten males. The janitors, whose job included fill-in witnessing,

162

would have to make up the remaining eight. There was a problem, however. The janitors were in the midst of a paint or plaster
job that would be ruined if it dried, and they were extremely
annoyed at being called down for a wedding. They protested
loudly, but to no avail, and as they stood there in their paint-
splattered overalls, they were jittery with impatience. Luckily for
them, the ceremony was short, though there was a slight holdup
when Yaron was asked what he would give me if we divorced.
"Nothing," he said, fuming. "Say anything," I whispered, but the
rabbis were horrified and shushed me; apparently religious law
forbids the bride from speaking during the ceremony. "Five
pounds," Yaron said. The rabbis muttered something, the ceremony proceeded, and as soon as it was over, the janitors ran back
upstairs with their pails.

The shtetl-like atmosphere of burlesque and improvisation
suited me perfectly. Clearly I wasn't the only one for whom this
ritual lacked solemnity. In fact, the rabbinate was essentially on
the same wavelength as us: the main thing was for us to be married. I was relieved that they hadn't tried to impose a sense of
sombre sanctity on us. Judaism, I have always felt, is far more
flexible than some of its practitioners would have us think.

We went upstairs to sign the marriage document. I didn't
notice until later that for the amount I was to be given in case of
divorce the rabbis had written "5,000" instead of "5," either to
protect me from my cruel, parsimonious husband, or for the sake
of religious propriety, or both. It didn't much matter. Inflation
was so high at the time that within months 5,000 pounds would
probably be worth as much as 5.

When we were through signing, one of the rabbis approached
Yaron and told him a tip was expected. Because the government
continually yielded to the financial demands of the religious parties, Yaron saw this as yet another attempt at extortion, and he

said, "Thanks for the information." I was shocked at his chutz-
pah but could not help being amused, and I used the line in *Ten
Thousand Lovers*.

The beautiful ring was part of the ceremony. I liked the Jewish
custom of wearing the marriage ring on the right hand rather than
the left, and I surprised the rabbis by knowing which finger (right
index) to extend. I treasured my ring as a symbol of our love, and
until recently, when it wasn't on the third finger of my right hand
it was in my night-table drawer. But last year, when my daughter
and I relocated to Guelph, the ring vanished mysteriously during
the move. I spent days turning the house upside down, trying to
find it. I finally had to accept that it was lost forever. My regret
surprised me—I am not usually attached to objects. I have since
discovered that the design of this ring was extremely unusual, and
the ring may well be irreplaceable.

In the end, it was a good thing we were married, as shortly
afterwards Yaron decided to escape the Israeli sun and pursue
his music career in Canada. Our marriage made his immigration
process far easier. Once again I was questioned. This time, however, I had to give a bored official an account of our courtship,
and Yaron had to give his version in a separate room. We both
felt like crime suspects, but the process was meant to ensure that
Yaron and I had married for love, and not so that Yaron could
qualify for Canadian citizenship.

Being married meant that when we parted ways we had to
divorce. Our divorce eight years later in Montreal was far more
emotional than our marriage. We entered the courtroom, did not
contest, and a few minutes later were free to go. We hugged in the
lobby, heartbroken. Yaron didn't want a child, I did, and so I left.
It was the right thing to do, but I would never be loved again as
I was loved then, and parting was agony. We both wore jeans.

EDEET RAVEL is a Canadian-Israeli mother, writer, house slave, ex-wife and ex–deep sleeper. She lives in Guelph, Ontario, with her nineteen-year-old daughter, Larissa. She has written an anti-war trilogy about the Israeli-Palestinian conflict that was met with enthusiasm by some, ire by others, and was applauded by the former head of the Israeli Mossad—although her mail is still being opened by the censor. Her first three Pauline novels, written for young adults and old parents, will be coming out this year with Raincoast Books.

A Small Ceremony

My first thought was to borrow a dress. After all, it was just a small ceremony with witnesses so we could start the immigration process for Clay. We weren't going to tell many people about this wedding; later, we'd have the *real* wedding, with friends and family from out of town.

The day I met Clay, I wasn't looking for a husband. I was looking for my running shoes, which I'd left on the front porch. He just happened to be across the street, watering his lawn. "Who is that handsome man?" I wondered, pulling on my shoes and walking my dog past his house. "Hello," he called out.

In that first meeting, I learned that he was from California and that he'd just bought the house across from mine as a second home, somewhere he could visit during the summer months. Over the next few days, we waved to one another and I slipped a potted sunflower on his porch. Just a housewarming greeting, I told myself.

In my forties, I was open to the idea of a serious relationship in a way that I hadn't been in my twenties or thirties. At that time, I was too independent, too focused on graduate studies and a career. Within weeks of meeting, Clay and I took a road trip to California and fell in love. Marriage was something we both wanted.

I didn't know what kind of wedding dress I would find in my friends' closets, but I hoped there might be one suitable for a casual oceanside wedding. I started with Sara, my friend of ten years.

"Sure," she said over the phone. "I've got a dress. It's not traditional, though."

"That's all right," I said, picturing her usual West Coast attire of capri pants and sandals. "I wasn't looking for a long train or anything."

"No train," she said. "Mid-calf length."

She didn't tell me the dress was red.

"No, not red," she said, shaking it out of its protective plastic. "It's shot silk—red threads one way, green threads the other."

She held it up to the front window, where the dress shimmered green in the light and burgundy in the shadows. Sara's parents had purchased the fabric on one of their trips to India, and she and her mother had sewn it into an elegant wedding dress. I stepped into the full skirt, while Sara fastened it at the back. Her six-year-old son stared at me as I picked my way through Lego and helicopter parts to the full-length mirror in the hall.

I gazed at my reflection as Sara straightened the straps on my shoulders. I tried to think ballerina, even rose on tiptoe in my socks to see what a more elongated leg might achieve, but all I could see were scrawny arms and legs, my skin looking pale against the rich colours of the dress.

"It's a unique wedding dress," I said, choosing my words carefully.

167

"I wanted something I could wear again," explained Sara.

"And have you?"

"Not since Ryan was born," she sighed dreamily. "But once, on our anniversary, Mark and I got all dressed up." She stood behind me, scooping her dark hair into loose curls on top of her head. In that moment, I could see how the dress must have looked on her, the silk shimmering from red to green. I could imagine her long neck adorned with heavy jewellery—rubies in an antique gold setting. And then she stepped away from the mirror, and it was just me again.

"It's beautiful," I said, slipping the dress off my shoulders. "Just not what I had in mind."

A few days later, Clay and I met with the immigration lawyer and told him about our wedding plans—a small ceremony with a Justice of the Peace, maybe a quiet dinner with a few friends. We'd already told Clay's children in California that it would be just a small ceremony and they needn't fly to Victoria. It wasn't a good time for them to visit, two of them still in exams and the eldest already in his busy season as a firefighter with the forestry service. Next year, we promised to do something big at a time they could all come.

The lawyer suggested we do something more *this* year. Have a party, send out invitations, create a paper trail. We would need documentation for the application to make my American hus-band a permanent resident of Canada. "You'll need to hire a photographer," he said. "You'll want some wedding photos of the guests, and photos from any trips you've taken before and after the wedding."

"Trips?" I asked.

"You are going on a honeymoon?"

We looked at each other blankly. *A honeymoon?*

"I'll need a list of all the guests in attendance." He made it sound like there were hundreds.

"We weren't going to invite any guests," I said. "We weren't even going to tell anyone."

He shook his head. "You must tell everyone. How will it look if you keep it secret?"

Clay and I bumped up the guest list to twelve. The next day, I bought invitations. I didn't buy the formal wedding package, thick with envelopes and reply cards; instead, I chose a small blank card with violets on the front. I planned to hand-write each message, but Clay, worried that the lawyer might want something more professional, suggested a calligrapher. I found a woman in the Yellow Pages who agreed to meet me the next day.

I showed her the simple cards and the brief message I had written out. With a small silver ruler, she measured the card, jotted some notes and punched the keys on her calculator. "I charge by the letter," she said.

I looked around the room nervously. I wanted to tell her that I'd made a mistake, that this wedding didn't need fancy invitations. Maybe for the *next* wedding I'd engage her services. But she was already dipping her pen and showing me how our names would look: *Clay and Laurie invite you to our wedding day*—the final "y" trailing into a delicate vine.

She blew softly on the ink. "In my experience, it's best to have a few extra invitations on hand. You'll want one for a keepsake."

I nodded.

"How about envelopes? Do you want your friends' names on them?"

I handed her the guest list, and while she counted each letter, I thought of my friends, the ones with hyphenated names or different last names than their husbands. I tried not to think of them opening their invitations, smiling and tossing their envelopes in the trash. Instead, I looked at the freshly lettered page, perfect in its simplicity and elegance. "Yes," I said. "Their names on the envelopes, please."

With invitations going out in the mail, it was time to tell my family in Ontario. I started with my sister, Kate, in Toronto. Picking up the phone, I hesitated. For the first time, I wasn't sure how I was going to explain. It was no longer a secret wedding, nor a wedding with just a few witnesses. But I didn't expect my sister or any of my family to fly in. For them to come to Victoria, I would have wanted to give them so much more than this small ceremony with a buffet lunch.

"What's up?" asked Kate, detecting something in my voice.

"I'm getting married," I said.

She was the only member of my family to have met Clay. The previous summer, she'd flown to the Coast and we'd met for breakfast in Vancouver. It had meant a lot to me, my older sister flying out to meet the man I'd recently met from California. I had no doubts about him, and I wanted to make sure she didn't either. All I remember about that visit was Kate whispering in my ear as she hugged me goodbye, "I'm so happy for you."

Eight months later, she was not surprised to hear we were getting married. "But in two months?" The exasperation in her voice was apparent. "I don't know if I can get the time off."

I hurried to explain. "That's okay. It's not the real wedding. It's just a small wedding with witnesses."

"Witnesses?"

"The real wedding will be next summer."

"Are you saying vows?" she asked.

"Yes."

"Exchanging rings?"

"Yes."

"Going on a honeymoon?"

"A small honeymoon."

"Sounds like a real wedding to me."

I didn't know what to say.

"It's just that . . . I would like to be there," she said.

After hanging up the phone, I took a deep breath. If my sister was tough, I could only imagine what my mother would say. I went over the words in my head as I made the call, "Just a small ceremony, but next year . . ."

She was in the middle of making pastry. "Hi, hon," she said. "Wait a minute till I get my hands wiped." To my surprise she took the news of the small ceremony in stride. No tremor in her voice, like in Kate's. More like a hint of relief. "We'd like to come to this one," she said, "but your father's not in the best health. Maybe next summer he'll be feeling better."

"Yes, next summer—"

"Wait a minute, your father's yelling something in the background."

Then his voice came on the line. "Tell him he was lucky to find you. A woman with a good job and a house. Not like they come along every day."

"He knows, Dad."

As I drove to work the next morning, I passed a bridal boutique on Fort Street, an ivory gown in the window reminding me that I hadn't found a dress. I still didn't know what I was looking for. Those kinds of wedding dresses, the ones with hand-beading, A-line skirts and panels of lace, were for *real* weddings. I needed a dress, but not *the* dress.

"I bought my gown at Victoria's Secret," said a colleague.

"I thought they only made lingerie."

She laughed at my naïveté and invited me to come to her house after work. "I'll make us some martinis and you can try on the dress."

It was white lace and clung to my body like spandex. It was what my mother would have called a "number," as in, "That number looks a little tight on you." With my martini glass in one hand, I turned to get a better look at the back, to admire curves I hadn't known existed. I was pretty sure Clay would like this dress. I held out an imaginary bouquet to see what effect it would have.

"You'll need one of those push-up bras," suggested my colleague. "Perhaps a merry widow."

I had no idea what a merry widow was. The extent of my lingerie expertise was the teddy. I had one in black lace and one in white.

"And stilettos. White power pumps."

She opened a door to reveal one of those ceiling-to-floor shoe organizers, every slot filled with a different style. She withdrew a pair of white satin pumps with two-and-a-half-inch heels. "Try them on," she urged.

I wobbled over the smooth hardwood flooring.

"You'll get used to them after you've worn them for a while."

The ceremony was to take place on a rocky shore. I imagined teetering down the steep flight of wooden steps. "I'm not sure about the shoes. There's going to be rocks and driftwood."

"Maybe you should change the venue." My colleague poured herself another martini.

The beach where Clay and I planned to say our vows was directly across the street from a house we had just purchased in Fairfield, a funky part of Victoria with houses that dated back to the early 1900s. In the years ahead, we would be able to walk out our front porch, cross the street to the place where we married and watch the sun go down.

I slipped off the high heels. "My friend Paula got married in Keds," I told her.

"I couldn't imagine," she said, sipping her drink.

I wriggled out of the dress and handed it back to her. "I just don't think I can carry it off. Fabulous dress, though."

When they received their invitations in the mail, some of our friends expressed surprise: "You mean *this* May 10th?" But they thought the idea of saying vows beside the water was beautiful and that a small reception at our friends' house with champagne and cake was a good way to begin a life together.

Because my family couldn't come, they did the next best thing: they made a video. Assembled on the front lawn in front of the lilac bushes, they introduced themselves to the man I was marrying. "We're your typical dysfunctional family," said my father, "but we'd like to welcome you aboard." He forgot to introduce the grandchildren, so my brother went down the line, all of the four kids nervously fidgeting as he called their names. At the end, my sister-in-law and mother said a huge "Congratulations," pulling everyone together.

After watching the video, Clay rose to take the tape out. "Maybe everyone will be able to come out next summer."

I knew he was thinking of his kids. There had to be a way to get them all together to help us celebrate. But it wouldn't be easy. When Adam wasn't taking classes, he was working at his summer construction job. Caitlin was in water polo tournaments or teaching swimming classes. And Nic? Summer was fire season in California, and he rarely got time off.

"We'll find a way," I told him.

Six weeks before the wedding, I still didn't have a dress, and the thought of going into bridal shops filled me with dread. Then I got a call from a friend: "Heard you were looking for a dress?" She promised to drop it off at my house the next day.

I heard her car pull into my driveway and the sound of boots running up my front steps. She was always in a rush, and today was no exception. As I opened my front door, she pushed a bundle into my arms.

"It will have to be dry cleaned," she said over her shoulder. "Let me know how it works out."

I closed the front door and looked down at the heap in my hands. I shook out a short dress with layers of chiffon and a sleeveless silk bodice. I liked the playfulness of the style, the short skirt that came alive with the slightest movement. Eager to try it on, I pulled off my jeans and shirt, slipped the dress over my head and stood in front of the full-length mirror.

The princess transformation I had expected didn't happen. The dress hung off my body, several sizes too big. My feet in their socks became ridiculous. I looked like I was trying on someone else's dress. But still . . . I cinched the waist in the back. I tugged off my socks and slipped into a pair of heels. I twirled in front of the mirror. The layers of chiffon danced.

If only I were bigger. If only I had a bust to fill out the darts on the silk bodice. If only I had taken up rowing on Elk Lake, something I'd been meaning to do after admiring a colleague's broad shoulders. I found a hanger for the dress and hooked it to the back of the door. I couldn't remake my body in six weeks.

At the hairdresser's I asked for advice. "Debra, if you needed a dress—a really fancy dress—where would you go in Victoria?"

She held up two bottles of oil. "Relaxing rose petals or rejuvenating peppermint?"

"Rose petals."

"There's a couple good dressmakers in town." She poured a few drops of the essential oil into her palm and rubbed it into my scalp.

"Could they make a dress in six weeks?"

"You don't make it easy." She scribbled a name on the back of a card and handed it to me. "Iris Moon. She's got a website."

I'd never been to a dressmaker before, but after visiting the website and seeing photos of the beautiful gowns, I called for an appointment. Perhaps I could show Iris Moon the chiffon dress and have her make a similar design.

Iris stood about five feet high. A woman in her mid-fifties, she wore a shimmering silver wraparound skirt over black military boots. She had cleavage at ten in the morning. She ushered me into a room with full-length mirrors, rows of shoes and racks of dresses. Everywhere I looked were beautiful gowns in magenta, emerald and fuchsia.

"Grad dresses," she said. "I've got fittings all day." She nodded towards the dress I'd brought with me. "Let's see what you've got."

I held it out to her.

"Put it on while I get my measuring tape." She slipped out of the room.

I stepped into the dress and slid my bare feet into the pumps I'd brought. I straightened my shoulders.

Iris returned with her clipboard and a measuring tape around her neck. She took one look at me and said, "That dress looks like hell on you."

My shoulders sagged.

"But let's see what we can do." She took the square neckline and folded some of the material under, transforming it into a round neckline. "See how much softer?"

I nodded.

"You have good collarbones. Let's show them off."

In Iris's hands I felt like Audrey Hepburn in *My Fair Lady*. She pulled the silk bodice tighter, emphasizing my waistline. She couldn't make my bust any bigger, but she knew how to show off a neck and collarbones like nobody's business. Then she ran her hands over the chiffon skirt. "Feminine and pretty," she muttered, "but too short. You want a wedding dress, not baby-doll pajamas."

She sketched a design on the clipboard, showing me how she would make the skirt longer and have it brush the top of my knees in a way that was elegant but still playful. The dress would be two layers of chiffon over a satin slip. She led me into the fabric room,

175

where she ran her hands over bolts of cloth, snipping small samples of material and stapling them to the sketch: a cream chiffon and an ivory satin. "What do you think of this for the bodice?" She unrolled a bolt of silk embroidered with a delicate silver thread.

"Yes," I said. "That's prettier than the original."

She scoffed. "*Yours* will be an original."

Until that moment, I had pushed all thoughts of cost aside, but now I worried that I might not be able to afford these fine materials or Iris's unique design.

I watched her sketch the rest of the dress, drawing a row of tiny buttons down the back.

"Covered buttons," she said.

"Are they very expensive?"

She lifted her pencil. "How much do you want to spend?"

"On buttons?"

"On the dress."

I knew that this was the dress I wanted, not just for *this* wedding but for the next one. I was willing to pay the price. But how much? I thought about what my friend had spent on her dress and offered the same amount. "I can pay you $450."

She nodded. "That's a fair price."

I was relieved. The last thing I wanted to do was haggle.

She took a photocopy of the sketches she had made, then handed me the originals. "This is for you to take away and show your girlfriends. The next time I see you will be for a fitting."

I left just as a young girl was arriving with her father. I wondered which dress was hers, and what her father would think when he saw her wearing it. As I got into my car, I thought about my own father and how he wouldn't be at this first wedding. I wondered about the haste of our plans, but I pushed these thoughts away. They would see it all next summer, the dress just as beautiful a year from now.

When I arrived home, there was a message on my voice mail. "I'm coming for the wedding," announced a friend who had been in Korea for two years teaching English. "And to meet this man of yours." The guest list that had begun as two people had now grown to fifteen.

"Are you sure it's all right to add another?" I asked the friends who had volunteered their home for the reception.

"What's another bottle of champagne?" they said.

Then there were Clay's last-minute additions, such as a friend's father who had made it possible for him to visit Vancouver Island over the years. At seventeen, Clay had arrived on his doorstep, and this man took him in, giving him a job and a place to stay so he could spend the summer in Sooke rather than Los Angeles. "He's been like a father to me, and it just wouldn't be the same without him."

"It's a big wedding cake," our friends said. "We'll just rent a few more plates and forks."

People around me, especially friends who had been through it before, tried to talk to me about the importance of the day. "It's your wedding," said Sara. "It's going to be something you'll never forget."

I was reluctant to say it out loud—to name any of the hope, the love, the tenderness I felt. I was afraid to say that any of this was important to me, because it might be taken away. I didn't have a clear idea of who would take it away or why—jealous gods, Murphy's Law, simple bad luck. I just didn't want to "tempt the fates," as my mother would say.

"Have you thought about flowers?" asked a friend whose mother owned a florist shop in Victoria.

I had always wanted lilacs on my wedding day. As a young girl I had imagined I would be married in Ontario, cutting flowers from the two old lilac trees that grew next to my parents' house.

"I was thinking of lilacs," I told her. I had planned on raiding my neighbour's bushes in the wee hours of the morning.

"I'll see what I can do," she said.

The day of my dress fitting, I was nervous. I flew by Iris's house without even seeing it and had to turn around in a neighbour's driveway. A black dog barked at me, showing his wolfish teeth. Inside the dressmaker's shop, I waited with two anxious teens, their hair swirled on top of their heads like meringue. Apparently today was their grad day, and also the day of their final fittings.

Iris was not to be seen, but I could hear her voice coming from the fitting room. "You've lost weight. I told you, no dieting. You've been living on pretzels by the look of you."

The girls in the waiting area looked guiltily at one another.

After a few minutes, Iris emerged with a gown wrapped in white plastic and a red-haired girl in tow.

"Hello," she greeted us. She did not look the least bit ruffled to find three customers in her small waiting room.

"This will not take a minute," she said to the girls as she took my arm and led me to the fitting room. My dress was hanging in front of a large mirror.

"Take your time," she said.

I drew out the new bra that Iris had instructed me to purchase. She had specifically said it was to have no seams and should have a bit of oomph—some extra lift and padding. I clasped it in placed, amazed at what a good bra could do. I pulled on nylons and laid out my new shoes, a pair of slingbacks with a low heel.

178

I took the dress down from where it hung, admiring the beautiful bodice. The delicate silver threads blossomed into yellow flowers, so pale you could hardly make them out. I was almost afraid to put it on, it was so lovely. Stepping into the dress, I kept my back to the mirror. I didn't want to see it until everything was in place. Iris glided into the room to help me with the buttons. I looked in her eyes and saw that she was pleased. Then I turned around. It was everything I had hoped for—feminine, sexy and elegant. I twirled in front of the mirror.

"I'm getting married," I said, as if realizing it for the first time.

"I hope so," said Iris, smiling at me. "That's a wedding dress you're wearing."

Two days before the ceremony, the guest list had grown to twenty. My dress was hanging in the closet beside Clay's new suit, and we were just slipping into bed when the phone rang. It was my sister.

"I've sent you a package," Kate said.

"What time is it there?" I asked, thinking it must be about 2:00 a.m. in Toronto.

"It's late," she said, "but never mind. I've sent you and Clay a wedding present, and it's on your porch."

"It's on the porch now?" We'd been at home all evening and I hadn't heard anything being delivered.

"It's there," she said.

"I'll get Clay to look."

"No, you have to look."

I switched on the light, shoved my feet into some slippers and headed for the door, still talking to Kate and wondering what she had sent us.

When I opened the door, she was standing on the porch with her cellphone in one hand and a huge wrapped package at her feet. "Well, did you think I was going to miss my own sister's wedding?" she asked.

Her arrival was more than I had hoped for. In fact, everything was more than I had hoped for. When I told the hosts of the reception that my sister had flown in from Ontario, they said, "What's one more?"

On the morning of the wedding, my friend delivered a bouquet of white and purple blossoms tied with a silk ribbon. The card read, *I know it's not the same as lilacs from your parents' trees, but these are from my garden, well . . . the purple ones. The white ones are from my mother's.*

At the ceremony, Clay and I stood with our backs to the ocean and our faces to all the friends who had come to wish us well. In our hearts we held the ones who couldn't be there, especially Clay's three children. As my sister took her place against the railing, I thought how in spite of all our attempts to keep the wedding a prologue to the main event, we failed. This was the wedding, the *real* wedding. With the sun on our faces and the air scented with lilac, we began to say our vows.

On the evening of our first anniversary, Clay and I walked across the street to the beach where we were married. We toasted our year together and watched the sky turn a vibrant red.

"Do you think we need to tell anyone there isn't going to be a *real* wedding?" I asked, breaking the silence.

He looked at me in surprise, as if the idea of another wedding had never occurred to him.

LAURIE ELMQUIST has had short stories, memoirs and poetry published in literary journals and anthologies. She holds an M.A. in English literature and creative writing from the University of Windsor, and lives in Victoria, British Columbia, where she teaches creative writing and literature at Camosun College. She lives across from the spot where she and her husband married, and often walks along the rocky shore.

Mary T. Malone

Bride of Christ, Bride of Mike

The aroma of mothballs wafted around the chapel of the mother house as the six brides walked as solemnly as they could up the aisle, marking their steps carefully to the background music of Handel's Largo. It was important to concentrate on walking, on keeping our eyes fixed somewhere between our feet and the shoulders of the one in front, because otherwise the temptation would have been too great. "Do not look out for your family," we had been warned. "It will destroy your concentration on the real meaning of this day." Of course, that was the crux of the day. What was the real meaning of what we six were doing, dressed as brides in borrowed finery? I did look for my mother's hat, and having located it, I felt strong enough to continue my mothball-scented way up the aisle with some greater degree of courage.

We were three English and three Irish young women, all around eighteen years of age, walking to the altar, dressed as brides of the "world," to assume the habit of a bride of Christ. Our progress up the aisle was punctuated by sobs from the group of relatives. This was quite disconcerting because, having lived for the past six months in the cocoon of the novitiate, I assumed that everyone would feel the same way about what I was doing. Not that I quite knew what I felt, except that this was something I had to do. My motivations at the time were a mixture of the idealistic "giving everything up for God" and a much more psychologically confused sense that in order to make it through life I needed a sheltered environment. However, if I had actually seen my mother's tears, I am sure I would have abandoned the whole enterprise. At the back of my head was the story of the young woman, similar to us in every way, who had walked up the aisle as we were now doing, but when she reached the sanctuary, she turned around with the same solemn step and hands joined reverently, and walked down the other aisle, out the door, down the steps and across the garden towards the cliffs that bordered the novitiate garden. In my head I saw her still making her stately walk endlessly across the world. In reality, I gather that she married very happily and had a large family.

What had brought me to this solemn ceremony in beautiful Kent, on the southeast coast of England, on this July day in 1957, dressed in someone else's slightly stained and much-used moth-balled wedding dress? This particular ceremony marked the end of the six-month period of what was called the "postulancy." It was designed as a period where, theoretically, I tried out the religious community by living a diluted version of religious life. Meanwhile, they kept a watchful eye on me and my often ham-fisted attempts to act like a nun. The reception ceremony in the bridal dresses signalled my entry into the two-year period of novitiate training, a move to my new living quarters in the Novitiate House and a much more intensive formation period.

Back in 1957, the fact that this formation had not changed much from that offered by Hildegarde of Bingen to her novices in the twelfth century was not as easily apparent. From the perspective of 2006, it is almost impossible to re-enter that world in my imagination. My attempts usually end in tears: such life-altering decisions made with so little guidance.

I had left my home in Ballycanew, on the southeast coast of Ireland, on a dreadful January day in 1957. The fact that this was completely my choice, combined with my religious motivation, did not diminish the human emotion of the day. For all intents and purposes, I was severing all ties with my family and friends, and I did not expect to ever see them again.

I was eighteen, the third child and eldest girl in a family of eight. I had been a relatively pious child in a world where our whole life was absorbed, almost unconsciously, into the ethos of the Irish Catholic Church. Being a pious child was at that time similar to being what might be called a "bookish" child today. But there were very few books around, and all of us had read the six-volume set of the *Cassell's Book of Knowledge* a dozen times over. My mother's most frequent admonition to us, as small children, was "Go down the fields and play." It was a gentle, ordered, dependable childhood in which I, as eldest daughter, had to assume a certain amount of responsibility for the care of my younger siblings while my mother tended to my ailing but continuously working father. We prayed the rosary every night, with my eldest brother's ear glued to the radio in the corner to report to us children how the Top Twenty hit parade was doing. Our praying voices were raised and lowered as we sensed our parents' suspicions awakening. Food was plentiful and money was practically non-existent. Despite all my efforts to challenge this picture, I have had to come to the conclusion that I am the victim of a very happy childhood, without even a raised parental voice to signal some turbulence in the even tenor of our lives.

The turning point came for me when I won a scholarship to secondary school, which, of course, entailed leaving home to become a boarder in an all-girls school about twenty-five miles away. This turned out to be, in retrospect, one of the most important transitional moments of my life. Ties were broken definitively, not only with my parents, but also with my younger siblings and, in a most conclusive way, with life in a small Irish village. Of course, I returned for holidays, but now as one of the "ones who went away," an all-too-frequent experience in Ireland of the fifties.

Boarding school life was agreeably benign, with a huge emphasis on intellectual development, although sports, drama and music, both instrumental and choral, were not ignored. I sailed fairly unreflectively through the five years and was deemed to be headed for university, armed with a scholarship based on my final examinations. It was only at this juncture that I allowed the niggling notions of what was then called a "vocation" to surface. The idea of becoming a nun was not new to me; in some ways, I seemed to be ideal material: quiet, pious, academically successful and so appropriate for a teaching order of nuns. I had been seen as generous in helping the more academically challenged, or often just less interested, students with their studies. I was quietly popular, a model of punctuality, especially when it came to music practice, and usually stood academically at the head of my class.

I was astonished by my classmates' apparent clarity regarding their plans for the future, limited though they were at that time: teaching, nursing, clerical work, domestic science or "going into the family business." Their paths seemed clear. My path centred more on uncertainties, and I seemed to be consumed by a kind of inertia. I could not envisage myself where they were going—not at university, teacher's college or nursing school, and most certainly not in marriage. Once, when the local priest was visiting my mother, I heard him remark that, when I was old enough, he would provide money for my training as a teacher, and then I could provide an enduring teaching environment in the village for the foreseeable future. It was at a time when the long-standing village teachers had recently retired and a whole series of new and young teachers seemed to pass annually through the village school. Stability had gone, and I was seen as the one who would provide it. Something inside me balked at the idea.

So when I eventually told my mother that I thought I should be a nun, I seemed to be moving along the path of least resistance. In Ireland it was almost customary for one daughter to be a nun and one son to be a priest. I don't remember now whether I felt that "God was calling me," but no other option seemed to energize me sufficiently to the point of decision-making. Once decided, events proceeded with a predetermined pattern. There were three other young women from my class who had made the same decision, and towards the end of January 1957 we set out for Dún Laoghaire and the ferry for England. The final Christmas and the few weeks preceding my departure were shrouded in a kind of numbing sorrow. I went for a last jaunt alone on my bicycle around familiar haunts and forced myself to sing "Whenever I feel afraid, I whistle a happy tune" until finally I had to sit under a roadside hedge and just let the tears have their way. My mother and some older siblings travelled with me to the ferry, but I had to say goodbye to my ailing father at home, knowing I would never see him again. Nor did I. I did not, of course, expect to see the rest of my family again either, but somehow that did not seem so definitive. I was leaving home for God and did not expect to return. I did not know that families would be invited to the reception day six months later until a few days before it happened. And even then we were told that they were not invited every year to this event. It was all arbitrary and depended on the "Will of God."

Once the other girls and I were finally ensconced in our cabin on the ferry, a kind of wild giddiness overtook us, and we went around the ship, giving away money. Eventually we were persuaded to try a last cigarette before disappearing from the "world." It was my first and last cigarette, smoked on my first ferry trip. I was deathly ill, and I descended happily into sea-sickness, as it was less painful than my jumble of emotions.

We were so exhausted after an overnight sea crossing, a seem-ingly interminable train journey to London, an overnight in a large and draughty convent, and finally the train ride to Broadstairs, in Kent, where we were to enter into our postulancy, that we experi-enced nothing but relief at our final arrival.

The six-month period of transition passed in a whirlwind of religious formation, manual work, prayer, regular recreation and endless fits of uncontrollable giggling, all within a veil of silence. Conversation was reserved to occasional brief interludes, and was always supervised by a senior nun. "Whirlwind" is perhaps not the right word, as our days were nothing if not ordered. We knew where we should be at all times. There were very few breaks in the routine. Occasionally, one of our number disappeared. No words of explanation were given, no goodbyes said and, on our side, no questions asked. Subsequent religious instructions would refer obliquely to God's choice and God's fidelity and human weakness and inconsistency, which, of course, served their purpose in directing our attention heavenward and increasing our earthly insecurity. During this period, there was no contact at all with our families and, in accordance with the religious zeitgeist, we were given to understand that family memories and the heartache of absence would be our greatest temptation and obstacle to prayer.

In many ways, I realized early on that prayer was what I had come for. After our arrival, we entered almost immediately into a thirty-day retreat, in the style of the Jesuit founder, Ignatius of Loyola. I revelled in this. I revelled in the opportunity for reflection, introspection, spiritual reading and the ancient prayer of the breviary. I grew to love the daily and seasonal liturgical round of prayer and ritual and, on Sunday afternoon breaks, I set myself to memorizing all the ancient Latin hymns. I felt I had come home to my real self. It was not that I felt I was becoming more holy or anything like that, but I felt I was attending to a part of my being that was close to my essence. In a strange twist of events, I lost my childhood piety and grew in the ability to be self-critical and more demanding of myself in terms of honesty and integrity. My theological questions accumulated without any immediate outlet, but at this stage I seemed content to know that I was in the right place, more or less, to have these concerns attended to.

And so, finally, on July 25, 1957, there I was, taking another momentous step on this journey. The wedding dresses had come as a bit of a surprise. We had been well prepared for the religious dimensions of the ceremony, but our minds had been diverted from the human elements. Who would come? When would we see them? What on earth would we talk about? I had a real concern about money, as I was not sure my family could afford the journey. On the evening before the ceremony, we gathered in the novitiate kitchen to be fitted into our dresses and to have our hair primped, and we collapsed in giggles again as we allowed ourselves to dream of what might have been.

I know nothing of the provenance of my dress, but it was probably a long-ago gift from some nun's sister. My own sisters-in-law eventually donated their wedding dresses to the mother house. The dresses were produced out of storage, apparently had never been washed and smelled of mothballs. While the dresses were not identical, they all had long sleeves and were fastened tightly up to the neck. We six "postulants" were left in the care of a woman we had never met before, an elderly unmarried sister of one of the nuns. The discipline of silence and lowered eyes was relaxed for the last time. She more or less pinned us into our dresses. She had brought curling tongs, which were left to heat on the range, and we could smell the frizz as our hair was burned into shape. We admired one another and then proceeded to fall about while we practised walking in unaccustomed white shoes. I do not think that any one of us felt like a bride of Christ or of anyone else. We were more like children dressing up for a party.

"Bride of Christ" had been a traditional liturgical expression since about the fourth century of the Christian era. I never met anyone in the convent who felt she was married to Christ. Certainly I never did, nor did I ever wish I felt that way. It was a ritualistic expression, designed, I think, to describe the elevated position of nuns vis-à-vis married women, as was the teaching of the Church for centuries. My own desires had more to do with joining a particular group of women, some of whom I had come to know and love as friends. It was amazing how well you could get to know someone while living side by side in almost total silence. I felt that, once I was in the habit, the real life and work of a nun could begin: to become "holy," to learn to pray, to look for God and to try to figure out what God's designs were for us.

As the ceremony progressed, we were each summoned in our bridal finery to make an act of commitment and receive our habits as novices. Bearing these in our arms, we filed out of the chapel again, this time, of necessity, facing the congregation and our families, and making unobtrusive contact where we could. I knew my father would not be there, but once I had met my mother's eyes, a huge contentment enveloped me.

The next stage is usually the one that grabs attention in movie versions of religious life. We were each taken in hand by a group of older sisters, our hair was shaved off completely (I learned later that my long reddish gold locks were given to my mother), and we were fitted with our habits and given our new names. I was to be Sister Mary Bernard from that day forward. As we filed back to our seats, I realized immediately that the religious habit was doing its work: we were now indistinguishable, except for differences of height. My habit, the habit of the Faithful Companions of Jesus, was a religious adaptation of the dress of the French widow of the lower aristocracy, and its style, length and degree of cover-up of the female body was dictated by Roman decree. Our vision was restricted by the headgear. Now there was no surreptitious glancing at relatives, because, in order to look, I would have had to turn my body completely around. Dressed in the habit, I felt confident in my choice of vocation and was ready to begin the rest of my life, first for two years as a novice, then for six years as a junior professed nun and finally as a fully professed member of the community.

Eventually, the joyful reunion with our families took place on the lawn of the convent grounds, with tables laid for lunch, and as I sat with my mother, aunt and eldest brother, I was able to relax into the total bliss of the moment. I was with my family again, I had accomplished something, and I was on my way towards the next part of my religious life, which would eventually include university and travel. I had imagined that life had stood still, but of course it had not. After they left, I found that it was the little details they had told me—about what had changed at home, like the new paint in the kitchen, the shuffle of bedrooms in my absence, my baby sister's first days at school, my mother's new hairdo, and the small gifts they had brought (all eventually to be taken away), the village gossip and the flowers in the garden—that remained with me.

One more brief visit was allowed the following day, and then our two-year novitiate period began. We would eventually profess

three vows: poverty, chastity and obedience. My mother remarked that, having seen the circumstances of my new life, the
beauty of the grounds and the convent buildings, she knew
exactly who in the family was living the vow of poverty, and it was
not her novice daughter. Chastity was almost irrelevant at that
stage of my development. It was obedience that proved to be the
most difficult vow for me, and the one that eventually led to my
departure from the religious life, seventeen years later.

I have always felt some pity for those who did not have the
privilege of living through the sixties, with its turmoil of civil
rights, feminism, peace activism, social justice, sexual liberation and, within the Catholic Church and far beyond its borders,
the watershed of the Second Vatican Council. I feel even more
blessed that I spent a good part of the sixties on a university
campus right in the middle of Toronto, where I had arrived in
1964. As the first member of my religious community to pursue
a doctoral program, I spent those years more or less on my own,
leaving the convent early in the morning and returning late at
night. Even before I had heard of feminism, I had been acutely
aware that, as a woman, I had no history. It was only natural,
then, that my studies focused on the history of women within
Christianity, and that pursuit remained at the centre of my personal and professional life. I lived those years in a continuous
buzz of excitement, delving into the misogynistic attitudes
towards women and, at the same time, discovering the constant
and brilliant ingenuity and downright disobedience of so many
women in the pursuit of their own personhood.

It now seems only natural that I left the religious community
in 1974, four years after I had graduated from the University of
Toronto, doctorate in hand. There was very little ill will on either
part, as I remember, but the few pieces of correspondence that
remain with me from that time reveal a blush-making arrogance

on my part as I try to point out to my former sisters the superiority of my choice. The realities of life beyond the convent soon brought me firmly back to earth. At the time I had no great agenda, most certainly no marriage agenda. I had intermingled freely with my student and eventually professorial colleagues on the campus, but sexual excitement was the furthest thing from my mind. I loved teaching and the buzz of university life. In the early seventies I had come across the marvellous book *Beyond Mere Obedience,* by Dorothee Soelle, in which she illustrates the immorality and sinfulness of misused obedience, especially in connection with the Shoah. Soelle points out the persistent attitude in the Roman Catholic tradition that it is wrong to question superiors. This allows people to act with a total lack of responsibility, displacing their accountability by saying they are "only following orders." I was never able to simply "obey orders" and always struggled with this. Her message was a balm to my soul, and the last strings of the vow of obedience were severed.

Despite the high excitement of the period, I felt myself to be more a bystander than a participant. My involvement seemed to be at one remove. I was at the periphery of several movements: religious life, liturgical life, the academic life as a feminist, where male dominance and male interests still predominated, and also the feminist movement, where religious feminists were treated with a great deal of suspicion. (In fact, marginalization was one of the choice stances of an active feminist, especially in a Christian sense). I realized that my life's journey as a female Christian was never going to be mainstream, except inasmuch as I could immerse myself in the historical flow of women's lives throughout Christianity. This entailed, first of all, learning about the lives of these women in Christian history, as I came to realize that women had dropped through the cracks of the story, not by accident but by design. I was on the edge of Church life. As a single woman, still universally defined by the negative title "unmarried woman," I was on the edge of social life. I was on the edge of academic life as one of very few women professors and the only woman on my college faculty. Feminist scholarship was, at the best of times, described as "lightweight," and at the worst by the phrase "bitchy, brittle, batty feminism." I was on the edge of theological life, never having studied theology—my work on Christian women predated the founding of the Toronto School of Theology and was done in a secular environment—yet here I was teaching on a theological faculty. The edge was where I felt at home.

It was, then, no small surprise to me when, quite out of the blue, I fell in love for the first and only time in my life.

Our first encounter was not promising. We met in the context of a church event at which I was a guest speaker and he was the chairman of the evening, and intensely sure of his chairmanship. I was firmly told where to sit, when to speak, the kind of contribution that was expected of me and when to finish. His tone seemed to convey that, since not much was expected of me, I should make the event as short and painless as possible. I was actually quite intrigued. As a feminist, I was, by then, accustomed to hostility and opposition, but I had not met such a level of low expectation before. I came to the conclusion that he was the most discourteous man I had ever met. In any event, I apparently exceeded all expectations. Later that evening we tried to arrange a first date, but it was two months before I was able to oblige. He was in a humbler mode, and I was in a state of cautious curiosity.

Over the next two years our lives became more and more intertwined, and we both knew that our future lay together. Mike was fifty-two and I was forty-two, and we each brought very different life stories to our married life. Mike was from Detroit, had served two stints in the U.S. army and had benefited from the educational rewards granted to army veterans. He married and had four sons. When we met, he had been divorced for about twelve years. I was a former nun, now teaching in a Roman Catholic seminary and with several fairly high-profile Catholic diocesan involvements.

I was quite willing to marry at once and accept whatever the ecclesiastical consequences were. Mike, however, was not willing to be responsible for my inevitable rejection by the Church establishment as a woman in what was called an "irregular" marriage. So he went down the peculiarly Roman Catholic path of marriage annulment. The whole process—rushed, we were informed, because of our "elderly" status—took more than two years. Eventually, the wedding ceremony took place very quietly on November 1, 1980, with a group of about twelve friends and relatives present.

Rather than a wedding dress, I wore a multi-purpose suit of what the saleswoman called "winter white" and olive green. So this event holds no wedding-dress-related memories or emotions for me. We found that we were not even remotely interested in the usual details of a wedding ceremony, and any of the normal accompaniments that appeared on the day were the gifts of friends. Our local parish priest contributed the cake, suitably decorated, to my amazement, to match the colours of my outfit. Out of the blue, a group of young men from the seminary *schola* arrived to provide the music, beautifully and memorably. Mike and I had written our own wedding ceremony, and the ritual was punctuated by the humorous attempts of the presiding priest to get a word in. The whole event was joyous and, like my previous bridal adventure, was accompanied by sobs, this time my husband's. Mike wept his way through the ceremony and was barely able to articulate the words of commitment. They were tears of joy and relief that the rather sordid process of annulment had come to a benign conclusion and we could face our life together in peace.

The two-year wait for the finalization of our marriage commitment had exhausted both of us, and every part of the actual wedding seemed more or less irrelevant, except as a necessary formal expression required by both civil and ecclesiastical authorities. Our attention was focused on our relationship and our growing love for each other. We had not even thought of wedding rings, and when two rings fell out of a cereal package one morning at breakfast, we had decided that these would suffice. Friends persuaded us that we owed ourselves something more, and we eventually bought the minimum requirement.

I realize now that every moment of this wedding ceremony and subsequent celebratory meal is coloured in my memory by the life we eventually shared together. A little over a month later, we went to Ireland to celebrate Christmas with my family. On the way home from midnight Mass, we noticed that Mike was limping. It was the beginning of the gangrene that led, over the next seven years, to three amputations, kidney failure and blindness. We often remembered Mike's joyful tears on our wedding day and saw that as the key evocative moment of our married life. Despite the progressive disabilities brought on by his long-standing diabetes, our life was full of joy. The knowledge that our time together was to be abbreviated led us to focus intently on each gifted moment we had together. Certainly there was an abundance of sorrow, but we both felt that we were living life with a fullness we had not known before. Every moment was significant, and we seemed to be alive in every fibre of our being. All through the hair-raising experiences of the amputations and the life-threatening crises that accompanied the surgeries, we grew closer. After Mike's kidneys failed, dialysis became necessary, a service I performed at home for Mike four times a day for three years. This brought a level of intimacy to our relationship far beyond any kind of sexual encounter.

Of necessity, I continued with my teaching, and we were

determined not to allow our relationship as husband and wife to deteriorate into that of nurse and patient. During the day, a succession of home care nurses looked after Mike, but from four o'clock till the next morning we cared for each other. Eventually, a night nurse was deemed necessary, and the proposed plan was for me to get some sleep in an adjoining room while she looked after Mike's needs. The plan lasted for one night. The absolute ludicrousness of Mike spending the last nights of his life in the presence of a stranger sent us both into paroxysms of laughter. So the nurse was confined to the adjoining room, and Mike and I slept together as we had done. Sometimes we just sang our favourite songs together. Mike had a liking for sentimental love songs, such as Roger Whittaker's "The Last Farewell": "For you are beautiful, and I have loved you dearly / More dearly than the spoken word can tell." We would lie back on the bed and sing this at the top of our voices in the middle of the night. The night nurse would stumble in to see if we had both gone mad. Towards the end, all I could do was hold him as the spasms of kidney failure seized his frail body.

I had never been close to someone near death before and found the whole experience much less frightening than I had imagined. Mike's four sons were with us for the last few days, and each took his turn saying farewell.

The end came very quietly, with a final whispered word of love. We each seemed to know instinctively that this astonishing moment in and out of time was about to occur. I sat there in silence for about an hour, then called my stepsons. When they arrived, we drank a toast to their father and my husband, and then the usual rituals of death ran their course.

The weekend before we got married, Mike and I, in an unwonted fit of piety, decided to go to a retreat centre to prepare for our married life. We were consigned to different floors of the sleeping quarters and informed that a director had been assigned to us for the following day. We were, they told us, the first engaged couple to come for such a retreat. The next morning, after giggling in a most un-retreat-like way through our silent breakfast, we went to meet our director, a rather elderly nun. Without any effort to find out who we were or what we thought we were doing, she proceeded to describe to me, in particular, what marriage was all about. She told me that nuns, brides of Christ, walk up the aisle to their beloved and, without hesitation, walk straight into the sanctuary and into the arms of Jesus. You, on the other hand, she told me, will walk up the aisle, hesitate at the gate of the sanctuary and then turn away from Jesus into the arms of a mere human. We both burst into uncontrollable laughter, apologized to the baffled nun and left the room and the building as fast as we could. It was the contrast between her spirituality and ours that caused the laughter. We were mature human beings, always open to the discovery of the mysterious interweaving of the divine and human in our lives. We marvelled continuously at the transforming power of love, and knew that nothing could shatter the wholeness and beauty we found in each other. And nothing did.

MARY T. MALONE retired and went home to Ireland in 1998 after thirty-four years spent in Canada teaching feminist theology and women's Christian history in academic institutions in the Toronto area. She is the author of several books, most recently the three-volume *Women and Christianity*. She lives in Wexford, where she continues to pick up the broken threads of memory and to write, garden, search, pray and enjoy family and friends. When asked to provide a photo of herself at her reception in 1957, she was unable to, as only one had been taken and it was buried with her father, who died 9 months after she left home. It was years before she was able to visit his grave. She now lives close by.

Sandra Campbell

What the Photographer Didn't See

On that snowy mid-January morning in 1965, I jumped when the doorbell rang. I was shivering in my underwear, upstairs in my bedroom. My sister, her brow deeply furrowed, stood before me in the blue silk dress she'd had made especially for this day. In her outstretched arms she held my wedding dress, which had been her wedding dress four years before. She was waiting for me to step in.

"Hurry," she said. "The photographer! Step in!" Her smile was tight, her voice tense and sharp. I wanted to alleviate her feeling of urgency; indeed, I longed to please her in all things. She was eight years older, the fount of all knowledge of how things *should* be, and I was the fumbler, the mumbler, the stumbler, who longed to be just like her. In that moment, I felt a sleepwalker with arms and legs bound in sandbags. Unable to rush, I turned away from her to look out my window. Despite the blowing snow,

I could make out the sign on the door of a navy Chevrolet parked on the street beneath my window: HORSDAL PHOTOGRAPHY STUDIO, 60 SPARKS STREET, OTTAWA.

I had been relieved when my sister offered to select a photographer. She'd done it once before and knew exactly what to do. Best of all, with Di in charge, we'd spare ourselves the prickly consequences of dislodging Mom from her perch, high above the toil and sweat of doing and deciding. Mom preferred to pass judgment after all was done. Di's selection had not taken long. As she explained, the portfolio of the photographer she chose was pretty good, and better still, he was intensely eager. He was a junior photographer in one of Ottawa's best studios and anxious to establish his worth. After she signed the contract, he told her that doing my wedding was a big break for him, and this pleased all of us.

Unable to deny the evidence, I turned back to my sister as if I'd been deaf to her words a moment earlier. "It really *is* the photographer." Together we listened to the stomp-stomping of his snowy boots in the vestibule, the gravelly voice of my mother as she directed him into the house and the clatter of his equipment in our large formal living room of creamy walls, chintz sofas and chairs and silk curtains.

"This is the most important day of your life." Di's voice filled the room. "Hurry! Step into your dress. We have to make everything just right."

Fifteen minutes later I felt the trembling of the photographer's hands as he arranged my veil and adjusted the angle of my shoulders. I wondered if he could see how my hands shook underneath my bouquet. I heard his voice quavering as he posed me, and I could offer no words of calm or comfort. My sister sat in a big stuffed chair, facing me, watching, cajoling, cheering. Suddenly everything changed. The photographer became absolutely still, and his eyes grew wide. I followed his gaze and was startled to see my barely clad brother, a cigarette in his hand, slouched against the living-room door frame. His arms were folded across his bare chest; his boxer shorts nearly touched his knees; his hair was a wild, dark circle of curls framing his unshaven face.

Di jumped up from her chair and flew towards him. "Hurry! Get dressed. You've got to be at the church in an hour!"

His arms fell to his sides, he straightened, and then he turned on his heel and headed up the stairs to his room. "Okay, okay, cool it!"

I'd wanted my brother to be an usher in spite of what the years had wrought between us. We were only a year apart in age, and we shared a bedroom for the first seven years of my life. Then, one day, my mother packed his clothes into a large suitcase, loaded it into the trunk of her car, dressed his scrawny eight-year-old body in a new grey flannel suit, white shirt and tie and drove him to a school five hundred miles away. After his departure, she explained that he had to leave because there was no accounting for his behaviour, and he was adopted, after all. His new, special school would provide all the right experts for his "learning difficulties." I loved my brother and missed him terribly. Besides a bedroom, I shared his friends and a passion for building forts and exploring woods and riverbanks, for stealing matches and starting fires. When he returned home on holidays, his pleas to be allowed to remain at home fell on my parents' deaf ears and twisted my stomach in knots. For the next six years, he was bumped from one school to another until, by the time he was fourteen, there was none left that would take him. After my parents' divorce, and at the time of my sister's wedding, he had settled back into our home, a brooding, dark, unpredictable presence.

Di didn't return to her chair. Instead she took my brother's place in the doorway and resumed her watching. The photographer moved silently about me, adjusting my shoulders, arms, dress ever so slightly. "Don't forget your smile," Di called out. "Remember, *he* is capturing your day. Forever."

Forever. Throughout the eight weeks of my precipitous engagement, my sister had said that word several times. Each time she did, I'd nod in agreement, then sicken as another wave of anxiety stalked my body. I feared that she, my wise, all-knowing star, might hear the sounding of the niggling narrative that I was unable to silence inside me: I'd marry until I divorced.

Forever. As a youngster I happily lay beside her on her bed and absorbed her musings: "If he notices me, if he likes me, and then if he loves me, and if I marry him—well then . . ." In her pause, I breathed in her belief that the way had been swept clear for a contentment that was beyond words, one that was forever. In that pause, I tumbled into her assumption that marriage was the end point of a woman's life, one that enabled her highest purpose, the care of husband and children. "Marriage is what every normal girl should aspire to," she said. I wasn't so sure, but I longed to be normal—just like her.

In 1961 she married the man who'd been her boyfriend since she was sixteen. She was twenty-three, which was considered a good-enough age for marriage, yet just on the cusp of running the risk of being left alone on the shelf, husbandless. She'd broken their engagement twice, then she'd finally relented. She said her decision was the result of simple logic: she could not live without him. To that she added the bottomless feeling of being needed, which gave meaning and purpose to life. Forever.

When I said yes to marriage I was eighteen, going on eighty, worn out and set adrift by loss. In the previous two years my closest friend had been killed by a drunk driver and then, a year later, my father's heart had stopped forever. He died when I was an ocean away, just beginning my studies at a Canadian school in Switzerland. I yearned to return home. "Not possible," my mother said. "You must not let him interrupt the best year of your life." My sister agreed. "It's all over. He didn't want a funeral." I didn't speak to my brother because Di said he'd disappeared, again. Then John, an older (than me) Canadian arrived at the house where I lodged and made my life bearable. He was studying languages. After my school year, he landed an exotic job in London, England. The plan was that, after a short stay in London, he'd be given a long posting in Paris. That's when he proposed. London sounded wonderful, Paris even better. I said yes.

When I told my sister, she whooped in joy. I longed to be able to join her. "You'll be needed," she said. I didn't tell her that being needed was a concept that never entered my head. I wanted only to belong. I wanted to join his family. His parents enjoyed robust good health (mine never did), laughed together, smiled and kissed whenever they reconnected after an absence. His mother never drank too much, and she cooked tasty dishes with exotic names like coq au vin and osso bucco. At his family's table, people talked about books, which they read in three languages, and travel and the wondrous idiosyncrasies of different cultures. At my family's table, we ate burnt sausage and creamed corn and cut people up with tongues as sharp as razors.

When I said yes, marriage was the only respectable way to run away from home. Respectability was paramount in my family, and extremely precarious. Dad, a prominent citizen, had shamed our family. Five years before he died, he left us for the woman next door at a time when divorce happened only in Hollywood and required an act of Parliament (and a five-year wait) to accomplish. Dad shunned Parliament and flew with his love to Mexico for a twenty-four-hour divorce. This too happened only in Hollywood. On their return, he and his new wife were hurled out of respectable society.

In our Ottawa, I'd observed that affairs often happened, but I was to be taught that marriage was sacrosanct. Shortly after Dad returned from his illicit honeymoon, the Anglican minister at my mother's church sat me down and explained solemnly that Dad had broken the moral law and was living in sin. If I visited or, even worse, if I stayed over at his new home, I'd be complicit in his transgression. Mom nodded emphatically, and when I did too, the minister beamed and clasped my hand and said he was glad I understood. My nod camouflaged my sudden awareness that I was heading straight to hell: I liked the woman my dad had married, had sat happily at her table, savoured her delicious meals, gobbled up the sweetness of her cookies and her welcome and wondered how she could make my Dad laugh and soften so. I fantasized a new family with her.

When I said yes to marriage, Mom was enjoying much acclaim as the stoical and innocent victim of more than one wayward man. While Dad's death had released her from the public shame of his deeds, she was left to contend with my brother, now a member of the Hells Angels. On my return from Switzerland, Mom's friends greeted me with clucks and sighs, saying that Mom was a stalwart woman and a darned good sport to boot, who didn't deserve such a son. When they remarked with raised eyebrows on the rumours of my "serious" boyfriend, I heard again Mom's constant refrain as I was growing up: "A man wants only one thing of a woman, and only a fool gives it before marriage." I could hardly add to her shame by becoming a sleazy daughter shacking up with a boyfriend. After I said yes, Mom pronounced that a sensible woman would never tell a man she loved him. "If you do, you'll lose all your power." I flushed and hid my face. I had said those words in moments of abandon.

Hand-me-downs were a tradition in my family, but not because we were short of cash. Frugality was a solid British Protestant virtue, and all that was British was highly esteemed. The story of the frugal Queen Victoria, who remade her wedding dress, with her own hands, into an evening dress, had been planted in both my sister and me when we were very young. As we grew, this story was embellished by an additional one: at the end of this most virtuous queen's life, at the time of her Silver Jubilee, when she was rich beyond belief from the spoils of Empire, she wore the ghost of this dress underneath her black gown. While my parents wouldn't consider hand-me-downs for themselves, they believed its practice crucial when it came to their children. A child quickly outgrew new clothes, and spending money on a child led to spoiling, and a spoiled child was a brat. As a youngster, I considered it a privilege to wear my sister's old clothes, and as an adult, given the fact that I had kept her on her pedestal, I was happy to continue the practice—we were the same size, or nearly so. To wear my sister's wedding dress made perfect sense.

My sister's dress was not entirely new—even for her. It was a hand-me-down of another sort, from Eaton's department store in Montreal. Its provenance was almost royal, as well, and most certainly British.

I had hoped to join my sister and Mom on their dress-shopping expedition to Montreal, but it happened on a school day and hooky was another sin that could not be countenanced. All day I counted the hours until their return, and when I heard the front door open, I ran to greet them, my eyes and ears sharpened to take in all the details of their day. I was surprised at how small Di seemed, almost slouched, while Mom was buzzing with excitement.

"A long, tedious day." She paused. My heart sank. "But then, a triumph!" Mom's voice rang throughout the house.

I followed them to the kitchen, where Mom poured a rye and water and Di dropped down into a chair at the kitchen table. I sat beside her. Mom stood in the middle of the room, her drink in one hand and a cigarette in the other.

"We tried on one dress after another—the saleslady had racks of them—mostly mediocre, I have to say, and the prices outrageous! Some in the hundreds and one, a tidy one thousand dollars, if you please! Not one caught our fancy, not really, wouldn't you say, Di?"

Di shrugged, then nodded. Then she pulled herself up. "Well, there was that one with a rosy hue."

"Ah yes, that one. But rose is hardly a suitable colour for a proper dress. And the price. Never forget that we can't predict what your father will agree to pay for."

I watched Di shrink down again.

"We took a lunch break, didn't we, Di, before beginning again. We'd narrowed the selection down some, but the prices, really, and for such mediocrity. Finally I'd had it. 'Enough is enough,' I said to the saleslady, who quickly disappeared from the dressing room. She looked quite bright when she reappeared and asked us to follow her. We ended up in the store basement, where another saleslady was waiting for us. She led us into a small change room, and hanging on the wall was this dress. Beautiful fabric, silk organza, the bodice without any ornamentation, but piped in satin, the waist cinched—perfect for Di's figure—and a voluminous skirt atop a generous crinoline, which was included in the price, of course."

The dress, a bit weary but only slightly limp, as Mom said, had once adorned a mannequin in the store's Sherbrooke Street window. It was "the" celebratory window, one that was framed by a luscious purple satin banner that proudly proclaimed the dress as Canada's first and only one hundred percent authentic reproduction of the wedding dress of HRH Princess Margaret for her marriage to her commoner-prince, Anthony Armstrong-Jones on May 2, 1960.

As Mom spoke, I easily imagined a crisp white dress with a billowing skirt because I'd watched the wedding on television, the first royal wedding ever broadcast. Di had roused me at the crack of dawn to watch on our small television.

Mom's face opened into a gleeful smile. "Guess how much?"

I shrugged. Di groaned, then covered her face with her hands. "69.95! And a near perfect fit!"

Di shook her head. "Mom, you promised you wouldn't . . ."

"Yes, yes, but honestly, that price. You can't look a gift horse in the mouth!"

When the phone rang, Mom disappeared into another room. Di's elbows slid out from under her, and her head dropped onto the tabletop, where it rested, face down. "Promise you won't tell. Please. It has to be a secret." Her voice was muffled.

"Of course, but I bet it's a pretty nice dress. I saw it on TV. You did too! Remember?"

Mom had handed over the cheque in that small basement change room, while a dressmaker pinned the dress as preparation for her minor adjustments. Later, Eaton's boxed the dress and sent it to our home. When the box arrived, Di took it directly to the cleaners without unpacking it. Weeks later, I was standing on the front steps when the cleaners delivered it to our home in a big white cotton bag. Mom received it exuberantly, then announced that the dress had to hang in her walk-in closet and no one was to peek. I followed her orders.

A few days before the wedding, I came home from school and heard my sister sobbing behind the closed door of her bedroom.

I called out to her and entered her room. The wedding dress lay fully exposed on her bed. "Sun streaks," she sobbed as she gathered up the dress, brought it to the window and pointed to long streaks of yellowing fabric that lined the folds of the ample skirt.

I tried to persuade her that the streaks were hardly noticeable; with any luck, her wedding day would be cloudy and then, for certain, no one would ever notice. When Mom joined us, she shrugged and said a few streaks might be the price of a gift horse. Besides, there was no time for an alternative. "What will be, will be."

Four years later, when I was still silently reeling from the fact that I'd said yes, Di caught me unawares. "We could fix the sun streaks," she said.

"Sun streaks?"

"My dress. We could try."

I nodded. I couldn't admit that the prospect of a wedding dress had not even entered my mind.

"We could find a good dressmaker who'd know exactly what to do. There's enough time." I nodded again and she began a round of phone calls to friends everywhere.

My sister chose Madame Trepanier because she had made her friend Sally's wedding dress, which Di said was fabulous. At 10:00 a.m. on a crisp November morning, we mounted in tandem the stairway of Madame's front porch, carrying the white cotton bag. On our drive to Madame's house, Di had said the dress was just as she remembered. A flood of memories burst open inside me: first, an almost cloudy June day; I softened the focus of my eyes as I gazed on the dress and made the sun streaks dissolve. Then a crowd of people, light and warm, laughing, embracing—my sister's friends from everywhere and my parents too, despite the seamy divorce—and the sun streaks vanished. Much later, without thought or will, I danced those sun streaks into oblivion after her bridesmaid Betsy hung the dress in my sister's bedroom, secure in its bag, and my sister and her new husband drove away in his sky blue Porsche. I danced with my brother, stiff and slow, but he was smiling his crooked half-smile all the while, and I melted with relief. Later I danced the samba with my dad, who'd acquiesced to Mom's demand that he leave his new wife at home. His body pulsed to the beat, his eyes sparkled as he taught me how to move my feet alongside his, and my cheeks ached with smiling. Then I jived with each of my sister's handsome male friends, and my fourteen-year-old self awakened in a way that was brand new.

I liked how Madame Trepanier's face seemed to glow as she ushered us into the front room of her home. Two headless, limbless mannequins stood in the far corner, one draped with a luscious purple satin that swept the floor, and the other stark naked. Bolts of silks, satins and velvets were arrayed neatly in open shelves along one wall; along the other wall, underneath a blazing side window, sat a long table for a sewing machine, spools of coloured thread, tissue paper, pencil drawings, a clipped Vogue photo of a black velvet evening dress. Madame unwrapped the dress, carried it to the window, turned on her work lamp, squinted her eyes, furrowed her brow. "Mmmm," she murmured, then, "*Ah, oui, oui.*"

Madame held the dress while I stepped into it for the first time, then she directed me to the window where she scrutinized it, her hand at her chin. She assured us that she could brew just the right concoction to mask the offending streaks and transform the fabric into a particular shade of off-white that would suit me well. I enjoyed how she dipped swatches of organza in various small baths and held them up to my face, and how she proposed other adjustments as well: the crinolines had to go— they were no longer in style—and as for the bodice, perhaps a large scoop at the neck to make the dress "*au courant.*"

Afterwards, I descended the stairway of her porch, feeling light and bright, and when I turned to my sister, her face matched my mood. "Sally called her a fabric artist," she said. "Too bad I didn't know about her before my wedding. But I'm glad we found her for you."

Di and I settled into her car and slowly began to pull away from the curb. Then a shout: "*Attend! Arrêt!*" Di looked in her rear-view mirror, then jammed on the brakes. In an instant, Madame Trepanier's face was at Di's window, her eyes wide, her fisted hand knocking on the glass. Di rolled down the window. Together we listened.

"Come. You must. 'Oles, many leetle 'oles." Madame was sputtering. "'Oles, but not an animal. Eeze deeferent. Like boolet, maybe, leetle boolet, so many." Madame's English dissipated completely, as did our French, as Di and I were flooded with the memory of a July night four years earlier.

"His BB gun!" I finally said. "The boxes in the basement, that steamy night." Di's face screwed up in anguish.

In silence we parked the car, followed Madame, then dropped down into her sofa. The dress hung in the corner of the room. Madame stood before it, her eyebrows barely rising, then her shoulders in a most elegant shrug as she held up its skirt. Her finger marked a trail of small holes in the skirt. She clucked quietly. "I'm afraid to say . . . two trails, front to back. Two rows of tiny tears. They could get larger if . . ." Together we nodded, then averted our eyes and sank deeper into the sofa.

The damage had been done weeks after the wedding, just after my sister and her husband returned from their honeymoon. Earlier that day, they had stripped Di's bedroom, packed all her clothes and wedding presents into large shipping boxes and moved them to the basement to await transportation to their new home in Hamilton. Then they jumped into their car and drove away. I stood in front of our house and waved goodbye, my heart flip-flopping in my chest like a fish in a pail. My brother suddenly appeared and stood, dark and brooding and silent, beside me. He didn't wave. I longed to find a word or two, a gesture, perhaps, to reconnect us, orphaned brother and sister, but in the next instant he vanished.

Later that muggy night I sat alone on our back steps, desperate for a breath of fresh air. Mom had escaped to a friend's cottage, and I'd not detected a trace of my brother since Di's departure. Suddenly, short, sharp sounds cracked the air. They came from inside the house, from the basement. In the next instant, I was on my bike, racing to my friend's house. I recognized those sounds, imagined my brother surrounded by the shipping boxes, his arm raised and that small gun in his tight hand. I didn't return home until later the next day, after I'd determined that he wasn't there. You could never predict for certain what target my brother might choose.

When Madame thrust her closed hand forward to within inches of our faces, we lurched backwards. "*Attention!* See these!" Madame opened her hand to reveal a pair of magnifying glasses with lenses as thick as the bottom of a Coke bottle. "With these I can mend. No one will ever know. I do this. I mend your dress. I promise you."

Co-conspirators, we all sighed together.

The photographer dropped to his knees in front of me, his hands reaching for the hem of my dress. Suddenly he stopped and looked up. "May I? Your skirt needs to be flounced."

"Yes, of course," I said. I remembered Madame's promise, yet I averted my eyes as the skirt ballooned out in front of me. Just then, I was suddenly aware of the scent of Aqua Velva. I looked to the doorway to see my brother, now crisp and clean, shining black and white in his rented tuxedo, standing beside my sister. He was almost smiling, as was Di.

"Lookin' good," he murmured, with the slightest nod in my direction.

"Thanks," I said. "Madame Trepanier."

"The fabric artist," my sister added.

My mother, bustling in her new outfit, burst in between my sister and brother. "Is my hat on straight?" she blurted, turning to my sister. Then, in a half-whisper, "Any lipstick on my teeth?"

The photographer, still on his knees, looked at them, quickly stood up and gestured for them to join me in the middle of the room. Methodically he placed his hands on each of our shoulders and guided us into an artful line of four. Before he returned to his camera, he reached for my brother's hand to place it on my back.

We stood still and silent, barely breathing, as the photographer stooped behind his camera. I felt the warmth of my brother's hand on my back. He was shaking from head to toe, a steady vibration, as was I. On my other side, my sister stood calm and steady as an ancient oak, and then my mother, out of touch. My family of four.

The photographer burst into a formal smile and broke the nervous silence. "A handsome family. Very fine!" He continued to smile as he clicked the camera several times. And just before we stepped apart from each other again, he said, "Yes! Absolutely perfect!"

SANDRA CAMPBELL's wedding dress vanished within a year of her wedding when her mother sold the family house and its contents. Her breakaway marriage offered her the gift of two vibrant children and seventeen years of hearth and adventure, laughter and tears. Now, as a Toronto writer (*www.gettingtonormal.com*), teacher and gardener, she engages in her most passionate pursuit: rooting beneath the surface of things to explore what it means to be alive and awake on this planet without doing too much damage.

PART FOUR

Something Blue . . .
or Peach . . .
or Striped . . .
or Floral . . .

MICHELE LANDSBERG

Unbearable Whiteness

It was silk, with a scoop neck, short sleeves and a pattern of abstract pink and green swirls, and it had been run up swiftly by a seamstress in time for the wedding. It was a pleasant dress, but I was not very attached to it—the whole idea of marriage being sharply questionable in my mind—so I can't pretend that I was grieved when my mother gave it away several years later, on the grounds that it wouldn't fit me anymore, anyway. Just slightly aggrieved, maybe, at the gentle, habitual reproof to my fluctuating weightiness.

The most important thing about the dress was that it wasn't white, it wasn't long and it had not a whisper of tradition clinging about it. Wedding traditions had nauseated me since, at about the age of twelve or thirteen, I became aware of the concept of virginity. I turned twelve in the early 1950s, a decade of sickening hypocrisy, repression and conformity. You could say that our culture back then, if it could be personified, was formed in the likeness of a middle-aged white guy with crumbs in his moustache, candies in his suit pocket and the soul of a molester. Sticky sentimentality with a bitter undertaste of sadism.

It's hard to understand now the desperate importance of virginity in the 1950s. A girl's only worth (unless she had unusually educated parents) was in the man she might marry, and no man would want "used goods." (This phrase was carelessly tossed off in common parlance, and no one ever flinched at the idea of girls as merchandise.) Everyone knew that "boys only want one thing," and it was our most compelling task to manipulate that male lust to attract and enthrall boyfriends, without ever "going too far" and sacrificing our jewel of maidenhood.

Of course, the horror of losing one's virginity was just one link in the chain of patriarchy. Fear of illegitimate pregnancy was another, and it clanked even more fearsomely. A missed period meant weeks of heart-in-mouth lonely terror, thoughts of suicide and, eventually, a real possibility of death from an illegal abortion. Mothers began emphasizing the dangers to their daughters even before puberty, through hints and blushing reminders.

Thanks to the complete avoidance of frank talk about sex during that era, these hints mostly fell into the void of incomprehension. Virginity, because it existed independently of (prior to?) sexuality, could be described more explicitly, especially by one's high school health teacher. It was not true, she assured us, that leaping the wooden horse during gym would cause us to tear our hymens. However, we should think twice about real horseback riding, and under no circumstances might we use a tampon until after we were married. (Of course, we would all be married.) The school distributed little booklets from the makers of Kotex that assured us of the same wisdom.

The hymen, I learned, was a little flap of tissue in the vagina. This was what our worth amounted to; this was what all the fuss was about; this was what the purity of the white wedding dress proudly symbolized: a little scrap of flesh in the vagina. Your husband would be your first owner, and he would turn against you in fury and revulsion if his penis didn't meet the resistance of that barrier of tissue on your first night together, when it would be his mysterious pleasure and prerogative to "deflower" you. All the bright poetry and hot idealism in your head, all the powerful meeting of souls that they said was love, all would be nothing compared to the intact hymen.

Who wouldn't be disgusted by the concept? I was disgusted. Furthermore, as a daily witness to the hopeless mismatch that was my parents' marriage, I knew that marriage itself was a trap and a tragedy and that I would strenuously avoid it.

I would like to pretend that these early anti-patriarchal insights were all my own, springing from my keen and solitary intellect long before the second wave of feminism came rolling in to shore. I've always claimed that my early, ardent adoption of the feminist creed was informed by my reading of Simone de Beauvoir, and this is true, as far as it goes. I was still in pigtails and dirndl skirts and riding my bike on my weekly rounds of three libraries (you could borrow only three books at a time) when, having heard somehow of *The Second Sex,* I found it in the card catalogue of the Central Library on St. George Street. The librarian adamantly refused to let me borrow it: I still had a children's card, and the book was not even on the open shelves. Luckily, the children's library was then adjacent to the adult branch, so I noticed one day that the student librarian was alone on duty at the adult desk. As innocently as possible, I filled out a request slip. I remember my heart racing as I handed over the little paper square and tried to look nonchalant as the librarian went to the stacks to retrieve the book. I still remember my experience of reading it, electrified by knowing at last that there was someone else in the world who thought as I did about the universal use of the male pronoun to embrace (and obliterate) the female existence. I was by turns shocked, galvanized and baffled by ideas that met my need for an explanation for the discrimination girls suffered, ideas that were also frightening and sometimes wildly beyond my grasp. But why was I so wide open, so whole-heartedly responsive to these ideas? Long ago I concluded that emotion precedes ideology. If you're born into over-dogginess, you find a natural home among the conservative overlords. If family and economic circumstances make you identify early on with the underdogs, you're ready-made for the embrace of the left.

I might have gone on helplessly being the pretty little girl with dotted Swiss pinafores and glossy curls who so pleased my dainty mother. I remember sitting at her feet while she chatted with visitors (tea, Hadassah, where to buy patterns to make a smocked dress) and idly played with my hair, sending shivers of joy down my spine. To win her approval, I might well have simpered down the primrosy path all the way to the wedding altar, virginity intact between my legs.

My father, however, saved me from that ridiculous fate. I was kindergarten-age when my mother made the rare mistake of leaving him to babysit one afternoon while she and my brother were out on some errand. Shortly before this portentous day, I had disgraced myself by one afternoon arriving late for kindergarten. The door was so heavy, and the handle so high, that struggle as I might, I couldn't get in. Finally, sobbing and exhausted and frightened at being so alone, I trudged home again. Along the way, I wet my pants. This was not the first or last time. My mother, a model of hygienic practice, had so instilled in me a loathing of public washroom germs that I would try to "hold it in" past the mortifying point of no return.

The pants-wetting was a matter of consternation in the family, and on this particular afternoon my father decided to do some spontaneous re-education. He was noted for his sense of humour.

Less noted, or perhaps noticed, was his streak of cruelty. He began by predicting that I would never stop wetting my pants. In fact, he said, warming to his theme and chuckling a little at the image, "You'll be walking down the aisle on your wedding day and you'll wet your pants. Hoo-ha, will people laugh!"

Up till then, I'd been standing a little at bay, braced against his criticism but hopeful that he would turn playful at any moment. Now my blood froze.

"I will not!" I wanted him to admit that it was a joke, so that the horrid image would vanish and I could join in his amusement.

"Oh yes you will, wait and see!" He was so tickled by his success in shocking me that he was carried further on the crest of invention. "There's only one way to stop you from wetting your pants, and I know the way. I'm going to put a cork in you so you'll never pee-pee again!"

"You are not!" I squeaked, barely able to breathe.

"In fact," he surged onward, "I put in a special order at the factory, and I bet that cork is ready now."

My father, a travelling salesman in "ladies' frocks," made weekly trips to the factories on Spadina Avenue to pick up his samples for the week ahead. He wore white shirts that my mother had to iron, and suspenders. He snapped his suspenders now as he dialled the phone. "Sam, it's Jack Landsberg calling," he said, all jovial.

I was halfway down the hall to the bedroom.

"Listen, you know that special order I put in last week? It's ready? Oh good . . ."

I remember that the only place I could think of to hide in our tiny rented duplex was—how symbolic—under my parents' double bed. I could scrape under the low-hanging bedsprings by flattening myself excruciatingly and worming my way to the farthest corner. It was dusty. My heart was hammering. I wanted never to be found.

It was after dark when they finally unearthed me, and I can't remember what I said when I was dragged forth and scolded. I don't know how my father explained away my bizarre disappearance that afternoon. I never told, couldn't possibly repeat the threat, assumed perhaps that my mother was in on the plot. All I can recall from that moment was her fear, her bewilderment. Her words poured over me, unheard, as she knelt by the bed and held me by my upper arms. As I wordlessly cried, longing for comfort, a resolve formed in me. I knew from that moment that I would absolutely, positively, without question, never get married. Just in case.

Most of the negative things that happened to me in childhood served me in good stead. The anti-Semitism so casually doled out on the playground and in the classroom ("Jews ki-illed Jesus, nyah nyah nah nah nah!" or "You heathen children are going straight to hell") was painful but taught me at an early age to disbelieve all received wisdom and conventional authority. My father's joke inoculated me against wedding romanticism. My parents' mostly unhappy marriage warned me against marriage as a solution to anything. The conventional lower-middle-class culture in which I grew up, stifling as it was, goaded me into political rebelliousness.

My wedding dress, defiantly simple and non-white, stood for my rejection of a woman's role, my scorn for the concept of virginity and my reluctance to adopt, even for my mother's sake, any of the usual symbols of marital bliss. Nevertheless, in my months of grief after her death at age eighty-two, in a house fire, I betrayed most of my scornful hauteur about her conventional treasures. I scrubbed the soot from her Waterford crystal glasses, wept while I laboured for hours with a toothbrush to remove the black smoke from the folds of porcelain flowers on her little Belleek vases. And then a relative sent a package: my mother's long lace wedding veil, yellowed and torn. How innocently she had worn that costume; she once told me that, on the day of her wedding, she still believed that she could get pregnant from a man's kiss. Her marriage to my rough-tough father must have been one disillusioning shock after another—she so soft-voiced, a hazel-eyed beauty, so impeccably ladylike; he a former football player with a hot temper and a penchant for coarseness. I folded the veil into tissue paper and gently laid it in a drawer. Anything left of my mother's, no matter how I had rejected her beliefs during her lifetime, was now unbearably precious to me.

Never, neither then nor now, however, did those symbols and ceremonies hook me into their mystique. The day before our wedding, I dashed into Simpson's department store on my lunch hour and asked for "the cheapest wedding ring you've got," since the rabbi insisted on my having one. The sales clerk prissed up her mouth and held out a tray of rings, mutely pointing to the simplest; her expression said she just knew that my seventeen-dollar gold band was intended for a night of illicit sex at a motel. (I wore it for years until a sprained and swollen finger forced me to have it cut off; I happily ditched it and have never worn one since.)

My mother knew a seamstress who came up with a piece of silk in pink and green—that was fine, I said. Make it simple. Have it ready for next week.

As it turns out, I've been married to the man who talked me into a wedding (we were married six weeks after we met in an election campaign) for forty-three years. He won me over by making me laugh irresistibly, by his persuasive powers of language and by the dazzling fact that he was the first authentically egalitarian man I had ever met. Most seductive of all was his intelligence, and the fact of our perfectly shared ideals. None of these attractions has faded or changed in four decades. Our love is complicated, deep-rooted and profoundly satisfying to us both. We suit each other. We didn't need the wedding ring, the rabbi, a white dress or what it stood for. I still recoil inwardly when otherwise sensible young women plan elaborate "white weddings." I can't imagine why they care.

MICHELE LANDSBERG is a Toronto journalist and author whose award-winning feminist columns in *The Toronto Star* and *The Globe and Mail* provoked passionate debate, controversy and many readers' deep loyalty for twenty-five years. Since retiring, she has thrown herself into feminist volunteer work of all kinds, including serving on the Board of Directors of Nightwood Theatre and chairing the Board of Directors of Women's College Hospital. She and her husband, Stephen Lewis (former NDP leader, ambassador to the United Nations and now U.N. Special Envoy on HIV/AIDS in Africa), have three grown children and two adored grandsons (so far). Despite her early aversion to conventional roles, Michele turned into an extravagantly and joyously maternal adult who loves cooking and gardening.

ADWOA BADOE

Witness in Silk

In a dream, I saw the parade of wedding dresses—a mass of white, silver and cream satin, sateen, silk and organza—and gossamer veils in nylon netting, airy and discreet, coy and full of suggestion. There were no faces, no feet, just ghosts in dresses long and short, stepping lightly to a wedding march, played on a grand piano. White petals fell like confetti everywhere. But here and there a splash of colour protested in vain against the transparent colours of the sky. They say white is pure, as a bride ought to be. Virginal.

By 1996, I had lived in Canada for four years and was still enduring a difficult transition into Canadian living. I'd lived here four winters and had had two more children since landing, making me a married mother of three, holding down a part-time job at night so I could stay up, study and write exams to return to a career in medicine.

I shifted easily between hope and despair, between the joy of having children and the frustration of keeping house for three robust kids, with two still in diapers. I read anatomy as I breast-fed, surgery as I cooked dinner. The ordeal of my final degree exams in 1988 paled by comparison to the current challenge. In our stacked townhouse, with small living spaces heaped one upon the other on three floors, my hair was growing out of oily jheri curls into a medium-size afro quite untamable by the pre-scribed gel activator. The way I looked mattered less and less to me. Life puréed breakfast, lunch and dinner with pediatrics, pathology and diapers, wagon trips to the park and bus trips to the library with a baby wrap-tied on my back and one adven-turous little lad at each hand. Yet I was confident that God was good, and to my mind much more generous in the summertime.

One day in the fall, I was searching for something to wear, pushing through clothes hanging in two or three layers on plastic white coat hangers, and there at the far corner of my closet was my wedding dress. It hung all alone on a rose-print cushioned hanger under a clear polythene bag. Instinctively I reached for it, and in that moment I seemed to reach into the past.

I remembered that grey October day in 1988. How young I was at nearly twenty-five. I had arrived in London, England, only a week before, and I had seven days to plan my wedding, away from home and family. In the previous month, life itself had seemed to whirr and spin at unimaginable frequencies from its axis in Accra, Ghana. I had whizzed through exams, qualified as a physician and then been married off almost hastily by Akan tradition. Akan is what we call ourselves when we are inclusive of all members of the large language and ethnic group from which several distinct kingdoms arose in pre-colonial times and who make up nearly fifty percent of Ghana's population.

225

Identical traditions persist among Akan peoples of the old king-doms such as Ashanti, Fanti, Denkyira and Akyem.

Fulé and I had met and fallen in love at the University of Science and Technology, in Kumasi, while I was studying medicine and he was studying architecture. Two years into our relationship he had received his postgraduate diploma and left for England. Maintaining love across the Atlantic had its difficulties, but Ghana in the 1980s was a hard place to start adult professional life. Rent in Accra had more to do with the black market value of the U.S. dollar than with modest Ghanaian salaries, and it wasn't uncom-mon to find young professionals still living at home with their parents. So, like many other young Ghanaian graduates, Fulé had applied for and received the elusive British visa, his passport to independence. The general idea was to study and work in the United Kingdom in order to accrue enough money to start life comfortably in Ghana. And so we conducted two years of our relationship largely by letters and occasional phone calls.

At last I qualified. Fulé was working towards his membership in the Royal Institute of British Architects. We wanted to be married. He informed his parents and I informed mine. Then his family knocked formally on our door to propose marriage on his behalf. For some reason, we never called this tradition a "wedding." We saved that magical word for the larger, grander, veiled affair in a church, when we strutted by on high heels, supported on a father's arm, to the piano playing, "The Wedding March." We called this one a "customary marriage," and over the years some have demoted it to an "engagement."

The question of what I would wear to this ceremony seemed to be the last thing on anybody's mind. It seemed to me that a fashionable kaba blouse over a slit—ankle-length narrow skirt—in blue and white African wax print, with gold trimming, would be ideal. But I was coming to Akan culture a little late, growing up as I had in the city. I had nothing of the sort in my wardrobe, and there was no time to have them made. Kaba and slit were for mature women, always custom-made by overworked seamstresses who never kept to contract time. "Ready-made" was the term for European clothing one could buy in a shop. I ended up quite happily wearing a borrowed ready-made dress in white linen, with a wide red belt for a splash of fanciful colour. White—there was that colour again!

So it was that one early afternoon, surrounded by the two groups of family members, amidst feasting and proficient bargaining, I was married to my beloved but absent husband. My father explained the tradition. Two bottles of Kaiser Schnapps sealed the agreement. Money was given to my father, symbolizing the cost of his fatherhood. A smaller amount was given to my mother for the soiled cloth of childbirth. Money was also given to purchase salt for the extended family. Anyone who ate salt became a witness to my marriage. I was given a suitcase, six half-pieces of African wax print, four silk head scarves, a gold ring and a white leather-bound Bible from my husband.

Apart from these, my husband's representatives also presented crates of soft drinks to show his soft hand of generosity and his able hand of provision. Then there was the final fee of the brothers-in-law's pacification, which my brothers negotiated with good humour before the end of the marriage ceremony. Akan men consider a married sister to be a friend and helper gone from the household, and for this loss they argue loudly for restitution.

227

I was a little sad that my husband could not be present at our marriage, but as my father said, according to the old custom, the husband hid in his home waiting for news of a successful agreement. My parents were pleased with the ceremony, my husband's family was pleased with me and I was pleased with my ring. Yet we all knew there was more to be done.

One week later I had left family and custom behind. There I was in London, planning the next thing, a Christian wedding. My sister, my husband and I were hopping on and off buses and subway trains, running in and out of shops, appalled by the price tags on dresses meant to be worn only once and then left forever to hang in a closet.

In Accra, where I grew up, every bride yearns for white. In Accra all the cultures of Ghana mix and evolve. At the seaside, the old, dilapidated townships persist, overshadowed by European forts. In the suburbs, modest modern apartment buildings stand next to huge, opulent mansions, which stand across the street from gloomy old colonial bungalows. Like other teeming cities, Accra also has its sprawling slums and smelly markets. It has fine restaurants and five-star hotels. Large "roundabouts" strive in vain to control traffic during rush hour. Many are the rich businessmen and women who drive Mercedes-Benz cars and BMWs, but many more people stand in queues to board mammy lorries with wooden benches for the ride home from work. On the streets children sell everything from cigarettes to soccer jerseys. There, on our part of the coast of Africa, Western culture lies like a glaze on ancient, full-blooded West African rites of passage. After all, we have been colonized and neo-colonized for a century or more, taught Shakespeare as soon as we grow out of spider stories, and today, MTV is everywhere.

But I had already made up my mind to buy a dress I could wear again, and as I gazed at the array of dresses and fabrics this new world had to offer, I began to experience myself anew. Everything was out there, and I had the power of choice. I began

to awaken to this magical time of transition as a mature, independent and assertive woman, no longer under her father's
patronage or passion for tradition, nor under the restrictive
nouveau literate culture of middle-class Africa. To have arrived
as an African woman of substance is to have a university education and the great Christian white wedding, with veil and
train, bridesmaids and flower girls. As I said no to the allure
of white satin-sateen hanging long and elegant in shop windows, I became one who would live her life true to herself,

making her own unique way. I would, from that time on, pick and choose from two available cultures what I liked and discard what I did not like.

Once I saw the dress, I fell in love with it. When I wore the dress, I was smitten with myself. Who was this beautiful stranger, this enigma, whose dark brown irises gazed with curiosity and unbridled hope at a widening world that now included a husband and a new country, as well as positive energy from the old? With the unveiling of this great new power of choice, I knew that I would someday return to Ghana bold, changed and a revolutionary in my own eyes.

And so we bought the peach silk dress, a hairpiece, sheer white tights and matching peach shoes. After that we shopped for makeup and other accessories. A few days later, I was married in the dress with my friends and acquaintances surrounding me and I was happy and content.

Eight years later, there I was, rubbing the familiar soft silk between my fingers and watching memories rush in through the windows of my mind. I loved this dress. It was the prettiest dress I had ever owned. And I was still hoping I would wear it again to some fine affair such as . . . I stretched my imagination around the dress and smiled triumphantly at myself: "Someone else's wedding . . . dinner!"

Holding this dress again on its hanger, I wondered if it would fit after three kids and hundreds of questions about space, identity, time, immigration, expectation, motherhood, wifehood and career. My life had not turned out at all as I had expected. In place of the certainty I had discovered while choosing my wedding dress, I was filled with daily questions, which I answered a certain way on a given day, a different way on another.

I pulled the polythene bag off the dress. This dress had been the silent witness to the day of great contract-making, when promises were made between us and before God, his priests and our friends at Kensington Temple. This cool peach affair with its wide neck exposed to good effect my chocolate brown, youthful, smooth skin. Slim-fitting sleeves reached past my elbows. The dress hugged my hips ever so slightly and wrapped me up in a swath of puckered silk, delivering me to my husband with a wide bow to the side. I slipped it off the hanger and pulled the zipper down. On the label it read: 100 percent silk, Gianni Ballenti.

I stepped boldly into it. The house was quiet except for the puppets singing a letter and a number on *Sesame Street.* My two younger kids were engrossed in TV, and I could enjoy more closet time. This time, Gianni Ballenti-in-peach didn't fit so easily. But I sucked my belly in under a raised diaphragm and heaved until my body fell into the right places in the dress. I pulled the zipper up by sheer determination and exhaled ever so gently. The sight that greeted me as I looked in the mirror was less than inspiring. With narrowed eyes, I rose to the challenge. I reached for my afro pick and combed through my hair, fussing and patting it into some kind of shape. The result was somewhat disappointing. Indeed, I was beginning to feel a little desperate. I found the bottle of Pink on the dresser and squeezed much of it into my hands, then I rubbed the thick moisturizing oil vigorously into my hair. In the mirror, I noticed little beads of sweat forming on my nose. My hair shone as I combed through it again. I patted it even more firmly at the sides, but it wouldn't lie flat. My hair was springy and full of natural bounce. I found my wine-red lipstick and painted my lips, pressing them together again and again. I had always been uncertain about lipstick on my generous African lips. I stared at the mirror, opened my eyes wider

231

and batted my eyelids at my reflection, trying hard to retrieve innocence from its hiding place. "Mirror, mirror on the wall, I am not convinced and neither are you."

I felt worn out, used up and much older than the thirty-three years I had spent on planet Earth. Where was that vision I had seen eight years ago in the forgotten bridal shop in central London? I determined then to summon the energy of that other woman who several years ago stood before a full-length mirror, aware of destiny within her grasp. I would put some spirit into my living, in spite of babies in diapers and uphill skiing on the rugged slopes of various North American foreign medical graduate accreditation exams. I stood for a while, gazing at myself, caressing the silk wedding dress in which I had proclaimed my independence, my identity and my new-found assertiveness, far from family and home. Gianni Ballenti-in-peach fit with difficulty, and I looked different from the bride I had been.

I was still beautifying myself in the mirror, working hard on my eyes with dark blue eyeliner and dark shades of eyeshadow, when my husband came home. He watched, surprised, from the bedroom doorway. Then he turned away. He probably thinks I'm crazy, I thought. I was even more desperate to look perfect. When he returned soon after, he had in his hand a pink rose from the living-room centrepiece. "You look really good, and I can't believe this dress still fits," he said, as he handed me the artificial rose. He smiled. "Stand over there." Then he brought out the camera. "Smile," he said. He took several shots in succession. He directed me around the bedroom for different poses. I obliged, although I wondered: was this the kind of day to photograph? Yet I have always loved photographs, and I have tons of them organized in thick photo albums. The day was marked forever by a picture on paper, and I would remember it again and again.

Suddenly we were both laughing, and I realized that the dress was meant for this too: to remind me of the dream that had shone so clearly through the glass that day in a forgotten shop in London, England. There, at the beginning of a life journey, I had been blessed to see a beautiful picture of my maturing self. How clear the vision, and yet how blind to the twists and turns of the twin roads of time and place. This cluttering of the vision that had occurred over eight years I recognized as life: the daily events that bear down on dreams and shape them into biographies— wifehood, motherhood, migrations. From these arose the daily questions about previously known creeds of independence, identity, gender roles, time, space and career. The dress was a witness to the vision I had seen of one bold, strong black woman with dark brown irises, choosing her unique self confidently from at least two cultures.

Just the other day, when I was alone at home, I tried the dress on again. Nearly ten years have gone by since I last tried on Gianni Ballenti-in-peach, and I have been married nearly eighteen years. My kids have long since grown out of diapers, and instead of practising medicine, I practise the arts. I practise the arts that came to me from the depths of my African culture to sustain me during those early years in Canada when I was writing exam after exam while raising a young family. This time, the dress refused to climb past my hips, and I was laughing as I stepped out of it. The dress is still in good shape, and in the intervening years I have considered giving it up to one charity or another for sale. But I have always found other things easier to give away.

I placed the dress back in its clear polythene wrap and hung it up again between a blue and white kaba and slit and a lilac bubu gown. In spite of good intentions, it has been worn in pub-lic only once. It lives with me in silence, my witness in silk to

233

the promises I made to the vision of a woman I saw, a long time ago. I trust I am becoming this woman with each passing day as I live my life true to myself. I still hope to return to Ghana bold and revolutionary, but also patient and persevering. In the meantime, Gianni Ballenti-in-peach resides in my wardrobe with two cultures, new and old.

ADWOA BADOE has made many transitions in life since she wore her magical peach wedding dress. She became Fulé's wife and the mother of three creative children. Born a Ghanaian, she is now Canadian. A physician by qualification, she now tells stories as a writer, a storyteller and an African dance instructor, choreographer and producer of dance stories. She eagerly rides the circle of life, knowing that she will arrive where she began; but on the way she explores, participates and learns, often going off the path to make trails of her own.

MARGARET GOUDIE PARSONS

My Sophisticated Suit

I was born in Labrador in the mid-forties and grew up on Birch Island. When I was a child, my wilderness home was separated by the Hamilton River from Happy Valley, a town developed to support an air base during the Second World War. By the mid-seventies the growing town had been renamed Happy Valley–Goose Bay. Even the river had been given a new name.

Many years ago I watched with pride as my dad and the other men of the island built the bridge to connect our home to the mainland. At the time I was reading and loving *Little House on the Prairie*. Laura Ingalls Wilder could have been writing about the first settlers on Birch Island, who came from all parts of the world. There was a mixture of whites and Natives: Inuit descendants, Metis, an Innu family, Europeans, Newfoundlanders and other Canadians. Despite the diversity of races, we were a close-knit little community. Whenever help was needed, all hands chipped in. Some years after the building of that bridge, this way of life disappeared from Birch Island, as it had from the prairies a century earlier. The municipality of Happy Valley put a road through to Birch Island, and in the 1960s Premier Joey Smallwood brought in the resettlement program. The people of Birch Island, who originally came from the small coastal communities of northern and southern Labrador, plus other folks from away, were moved into town.

As a young girl growing up on Birch Island, I dreamed of wearing a floor-length white gown on my wedding day. The veil would be a matching white sheer, trailing down my back. My dress would be sleeveless, with my arms covered by elegant white gloves reaching past my elbows. Around my neck I'd wear a single string of white pearls, and on my feet, plain white satin pumps. I'd look like a fairy-tale princess as I walked down the church aisle on the arm of my father. Everyone's eyes would be fixed on me as I proceeded to the altar to unite with my groom while the organist played "The Wedding March." With my cold black hair, I'd be beautiful as Elizabeth Taylor, my heroine at the time. But it was not to be.

I was sixteen when my mother died of leukemia. I was devastated by her death. My family was poor, although my father took care of my brother and me as best he could. Dad worked as labourer for the RCAF and learned the trade of glass cutter in their carpentry shop. I can still picture him cutting firm, straight lines on glass. After he cut the lines, he carefully put down his glass cutter and gave the glass a quick snap, making a perfect window pane. He was very proud of his work. Dad worked for years on the base while my younger brother and I got an education. My brother's job was to light the wood stove each morning. I prepared breakfast, a scanty meal of bread and tea, before we walked to school on the mainland. It was rough going with Mum no longer with us. I missed her. A year after her passing, I became pregnant. I really missed her then.

When it became known that I was in the family way, my minister got involved. He told me how my baby would be born. I was so naive I thought the doctors would just cut my belly open. I was embarrassed by his explanation, but thankful that he cared; after all, I had committed the unforgivable sin.

During this confusing time, I didn't know whether I would marry my boyfriend, Lee, the father of my baby, or not. I felt so alone without my mother's guidance. In my generation, men ceased to exist when a girl became pregnant. They seemed to believe she had gotten into the situation all on her own. My minister didn't understand my feelings. He didn't include Lee in our discussions about my pregnancy, except to confirm that Lee was the father of my child. He didn't think marriage was the best option for us at this time. Lee and I wanted to get married but couldn't afford to. We were young and didn't know what to do. My father wasn't in any position to help. He was still in mourning for my mother.

There was one thing I knew I wanted: I wanted to be the perfect mother and do what was best for my child. My minister encouraged me to place my baby for adoption. He told me it would take more love to do this than to raise it myself, since I was still a child and would have lots of time for a family when I was married. He told me the story from the Holy Bible of the two mothers and the two babies. One baby was dead, and both women claimed the living child. King Solomon, in all his wisdom, said, "Take the sword and divide it." One woman said, "Yes, divide it," but the real mother replied, "No, let him live, give him to her." I would be making a similar sacrifice.

When I thought about keeping my child, I was afraid. How was I to care for a baby? Back then there was no financial assistance available. Deep down in my heart I wanted to keep my child. The maternal love that flowed within me was warm and beautiful, like my baby.

Giving my baby away wasn't the best option for me, even though my church felt it was. As the months passed, there was a wound inside my heart that left a permanent scar. My minister wanted to send me to a home for unwed mothers in Ontario, but I refused. I wanted my baby to be born in Labrador. I wanted to hold on to my child as long as I could. I weighed all the options and reluctantly agreed to adoption, thinking others knew best. After making this decision, I silently went into seclusion in my home on Birch Island until it was time for me to give birth. I ventured out weekly for my checkup at the hospital, then became a hermit again. I really didn't want to give my baby away to strangers. I cried myself to sleep every night, ashamed and lonely. I felt soiled, like the tears on my pillow.

The moment arrived when I gave birth to a beautiful baby boy. He was brought to me and placed in my arms. I cried, looking into the deepest blue eyes I'd ever seen. I kissed his cold black hair. I couldn't fathom how such a tiny life could so perfectly reflect his father and me. My tears would not stop flowing as I checked every finger and toe on his tiny body. I held him close to my heart. I thought I'd never let him go. The nurse on duty realized I shouldn't have seen my baby because he was being placed for adoption. He was snatched from my arms. I remember the sensation of his warm baby skin touching my skin and then leaving, even today.

I had only two visitors while I was in the hospital: my best friend, Marcella, and my boyfriend, Lee. I was too upset to talk with my dear friend very much, and held back my tears, but I appreciated the fact that she came. She understood my dilemma. When Lee and I were alone, I told him I had seen and held our son. It was very hard to hold back the tears this time, but I remained firm in my decision to give up the baby for adoption. Lee didn't make any comment, except to say that we had made the right choice, but I saw the pain in his heart. I wish we could have known the long-term consequences of our decision at that time, but we didn't.

Five days later I was discharged from the maternity ward. Before leaving the hospital, I signed the appropriate papers for adoption, with the assistance of a welfare officer. Naive as I was, I requested two things: that he remain in Canada, and that the adoptive parents be the ones to name him, for surely they would love him as much as I did. I prayed that these requests would be honoured. When I had completed this painful task, Lee came to take me home.

It took months for me to stop crying and get my strength back. Then, when I got my strength back with the aid of my minister, I entered the workforce. I was hired as a teller with the Royal Bank of Canada and moved from Birch Island into town with Lee. We purchased a business together called the Thrift Shop and entered the entrepreneurial world. We were on our way to independence. Our only problem was that we were living together, which wasn't approved of at that time. I felt like a Jezebel and a kept woman, even though I was contributing financially to our partnership. I felt ashamed, degraded and guilty. I knew I loved Lee, and I wanted to get married. I wanted my reputation back, and respect. Lee's reputation hadn't been affected. He could walk around town with his head held high.

Lee proposed when I turned nineteen, after we had been living together for a year. I readily accepted. I was elated to be getting married. At the same time, deep down in my heart, a part of me felt snapped off. I didn't feel like I would ever recover from the pain of giving my baby away.

240   Feeling all alone, I started to plan for my special day. I really didn't know how to plan a wedding, and I longed again for my mother's guidance. My dream of wearing white was gone. I didn't feel it would be honest to wear white before my Maker. White was reserved for virgins, who could claim the colour of purity. I could have worn a widow's black for the tears I'd cried. Purple and gold was for royalty. So what was left for me?

I flipped through the pages of Simpsons-Sears and Eaton's mail-order catalogues, past the bridal section, and turned to the suit department. I picked something pale and pink that I could use for work afterwards. It was beautiful and expensive, like nothing I'd owned before. The skirt was straight-cut, lined with matching pink satin. The jacket was long-sleeved, and the collar was embroidered with pink lace. It buttoned down the front with petite pink pearl buttons. Eureka! I had my pearls!

I ordered a headband-style hat typical of the sixties. It was decorated with pink silk flowers, intertwined with green leaves. I bought a soft multicoloured pink silk scarf to drape around my neck. My leather high heels were my one indulgence in white. Surely my feet were pure for my wedding day.

Now I had to approach my boss to ask for time off work to get married. The bank manager reluctantly agreed to one day. So I planned my wedding for a Friday evening, after work. I'd be serving customers again on Tuesday morning. Not a real honeymoon, but at least we'd have a long weekend.

Finally, my fiancé and I contacted a minister (not the one who had advised me to give up our baby). He agreed to marry us for a ten-dollar fee, which we thought was outrageous. I wish I'd tested his true calling and asked him to marry us for free.

February 16, 1966. I rushed home after a tiring day at work and donned my sophisticated pink suit. It seemed to blush as I put it on, telling me that I still lacked purity. Then I saw myself in the mirror. I couldn't help smiling. My suit was as stylish as anything Jackie Kennedy might wear. I looked lovely and could be counted among the elite.

I'd chosen navy dress pants for Lee and a burgundy sports coat to complement my pink. Lee looked so handsome—all spruced up, we called it, as the pungent smell of Old Spice cologne filled the room. We didn't have to leave right away, so I had a few moments

241

alone to meditate. I thought about my mother and wondered about her wedding day. She was born in northern Labrador and moved to Birch Island from Adlatuk Bay with my dad so he could work on the base. I had a black-and-white photograph of their wedding day. It was taken outside during the winter, a photo of two couples. My mum and her dear friend wore long wool coats. Their heads were covered by knitted caps. I'd seen pictures in magazines of ladies of the early thirties wearing similar caps. My mum could knit, so I'm sure she made hers. On their feet they wore white-bottomed sealskin boots. Again, I'm sure Mum made hers and Dad's, as I remember watching her chew sealskin to soften the hide for sewing when I was just a little tot in Adlatuk. She made all our clothes, using the Singer sewing machine I now call Old Betsy. My dad and the other gentleman wore dress pants and white shirts with ties. My dad wore a windbreaker and his friend a suit coat. As I thought about it, I became sure the photo was taken after the ceremony, because my mum and her friend weren't wearing their church caps. They were strong in the Moravian faith, so they would have worn their caps to church. Crocheted or knitted in strip fashion, the women's caps were trimmed on the sides with a ribbon and tied underneath the chin. A blue ribbon represented a married woman and a pink ribbon a single girl.

Looking at that picture, I grieved for my mother. I couldn't help thinking she'd be disappointed that I'd given up my baby for adoption. It was not the Aboriginal way. She would have raised my child as her own. I felt I had let her down, but what else could I have done? I imagined my mother in her casket at the front of the church. She wore her plain gold wedding band, which had belonged to my grandmother. During the funeral service, someone asked me, "Do you want the ring removed?" I didn't have the heart to say yes, but now I wished I had. I felt tears streaming down my face. I had to come back to reality and look to the future.

It was the mid-sixties. There were big changes happening in the world, but they were slow in reaching isolated Labrador. My world was still in the Victorian era.

My fiancé yelled, "Time to go." I dried my tears with my hanky, applied fresh lipstick, glanced at my face in the mirror and let the vision of my mum fade.

We arrived at the church and were married at six in the evening. It was a private ceremony, with my cousin and Lee's brother standing as witnesses. The guests were my dad, my brother, my brother's friend and my friend from work and her husband. There was not a celebration afterwards. Lee and I went back home to a chicken dinner I had prepared. There was no wedding cake.

Years passed. We had three children and a good marriage, but there was always that snapped-off piece missing from my heart. I felt proud on my wedding day, wearing my sophisticated pink, but I never forgot my private tears, or the feeling that I had disappointed my mother. I never forgot the baby I gave up for adoption. Being the determined woman I am, I had to find him.

More than fifteen years ago, my youngest daughter Paula and I became private detectives, embarking on what seemed an impossible task. We obtained the allowable information from post-adoption services and began our journey. One thing the government agency had lived up to: my son remained in Canada. I was thankful for that.

When I viewed the papers I had signed so many years ago, I saw things there that I hadn't been aware of. Being young and trusting, I'd signed where I was told. I wasn't advised that there was a six-month probationary period, during which I could have changed my mind. I'd believed that once I signed the papers there was no going back. There was never any follow-up to see how I was doing, as promised in the agreement. Placing my child for adoption hadn't been the right option for me. I had changed my mind the moment I saw and held my baby. Seeing those papers again, I felt like an object, not a human being with feelings (although I'd numbed my pain for many years). The papers didn't tell the real story. They made me a statistic from Labrador, where so many children were given away by unwed mothers.

My daughter and I searched for six months or more, making numerous phone calls with the little information we had. We searched church records and spoke to many people who remembered military families stationed in Goose Bay at the time my son was born. Through the process of elimination and the help of a good friend, we made a successful contact. What a day of rejoicing that was!

Paula was the first to meet her brother. When she met him, she thought she was seeing her younger brother, Phil. They could have been twins. Paula and her big brother bonded right away. Lee and I were the next to meet him. When we arrived at the Vancouver airport, I looked through the waiting crowd and immediately knew him. I called his name, and we embraced. I was never going to let him go again.

When I look back on my life, I wonder if everything that happened was meant to be. By finding my son, I was able to help his sister in his adopted family find her birth mother. Her mother was from my hometown. Broken pieces have come together for all of us.

I didn't wear a traditional white wedding dress. I don't regret it. My sophisticated pink suit turned out to be the most beautiful dress in the world, because I chose it. My life, surrounded by children, grandchildren and my husband, turned out to be more fulfilling than what the colour white, with all its purity, ever promised my generation.

MARGARET GOUDIE PARSONS is of Aboriginal background and a proud daughter of Labrador. She finds writing to be good therapy and has been her own private physician for years. She has been published in *Yuletide Preparations*, an annual Christmas book, and in the Slice of Life column for the St. John's *Evening Telegram*. Now a grandmother, she is pursuing her dream of writing full-time, in addition to raising one grandchild. She remains young at heart and eager to conquer the world. She has been known to tell her granddaughters, "I am the coolest grandma in town!"

JAMIE ZEPPA

Stripes

SUIT

In the photograph, my grandmother is wearing a dark suit in what appears to be machine-knit wool. It is belted, knee-length, undecorated—an ordinary workday outfit. She looks like she is on her way to the bank. Actually, she is going to get married.

"In that?" I wailed. I was twelve and appalled. "A—a *suit?*"

"It was the Depression," my grandmother said. "And I got a lot of wear out of that outfit, let me tell you."

How much wear you would get out of it was her primary selection criteria for any article of clothing. I knew this all too well: my paternal grandparents were raising my brother and me after our parents' spectacularly failed marriage, and my grandmother applied the "how much wear" rule to everything from winter coats to underwear. Apparently, not even wedding dresses were exempt.

"What did you do after the wedding?" I asked. A honeymoon was obviously out of the question, but I held out hope for a reception, possibly outdoors, with flowers and white tablecloths, a spray of stars against an inky sky.

"We ate supper at my parents' house," my grandmother said, "and then we all went to the show. A movie was a real treat in those days."

But it couldn't have been that much of a treat, I thought: she didn't even remember which movie. I handed back the photograph. It was all so unpromising: wearing the outfit you wore to church every Sunday, going to a movie after—with your *parents*. I tried to return to the subject of her engagement, which offered better material. "Your parents didn't want you to marry him, right? Because he was Polish and from the West End?" Her family was Protestant and English, and although they lived in a cramped, narrow house in a long row of cramped, narrow houses, they were still on the east side of Sault Ste. Marie's Gore Street, that border between the orderly, green-lawned land of the English and Scots and the broken-fenced, chicken-coop country of Everyone Else (Poles, Italians, Russians, Finns). I imagined my grandmother walking out to meet my grandfather at the dividing line, unable to hear the storm of shouted threats and outrage behind her over the pounding of her own heart. But there couldn't have been that much outrage if they all went to a movie together.

Still, the East End–West End part was romantic. Her parents had protested, especially when she started taking catechism lessons to become Catholic. Even better was the fact that my grandfather told his friends he was going to marry my grandmother the very first time he saw her, before he'd even spoken to her. He had been working in the yards at the tar plant when she walked past. She too was on her way to work: to wash dishes and sweep floors for a doctor's family. Still, she was not from his end of town.

People didn't cross Gore Street to shop, let alone marry. And my grandfather was not given to flights of fancy (his whole life, he refused to read fiction on the grounds that it was "all made up"), so what prompted this astonishing declaration?

I never saw my grandparents hold hands or exchange gifts. They never called each other anything except "Pete" and "Florence." On the surface, neither seemed the type to cross lines or defy convention or fall in love at first sight.

But I never heard them argue or speak in anger to each other, either; they appeared to be one person in two bodies. And maybe that was the thing about love, I thought. It could fell the most practical person. It could knit two people together so tightly you forgot where one started and the other began. It could make a lifelong story out of the most threadbare facts.

Maybe you didn't need a dress if you had the story.

SHIFT

My mother, Judy, had the dress: a knee-length satin shift with a lacy overlay. It came complete with veil, ring and groom in cream-coloured tux. In the pictures, her smile is dreamy and distracted. Beside her, my father is smiling so broadly it makes my face hurt.

It was a wedding that almost didn't happen. A few months earlier, my father had disappeared. It was not the first time Jim had run away. (The first time, he was thirteen. He got all the way to Sudbury before he was caught stealing a second car. The first one had run out of gas.) This time, ten years later, he took his own car and got all the way to Baton Rouge before his cousin, a police officer, tracked him down and brought him home. His parents (Pete and Florence) were at their wits' end. They couldn't understand

248

(for the life of them!) why a young man all set to settle down would get in his car to go to work one day, cross the bridge-slash-border and drive all the way down to Louisiana without so much as a phone call to say he might be late for dinner.

My mother was just as bewildered. A man had proposed to her and then run away. It made no sense, not even as an ending. Especially as an ending. The story was supposed to start with a date, build to a proposal, float through an engagement and end with a walk down the aisle in a white dress. And it wasn't just her ending. That was *the* ending. Even if you didn't literally *have* to get married, the way *some* girls had to, you eventually had to because what else were you going to do? Sooner or later, the story ended with a dress and a wedding.

After the ending, of course, it didn't always work out well, as my mother's own mother could attest. My maternal grandmother had to take in sewing to feed her five kids and pay the rent on their tiny two-bedroom apartment above a store. She specialized in wedding gowns and all their precursors: elaborate First Communion dresses and veils, evening frocks trailing pale layers of gauze. While she sewed lace and tulle promises of happily-ever-after, her husband staggered from card game to tavern, pay-cheque gone, luck unchanged, temper charged.

But even if it didn't work out well, even if it worked out that you were miserable, it had still worked out in the sense that you were married, which is what everyone expected you to be.

My mother intended to be married, but what did her intended expect? Pete and Florence had their theories: *Jim was always on his way to someplace else, he was going to go out west, or to Toronto, to do heaven knows what, always some scheme cooked up with some guy he'd just met on a train or in a barroom, a lot of foolishness, if you ask us.* They couldn't abide foolishness, whether you asked them or not.

The groom disappeared. The wedding was off. He came back.

249

The wedding was still off. They circled each other warily. They went out to talk. Nothing. Nothing. Then, lo! The wedding was on! Her mother sewed the dress. His parents, out of sheer relief, paid for the dinner.

In the church, there was the usual hush as the bride appeared. The groom waited in his place at the altar. Pete and Florence, in their Sunday clothes, were relieved. They weren't sure how Judy had done it, but she had obviously talked some sense into their son. He had put aside his pipe dreams, turned over a new leaf. It had all worked out in the end.

A woman beside Florence whispered, "Doesn't Judy look lovely?"

My grandmother agreed that she did.

"And we were all just saying: What a clever dress!"

My grandmother must have looked confused. The woman leaned closer to clarify. "You can't even tell she's pregnant!"

Of course, it did not work out well, or at all. Two years and two children later, they separated, then divorced. The ring was returned (bounced across the kitchen floor), the photos were lost, the dress ended up, for reasons unknown, bundled into a back bedroom closet of an elderly neighbour's house. (One can only imagine her perplexed children after her death: "Now who on earth got married in this?") My parents ended up in separate cities, and my brother and I ended up with Pete and Florence.

When I was twenty-three, someone moved something in the basement, and an album was dragged out of the bottom of a trunk. It was a shock to see them: two people, now unable to sit in the same room together, standing up in full wedding regalia, promising to love and to cherish until death did them part.

What good was the dress if that was the ending? I wanted nothing to do with that kind of story.

KIRA

Instead of falling in love and getting married, I went to Bhutan, a country in the mountains on the other side of the planet, where everything was so different that it was okay to fall in love, because no matter what happened, I wouldn't end up in a stupid lie of a wedding dress, in the back seat of a car covered with Kleenex flowers.

I returned home a few years later to break the news to Pete. My grandmother had died by then, and my grandfather could not (for the life of him!) understand what I was saying. I was going to have a baby? Before I was married? I wasn't going to *get* married? *At all?* And then, I was going to take the baby and return to a Third-World country, to the baby's father, who wasn't just non-Catholic but not even Christian? And live there? How would I ever fit in there? How would we overcome the differences between us? It was like some crazy novel he had never read.

It seemed pointless to explain that we were writing a different kind of story, that we were together because we wanted to be, that we did not have to get married (and anyway, I could barely hear him over the pounding of my heart).

But then, it turned out, we *did* have to get married, for administrative reasons, and quickly. There was no time to plan anything. Perfect! We got out of bed and into the national dress of Bhutan: for Tshewang, a gho, a long-sleeved, knee-length robe, and for me, a kira, a floor-length rectangle of cloth wrapped around the body and belted at the waist. They were both cut from a single piece of material woven by his mother as a present for us. The design, a gold pattern of small geometric flowers woven into thin red and blue stripes, was not one I would have chosen, but that in itself pleased me. I liked the suddenness of this material, the randomness of the whole wedding. *Here! Put this on! My mom wove it! We gotta get married before your visa expires!*

251

You don't need the dress if you have the story.

In Bhutanese fashion, men's stripes are always vertical, women's horizontal. I hadn't really noticed this until the day we got married, and then I wanted to believe that it would mean something: *Our stripes go in different directions, but really we're cut from the same piece of cloth.*

In the beginning, though, it was the differences that were most apparent. They were apparent in the smallest things: where we wanted to live, how we wanted to travel, whether it was insane to spend more money on a quilt cover than on the quilt itself just because the colour of the cover was the colour of the sky, which you hadn't seen since the monsoon let loose and clogged up everything with mist and rain.

They were apparent in the bigger things: when we wanted to be apart and what we wanted to do together, what we believed should be said and not said, what I meant when I said family and what he meant. What I meant was the three of us living together, with occasional, brief and announced-well-in-advance visits from his immediate family. What he meant was Family, immediate, extended and mythic (the last comprising cousins-in-law, cousins of cousins and friends of acquaintances), stopping by any time, all the time, to stay for however long they needed.

The differences grew more apparent as I struggled to belong to a place I loved. (*I love this place! Why isn't that enough?*)

If I had been paying attention to the dress instead of the story, I might have noticed the important differences the day we put on our wedding clothes. Tshewang slid into a garment he had worn all his life. I struggled into another country's national dress. It felt like a costume, but when I took it off there was nothing I could put on to help me belong.

I told myself: *These differences will not unravel us. His stripes go one way, mine another, but it's the same material.*

252

I stretched the metaphor until it tore.

Misery beset us, but ending it was unthinkable. I did not want to have written a story of regret, the wrong love, a ruined ending, photos hidden at the bottom of a trunk. What were you supposed to do with a story after it broke down? What did you do with all the earlier chapters? What to do with the moment we realized we were in love (wrapped in each other's arms in a candlelit room, unable to tell where one person ended and the other began, while the mountains outside dissolved in the night and the night dissolved in the rain)? What to do with all our shared things, the music we recorded, our letters with all their wild declarations of love? What to do with my wedding kira, a single piece of cloth cut in half?

I took the kira back to Canada. For a long time, it stayed in a closet, under a stack of towels. I pulled it out one night and studied it. By then, Tshewang and I were rewriting the ending by forgiving each other for failing to cross the most important boundaries, and perhaps that is why I did not think, *Here is the unhappy symbol of a torn union, stripes going in the wrong direction, a story I couldn't finish.* I was more struck by the brightness of the cloth: unlike my other Bhutanese weavings, it had remained curiously unfaded, the gold still vivid, the reds and blues still dark and bright. I used it as a curtain for a while, and then as a bedspread. When I see it now, I hardly ever think, *There is the dress I wore to get married.* It is so much a part of the here and now that I rarely notice it at all. But I have gotten a lot of wear out of it, let me tell you.

253

JAMIE ZEPPA is the author of *Beyond the Sky and the Earth: A Journey into Bhutan.* She teaches English at Seneca College in Toronto. She doesn't know how long she can resist the urge to turn her wedding dress into cushion covers.

Darla Tenold

Journeys of Hearts and Second Halves

When love beckons to you, follow him,
Though his ways are hard and steep.

— Kahlil Gibran, *The Prophet*

The most important thing about my blue flowered wedding dress was that it rolled up snugly to fit in my backpack and rolled out wrinkle-free after an overseas flight. You see, a year earlier, I'd fallen in love with a handsome Egyptian stranger who lived in the seductive city of Amsterdam and came from a different world.

When I met him, I wasn't looking for love, and I didn't consider myself romantic. I hadn't given much thought to the concepts of fate or destiny. Already approaching my thirties, life experiences and three years of law school had led me to value rational decision-making over following my heart. So when, in the middle of the Amsterdam sidewalk that fateful evening, Hamada kissed me so passionately on the lips and said, "I'm loving you. I wanna be with you forever. I want all of you," I came up with the only response I could: "But you don't even *know* me."

His reply: "Yes, but this is my feeling. I don't know what's happened, but you got in my heart. I'm honouring you."

I didn't know how to respond to something that seemed to happen only in movies. I suddenly became intimately aware of all of our surroundings: the sound of trams grating along the steel tracks that criss-crossed the cobblestone streets; the bikes everywhere and the accompanying sound of bicycle bells ringing randomly. It seemed as if a movie camera had panned across this Sunday at dusk in Amsterdam, where the streets were almost deserted except for extras hired by movie-makers to stroll by, pretending not to notice the drama unfolding around them.

I insisted on using logic. "You met me only yesterday. How can you love me? You don't know me."

He bared himself again: "I'm honouring you. It's more than pleasure. The love is in my heart. It's not in my head. I'm loving you. I wanna spend the rest of my life with you."

"I'm not getting married," I said, attempting to prove how much he didn't know me.

"It's not important, married or not. You are my second half. Please, will you live with me to see if we can be together forever?"

I gave up and kissed him. I liked kissing him. I liked the warm glow his soft lips gave me. I grabbed his hand and we continued to walk. I thought, "This is flattering." I thought of how much I liked him, and the kisses. Even if he insisted on the overwhelming concepts of love and the rest of our lives, I could enjoy this for just what it was—a thrilling adventure, a great story. The pink and orange light of dusk coloured the cobblestones and glinted off the canal bridges. We walked and stopped every few blocks to kiss again. He kept saying, "I don't know what's happened, how you got in my heart."

Only the day before, I had arrived in Amsterdam, the last stop on my four-week backpacking trip to Western Europe. I had left home with a loose itinerary that only tentatively included Amsterdam. Having arrived by train in the early morning, I made my way, sleepy-eyed and unclean, to the accommodations desk in Amsterdam's Centraal Station. I flipped open my trusty guidebook, pointed to the first hostel I had circled and smiled. The kind man behind the desk smiled back and shook his head, no. After going through these motions several more times, I discovered that all of my preferred options were already booked. At my confused look, the man suggested a hostel. I thought for a moment and glanced at the big black X through the entry for this hostel in my guidebook: it had too much of a party reputation. Now, in light of all the X's through every other hostel I deemed desirable, I agreed to go there.

At the hostel, the dimly lit reception area was hazy with marijuana and cigarette smoke. I carried my bags up the narrow and winding staircase to Room C, where large windows filled most of the wall looking out over the Amsterdam street. The dorm-style room contained half a dozen bunk beds lining the white walls. I grabbed a bunk on the top and took my time settling in while the two other young women in the room set about enthusiastically getting ready for an afternoon on the town.

While I was settling in, a man with chocolate skin, wearing a snug white T-shirt, entered the room. He began changing the sheets on one of the beds. He asked the two young women their names and where they were from. He said, "My name is Hamada. I'm from Egypt." He had a very appealing accent. Hamada turned to me. "What is your name?"

"Darla. I'm from Canada."

"Did you just come here to Amsterdam?" Hamada asked all three of us.

One of the other women answered, and Hamada continued to chat with them. I watched him. He kept doing his job, stripping each unoccupied bed, putting on new sheets, all the while making light, friendly chit-chat with the other women. I stripped the used sheets from my bed, added them to his pile and set out to explore Amsterdam.

As I re-entered the hostel later that afternoon, my eyes adjusted to the dim light. I noticed Hamada sitting at one of the tables, sipping from a mug set on top of a saucer. His full lips stretched into a smile and he said, "Hi." I couldn't help but smile back.

"How was your time in Amsterdam?" he asked.

"It was very nice. The sun was shining and there are so many interesting things to see." The truth was that I had visited the Sex Museum. I had found it boring, so much repetition. How many pictures of naked people does someone need to see in one afternoon? I felt my face flush. "Then I spent some time strolling around. This is my first day in Amsterdam, so I'm just trying to figure out where everything is."

"Did you see Vondelpark?" he asked.

"No. I haven't heard of it."

"Can I show it to you?"

The invitation seemed a bit forward to me, and I wondered if I understood. "I'm not sure what I want to see in Amsterdam. Where is the park?" I replied.

"I can show you. It's very beautiful, with so many people walking or running or riding bikes. You'll find a lake and flowers and trees. It's very big, with so many paths. Today, it's very nice outside, and you'll find so many people there." Amsterdam was not known for its parks, and this sounded like a refreshing change of pace after my visit to the Sex Museum.

259

"Will you go to the Red Light District?" he asked.

Now that was a slightly more suspicious question. Of course I had thought about going there, even though my guidebook said it was no longer a safe place to visit, especially at night.

"Well, sure, I guess. Doesn't everybody go to the Red Light District?"

"You should be careful in the Red Light District, really, if you go at night. If you want to go there, I can show you."

In the dark recesses of my mind, the red flags popped up. They were: *You Are Alone. You Don't Know This Man. He Has an Accent. You've Never Met Anyone Like Him Before. You Are in a Strange City: Different Culture. Stick to Seeing Sights in the Daytime, By Yourself.* I ignored them. I ignored them because he was sitting alone, drinking from a mug that I couldn't imagine contained anything illicit. In fact, I later found out, it was tea, of all things to consume in Amsterdam, city of legal soft drugs, partying and casual sex. Tea added to the mystery and majesty of this Egyptian man. The lines on his face were soft and rounded. His eyes, a beautiful and shiny brown, were framed by dark, soft lashes. The tone of his voice conveyed only sweetness, a melting chocolate accent to match his beautiful skin.

While all these observations and thoughts were running in the background of my mind, I heard him say, "What are you gonna do now?"

"I don't know." I was so caught up in him and his offer.

"Okay," he said. "We can go to the park."

"Okay," I said, unable to refuse. The park seemed safe enough. It was daylight, and he had said there would be lots of people.

I pushed open the door to the street and was greeted by bright sunshine and a mess of bikes locked up just across the sidewalk from the hostel. As we stepped off the curb onto the cobblestone street, Hamada lightly pressed his hand into the small of my back. "Take care," he said softly, and my heart fluttered as he so gently guided me across the tram tracks.

Along the way, Hamada pointed to the sights, explaining where we were and what we were seeing. We came to a large square presided over by an immense stone building—Dam Square and the Royal Palace, explained Hamada. We walked down narrow pedestrian shopping streets and passed restaurants serving everything from Argentine to Tunisian food. The streets were filled with people of many cultural backgrounds. We admired the architecture of the tall and narrow canal houses.

I had no idea where we were or even in which direction we were travelling. If I had needed to, I would likely have had trouble finding my way back to the hostel, and I hadn't thought to bring my guidebook or maps. Each time we crossed a street or tram tracks, Hamada repeated, "Take care," guiding me gently either by the arm or by the small of my back. I certainly was not used to a man treating me this way. I wondered if I should feel scared or trapped or angry at Hamada for being overbearing. Instead, I felt as though whatever I wanted to see and do, Hamada was at my disposal to show me. Each time he touched me on my arm or my back, my skin tingled through to my core.

At the park we picked a stretch of grass to sit on. Earlier, along the way, Hamada had told me he was an accountant by profession but because he could not speak fluent Dutch he hadn't been able to get a job in his profession yet. He was attending university classes to learn the language. After two years in Amsterdam he was captivated by the city and felt very settled. He planned to stay, eventually finding a job in his profession. This was all well and good and, in fact, appealed to the logical part of me. But I wanted more. Hamada stirred another side of me, so I probed further. I got the information I was interested in when he said, "I'm looking for my second half so that I can have a family."

"Do you believe there is only one person for you?" I asked him. As soon as I said it, I was shocked at myself. The question seemed so personal. I wondered why I should want to know this about him.

"Yes. Fate will make sure I meet her," he said. "Do you believe in fate?"

"I'm not sure. I don't think about that. I make decisions using my head."

"Yes, but fate is an attraction from the heart, something not controlled in the head."

All this talk of fate and hearts and second halves was making me a little uncomfortable. Even so, the question floated, ever so briefly, through my mind: could I be his second half? I dismissed it in an instant. He lived impossibly far away. He wanted to get married and have children. Marriage and children had never been part of my plans.

I changed the subject and told Hamada about the European sights I'd seen before arriving in Amsterdam. Hamada asked why I was travelling alone. "I started out on this trip with two friends, but one week ago we parted ways. I wanted to travel for the last week by myself, to see if I could find more adventure. I like travelling alone and wish I could be away longer, but I have to return to Canada to start my articling job."

For all of my adult life, I had wanted to take at least a year to backpack alone. I wanted to prove to myself that I was not boring, that I would not live a conventional life. My need for security made me focus on getting a university degree and led me to an articling position. Now, my one-year trip had been pared down to only three weeks, and all I could see in my future was hard work at a nine-to-five, plus more, job. I wondered where I would fit in all of the adventure.

Hamada didn't understand. I said, "I like my independence." In truth, long ago I had decided there was no one with whom I could share my dreams and travels, let alone spend the rest of my life. I'd seen so many marriages fail. I saw marriage as standing in the way of an adventurous life. I could rely only on myself, and planned on doing most of my travel alone. I couldn't bring myself to say these things now to Hamada. In front of him, these beliefs seemed bleak and ugly.

Hamada asked me what I wanted to do next. I knew I didn't want to go back to the hostel. I was enjoying his company too much. Already, I was thinking about the next day, wondering if I could see him again. Hamada agreed to take me to the Red Light District, on the condition that I stick close to him.

Darkness had fallen as we entered this infamous area of Amsterdam. Hamada again placed his hand lightly on the small of my back and said, "Take care." This time there were no tram tracks or streets to cross. He said, "It's dangerous here. Try not to talk to anyone."

The street was lined with neon signs advertising videos, lingerie, sex toys. Store windows were filled with all manner of things associated with sex, many of which I had never seen or heard of before. Some establishments had no windows, only doors slightly ajar, loud music pouring out and people ducking in and out. Several large windows showcased women for hire, a pinkish red light glowing around them as they made pose after pose in their lingerie. I remembered that my guidebook suggested visiting this area only in the daylight. Here I was in the thick of it, in the night, with a strange man I had met only hours before. We wove our way in and out of people on the crowded street, filled mostly with tourists and, on some corners, small groups of men wearing open shirts and lots of gold jewellery around their necks.

After spending some time strolling the main Red Light street, we turned into a narrow side street. Here there were fewer people, and they kept their eyes averted. Out on the main drag there was lively conversation in many different languages. Here, it was eerily quiet. There were no neon signs, so it was darker. There were many more glowing pinkish windows with women on display. As I noticed an entire block of these windows, I began to wonder if I could be one of those naive young women wooed, or forced, into a situation I would be sorry about later. I recalled our earlier conversation at the hostel. Hamada had first brought up the idea of visiting this area. Now, he seemed to hurry us along, turning first one corner and then another. It seemed to me as if we were navigating a maze. His gentle guiding on the small of my back turned much more purposeful now.

Outside one building we paused and then entered the small covered entranceway. The area was square, with a tall concrete rectangular block in the centre and a little dark door at the back. The outer walls of the entranceway were covered with posters of nearly naked women and show times. As we made our way around the outer walls, the little dark door opened and I glanced inside. The smell of marijuana smoke mixed with alcohol wafted out. The dark hallway was lined with little booths. One man was dropping some coins into a box and opening the booth door. In a moment, Hamada pressed my back again, away from the little door and out of the entrance.

Back out on the main drag, I was a little disappointed that we were leaving the area already, but Hamada said he felt the Red Light District was a museum for tourists. He talked about Amsterdam Nord, where he lived, and the Harbour as being interesting places that most tourists never saw. We agreed to meet again the next day after he finished work so that he could take me there.

Later, as I fell asleep, I couldn't stop thinking about Hamada. He had been a perfect gentleman all evening, kindly showing me the sights and expecting nothing in return. He had safely led me through one of the most dangerous areas of the city. Although I had questioned his intentions, I had not felt unsafe for one moment. In his presence, I felt like royalty.

Then I remembered what he had told me about his plans for the future. He was planning on staying in Amsterdam. He had fallen in love with the city. He wanted to get married to his "second half." Everyone I knew had heard me say, "No house, no marriage, no kids." I knew that I would have to go back to Canada to make use of my expensive degree and, for the near future at least, this was standing in the way of my desire for a daring life of travel. Despite the apparent stark differences in our future plans, my heart beat wildly and I couldn't help but consider the possibility of a future with Hamada. Not just any future, but one as his second half. I came to my senses and deleted these musings from my mind. I chastised myself for lolling around in this type of romanticism. Still, that night I dreamt about him, one of those vivid dreams that seem so real. It was filled with bright colours and excitement and images of meeting his family. In the dream I kissed him and I knew I was his second half.

The next evening, Sunday, at dusk, just one day after we met and the evening before I was scheduled to travel back to Canada, Hamada suddenly declared, "I'm honouring you. The love is in my heart. It's not in my head. I wanna spend the rest of my life with you." My mind raced back over the past two days, the conversation about fate and futures in the park, the tour through the Red Light District, where I felt cocooned in his protection, the dream I had the night before, the afternoon we had just spent in Amsterdam Nord, Rembrandtplein and Leidseplein, getting closer, putting our arms around each other as we walked, lightly pecking each other's head and cheeks. But what could all of that mean—love at first sight? He said, "You are my second half, and it is destiny that we met."

Surely, I thought, *this can't be more than a passing but powerful fling.* There were too many obstacles to a forever ending. So I said, "But I live in Canada." It was all I could say because I wanted him to keep kissing me.

He said, "I will come to you wherever you live, even if it's cold."

At the hostel, we agreed that Hamada would accompany me to the train station the next day after he finished work. I had to travel to Frankfurt by train and, from there, take the plane back to Canada. Hamada never asked me to stay in Amsterdam.

The next morning, I went as planned to the Anne Frank Museum. As I made my way through the museum, I kept hearing Hamada's voice in my head saying I was his second half. The dreamy quality of the past two days with Hamada clashed with the tragedy of the place where Anne Frank and her family led a hidden life during the Second World War. How could love at first sight exist in a world as harsh as this? Near the exit to the museum, conflicting emotions of desire, hope, passion, sadness and despair all swirled around me as I stared at the maps plotting the concentration camps throughout Europe. A man in line in front of me pointed to Bergen-Belsen and said to his companion, "That's where I was." Hearing these words was too much, and I couldn't stay in the museum any longer; tears were now spilling down my cheeks. I pushed my way through to the exit and into the bright, sunshine-filled day.

266   On the way back to the hostel, I felt as though the world were spinning around me. Like leaves whirling in a windstorm, questions filled my head. What had happened in the past two days? I wondered if I was being spoofed by someone who wanted a ticket to Canada. Not likely, since Hamada clearly loved living in Amsterdam, was doing very well and had stated his intention to remain here. Not once had he suggested that

I change my plans and stay on in Amsterdam. Nor had he pressured me for contact information. We had exchanged addresses but not phone numbers.

I thought about how I had ended up in Amsterdam, a city not firmly on my original itinerary. I thought about the big black X through the hostel entry in my guidebook.

And what about me? What about the dream I'd had the first night after we met? What about the sadness and reticence I felt about leaving? How could I be taken in by such a thing as love at first sight? How could fate or destiny collide so dramatically in my life? None of this fit into my plans. Yet I realized I wanted Hamada's profession of love to be true, and this astounded me.

At the station, Hamada accompanied me onto the train, making sure I was seated comfortably. He kissed me goodbye, and I watched him make his way slowly down the steps from the train and then from the platform, head down. I bit my lip and watched. He didn't look back, and I was thankful because I would have run off the train into his arms in an instant.

And so, a year later I found myself picking out a wedding dress. I wasn't right when I said the most important thing about the dress was that it fit into my backpack. The most important thing about it was that I could wear it at all. Okay, it's not a traditional white, satiny wedding dress, but it's *my* wedding dress. It's powdery blue, with large soft pink, pastel yellow and deep purple flowers that look painted on. It's sleeveless and knee-length and sits easily and softly on my body, the sheer outer layer shimmering and floating freely around the light blue slip underneath.

This is the dress I wore on the most romantic and adventurous day of my life. I wore it as we hurtled through the streets of The Hague, seven of us squished into the Corolla, me lying across three passengers in the back seat, including my mother, Hamada and a friend, listening to the frantic Arabic chatter as the driver navigated through the pouring rain to find the Egyptian Embassy for our eleven o'clock appointment.

At the Egyptian Embassy, in the stark light of the reception area, the reality of the cultural divide struck me. Of course, I'd thought of it over the months since we'd first met. We'd discussed it, indirectly mind you, in our numerous letters and regular Saturday phone calls. Now, though, I looked at my mother, who had never been outside North America. Even though she had met Hamada only a few days before, she never said one word to discourage me from marrying him. I looked down at my sleeveless dress: its flattering cut, its hem wafting around my knees, revealing my lower legs and my bare feet in strappy shimmering pastel pink sandals. My eyes were then drawn to the woman staring at me, leaning on a table, chin resting in her palm, mouth a straight line, head covered in a dark scarf and body draped in ankle-length brown-and-cream–coloured fabric. My ears tuned in to the foreign Arabic chatter as I watched Hamada joking around with his good friends. I thought of Hamada's first profession of love and my reply: "But you don't even *know* me. How can you love me? I'm not getting married." I remembered all of my pre-Hamada plans: no marriage, travel alone, reliance only on myself.

Minutes later, in front of an embassy official, my mother and our Egyptian friends and witnesses, Hamada and I joined our right hands traditionally across the low coffee table, thumbs pointing up and touching. As Hamada repeated his marriage vows, I looked deeply into his eyes and into the reflection of myself there for any sign of doubt. I saw only all of my dreams coming true. When I repeated my marriage vows in Arabic, I felt fate continue to unfurl our paths before us, anchored by our hearts.

DARLA TENOLD lives in Saskatoon with her enchanting Egyptian-Canadian husband, Hamada. She works as a lawyer. Hamada and Darla were married in the summer of 1998, and Hamada immigrated to Canada in the spring of 1999. They have since travelled widely in Canada and, to a lesser extent, in Africa. Hamada's love and support was crucial to making Darla's dreams of travelling and becoming a published writer come true. This story is her first publication.

AMI McKay

No Shoes Required

Magical thinking was easy when I was sixteen. Everything was done heart-first. Songs were listened to, rewound and spooled forward on my trusty tape player until the lyrics were not only memorized but the words worn into everyday conversations. "Love Is a Battlefield," I'd declared to one of my girlfriends. "And if Ed Riley wears his Black Sabbath T-shirt on Wednesday, I'll know he's going to ask me to prom." He didn't. He wore it the following Monday. "Too late." I shrugged. "I heard 'Jenny (867–5309)' ten times on Z-96 over the weekend. He'll ask Jen Baxter." By lunch Jen was jumping around the cafeteria, talking about dresses, matching cummerbunds and corsages. My pop-song formula for predicting the future, confirmed.

That same spring, Mrs. E. had begun reading poetry at the start of each English class. She started with sonnets, Shakespeare and Browning, then moved on to Keats and Byron. Something important snapped inside me the day she read Byron's "She Walks in Beauty." Having grown up in a small town where blonde hair and blue eyes ruled the high school hallways, I sighed at the club-footed poet's devotion to his raven-haired love. Move over, Belinda Carlisle, your Top 40 hits have nothing on this guy. Poetry can move mountains. I scrawled in the back of my notebook, *If someone ever recites Lord Byron's "She Walks in Beauty" to me from memory, that's the man I'll marry. I'll wear a beautiful dress, carry wildflowers and go barefoot. No shoes required.*

Somewhere between sixteen and twenty-five, poetry and magical thinking gave way to my newly acquired talent of falling (several times) into the rabbit hole of "What's Love Got to Do with It?" relationships. I spent my university years in music school, giving my heart and soul to Bach, Beethoven and the boys of the brass section. These were hot and heavy times when every steamy embrace meant falling in lust. In all the excitement, I gave up my girlhood dreams and forgot about Byron. By the time I got to graduate school, the French horn player I'd been dating for over a year said it was time we stopped fooling around and got married. He didn't know a thing about poetry, but he was sincere and I adored him. I found myself saying, "I do," wearing a lovely, but predictable dress and a pair of lace-covered, toe-crushing heels.

Only a few months after the wedding, things began to fall apart. Exams, thesis research, concert schedules and a heavy teaching load didn't leave much room for relationship building. We soon realized we hadn't been ready for any of it. Love under pressure is an endangered species at best.

When the marriage ended, I spent a lot of my time feeling sad and sorry for myself. I packed my bags and took a teaching position in Chicago. Some said they had seen it coming. My best friend from university, Dawn, said it was time to get back out

271

there and try again. So I did. Double dates, an old classmate from university, the friend of a friend's brother whom I'd first met on the Internet. What did it matter? I'd had my shot at the white dress and it didn't work out. "Everybody Hurts."

Then, during a long weekend in Toronto, my sixteen-year-old self came back to haunt me. I was with a friend in a restaurant in Chinatown, sitting with four guys, listening to them boast about favourite pickup lines. My friend's brother John swore by quoting from movies: "I've got my top five on the tip of my tongue at all times. One to get her laughing, one to make her blush, one that gets her into bed, you get the idea . . . if the girl doesn't get it, then I didn't want her anyway. I mean, any chick who doesn't know *Blade Runner* from *Casablanca* isn't worth my time." His best friend, Ian—someone I'd met only a couple of times in passing—shook his head. "You've got it all wrong. Poetry, that's what works. Why is poetry written? To woo women." He cleared his throat and began to recite, "'She walks in beauty, like the night / Of cloudless climbs and starry skies . . . '"

My face went red. "That's enough. We get the idea."

He grinned, seeing that I was responding to his efforts. "'And all that's best of dark and bright . . . '"

Just before the last line I blurted out, "Stop. Please."

He looked a little hurt. "Okay. Sorry."

I threw some money on the table and got up to leave.

272   John resumed his movie shtick. "You can't leave. All the plants will die!"

I bumped into John's friend Ian only a few times over the next couple of years. I was still in Chicago, and he had moved to Nova Scotia to get an education degree at Acadia University. Despite the distance, we became good friends. We exchanged emails and phone calls, and then began chatting via Instant Messenger online almost every day. We talked about poetry and music and novels and our relationships of the moment.

"What R U doing tonight? Got a hot date?"

"Well, actually—yes."

"How very *When Harry Met Sally* of you—What's he like?"

"Tall."

"How tall?"

"Umm, maybe 6'4"?"

"Too tall for you, it will never work."

"Shut up. He says he loves me. How's the Catholic girl who won't put out?"

"She's lovely to cuddle with."

"You'll have to marry her if you want to get in her pants."

"Ugh."

Eventually, while nursing each other through simultaneous breakups, we fell in love.

"How R U?"

"Sad."

"I told you he was too tall."

"Right. How are you?"

"Lonely."

"She was too much trouble. The worst kind. She thinks she's low maintenance, but she's really high maintenance."

"You have a long weekend coming up, right?"

"Yes. Thank God."

"Come to Nova Scotia?"

"Really?"

"I dare you."

Ian picked me up at the Halifax airport, all smiles and hugs. "Let's see what happens when we're in the same place for more than a couple of hours." We spent the weekend talking and laughing (among other things). When we stood together holding hands on the rocky shores of Scots Bay and Cape Split, I felt like I'd come home to a place I'd never been. I finally understood what my mother meant when she would tell me the story of the first time she met my father.

She was a young coed at the University of Michigan. He was a sailor in the U.S. Navy, home on leave. Her roommate, Izzy, had set them up on a blind date. They talked for hours; they sat at a diner until the owner kicked them out. My dad was so smitten with my mother that he almost forgot to pay. The jukebox was playing "Hold That Tiger" when the owner grabbed my dad by the arm and said, "Hey, buddy, pay up." After fifty-two years of marriage, she still says, "It was like I was at home with him, like my feet were planted firmly on the ground. That's when you know you're in it for keeps."

On the last night of my visit, Ian sat me down and told me there was something he'd started long ago that he needed to finish. He took my hand and recited the Byron poem from beginning to end. *A heart whose love is innocent . . .*

His family was in Ontario, my family scattered across the States. Where would we have the wedding? What would it cost to get everyone together in one place? How many bridesmaids? How many groomsmen? Sit-down dinner or buffet? Solo harpist? String quartet? Spring, summer, fall, winter? This madness went on for nearly a month before we realized that the cost of putting together a cross-border matrimonial extravaganza equalled a sizeable down payment on the sweet little Scots Bay farmhouse we'd been dreaming of.

Elope. We whispered the idea back and forth between us, the word sounding mysterious, dangerous and sexy. Las Vegas? No, too campy. The Caribbean? No, too cliché. We settled on getting

274

married in Nova Scotia, in early June (just six months after our long weekend together). The lupins would be in bloom, the apple blossoms fluttering to the ground.

A couple of meet-the-parents trips and many questions later, our families saw that we were serious, wished us well and got out of the way. Miraculously, no tears were shed, the plans went together and the date was set. With two weeks to go, only one problem remained. I hadn't been able to find a dress.

Not long after we'd gotten engaged, I'd walked into a Chicago bridal boutique, just to look around. The two women working there leaned their heads together in conversation . . . a verbal rock-paper-scissors to see who would have to wait on me. Evidently, brides-to-be in Birkenstocks don't hold much promise of a fat commission. Four tries at drowning in tulle skirts and pearl-strewn bodices later, and we'd all given up.

Next, I tried the vintage shops along Clark and Belmont. One store had a sleek ivory satin gown, circa 1940, hanging on a rack near the dressing rooms. The skirt pooled around my feet. The shopkeeper commented, "With a little alteration and the right pair of shoes, you'll be stunning." When I explained that I wasn't going to wear shoes, she stammered, "But that dress cries out for shoes. It's a look. A feel."

"Sorry, I guess I just don't feel it."

In desperation, I went through at least seven of my closest friends' and their sisters' closets and came back with nothing. With three days to go, and aside from the fact that it had to be a dress I could wear without shoes, I couldn't even describe what I wanted. I sat on the phone with my friend Dawn and cried.

"What am I going to do?"

"If you can't tell me what you want, tell me what you *don't* want."

I sighed. "Okay. I don't want to wear shoes."

"Yeah, got that. A while ago."

"And I don't want it to look traditional. No white, no sequins, no pearls . . ."

"Nothing out of *Modern Bride.*"

"Right."

"What else don't you want?"

"I don't want a dress I'll never wear again."

"Makes sense. Anything else?"

I paused, my throat getting tight. "Does this mean it's not going to work?"

"Come on . . . you don't mean that. You love him. He loves you. He did that whole kooky poem thing you told me you'd been dreaming of half your life. I barely know the guy and I love him. You'll find a dress."

"In two days?"

"I thought it was three."

"I'm tired and today's more than half over. So there's only two days left."

"Meet me at Star of India in twenty minutes. We'll get some curry. Curry always helps."

The Star of India was on Devon Avenue, a street lined with sari shops, video rental stores specializing in Bollywood films, beauty salons offering henna treatments and several East Indian restaurants. Having missed the lunch buffet, Dawn and I wandered the neighbourhood while we waited for the restaurant to reopen for dinner.

We stood in front of a shop, looking at the colourful posters in the window. One of them featured a close-up of a woman's hands, beautifully covered in swirling patterns of deep red.

"You should have someone mendhi your feet. Since you're hell-bent on not wearing shoes."

"Hey, don't poke fun. I just want to have my feet on the ground this time. Literally."

She took my hand and squeezed it. "I get it. That's why I suggested the mendhi. It's a beautiful ritual and I think your feet would look gorgeous."

"But I'd have to have the right dress to pull it off."

We stopped talking and kept walking. Towards the end of the block was a small shop, its storefront filled with images of Krishna, carved wooden elephants, strings of beads and bells.

Dawn pulled me through the door. "Come inside for a second. I think I saw some do-it-yourself mendhi kits in here once."

The air was filled with the heavy scent of incense. Sandalwood. Cedar. Jasmine. I followed as she ducked past a row of ornate tapestries hanging from the ceiling. My hand brushed across a display of silk scarves, my bracelet catching the rack and pulling it over into a heap on the floor. As I bent to pick up the mess, I noticed the hem of a dress on the wall next to where the scarves had been. I stood up, slowly inspecting the dress from bottom to top, taking in the hand-dyed green fabric, tracing the embroidered patterns with my fingers. It was a simple cut, sleeveless and light, with the weight of a sundress, but the stitching flowed down the bodice and skirt in thread that looked as if it had been spun from antique gold. The store's owner came up behind me to help gather the rest of the scarves. "My sister buys for the shop. She fell in love with that dress as soon as she saw it."

I nodded, still clutching the skirt. "It's beautiful."

Dawn appeared from the back of the store, holding a mendhi kit out to me. "Found it—" She paused when she finally noticed the dress, whispering, "That's it."

I lowered my voice to a whisper. "Yes."

The owner gently unhooked it from the wall. "I've got a room in the back for you to try it on."

Three large wall hangings had been fashioned into a small dressing area in one corner of the storage room. I kicked off my

277

sandals, shrugged out of my clothes and pulled the dress over my head. I stared at myself in a long mirror that was propped against the wall. The bodice hugged smooth against my breasts and my ribs, then gave way to a flowing skirt, the hem resting just above my ankles. Perfect. "I'll take it." We took home the dress, the mendhi kit, four kinds of curry and a bottle of wine. By the end of the night, I was feeling relieved and excited (and a little lit), my feet covered in red dye and wrapped in cellophane, my bags packed for Nova Scotia.

On our wedding day, we took care of the civil ceremony first. Ian and I stood with two of his friends from Acadia at the Kings County courthouse, trying not to laugh when the judge walked in sporting the worst black eye we'd ever seen. I slipped out of my sandals; we nodded, affirmed and signed the papers, choosing to save our vows and our rings for an afternoon hike at Blomidon Provincial Park, just the two of us.

It's been seven years since I married an amazing man who knew the poetry of my heart, who dared me to come to Nova Scotia, who brought me home. Together we've made our home in an old farmhouse by the sea, his love and this place leading me to a life filled with magic at every turn. I wear my wedding dress each year for our anniversary, our two sons now following behind, chasing after my hem and laughing as we make our way up the trails at Blomidon. Each time I pull it over my head, I swear I still smell incense and a hint of curry. Each time the dress falls around my body, I remember the day I first stood on red cliffs overlooking the Bay of Fundy, with a bouquet of lupins in my hand, my feet to the earth. Witnessed by the sky, the sea and a few bell-collared cows in the meadow nearby, my husband once again whispers "She Walks in Beauty" in my ear and promises he'll always have poems for me. I promise I'll always believe in magic.

AMI MCKAY is the author of *The Birth House,* a novel brought about by a wild cosmic soup of destiny, true love and magical thinking. She believes wedding dresses are absurd and sublime all at once. The same can be said about her feet.

GIANNA PATRIARCA

Undressing the Brides

"Re-entering the past is a dangerous adventure."
—Elizabeth Smart

As time so unashamedly crashes your party, some things begin to take on a different meaning. I don't know how well I really know my mother, but in her eightieth year I find myself scrubbing her back in the shower and noticing that her breasts are firmer and more beautifully shaped than her years would prescribe. I notice that her skin is blemish free, white and smoother than it deserves to be. I compare it to my own dark and weathered flesh and wonder how much of me my mother does not know. Her small frame, so unlike my own body shape, makes me fantasize that I may not be her daughter at all, but there is no mistaking our eyes, the shape of our lips, the round of our bellies, all proof enough that there are genes we share. I rub cream into her delicate hands streamed with blue veins and realize that this woman I have taken for granted most of my life, this small, beautifully preserved creature has taken my imagination captive. I feel a need to discover all that I can about her, a need that has come over me like a menopausal heat wave, reminding me how quickly all things become temporary.

My mother's memories are strange pieces of scattered jewellery, earrings missing a mate, bracelets with broken clasps, lovely brooches with shiny stones gone astray. As I speak to Mamma, I try to put the strewn pieces together. She offers them willingly, but they are hidden in different compartments, and even my enthusiasm to restore them to their original state, to their unique beauty, is a little suspect. Whether it is possible or even desirable to plunge into my mother's past is questionable, but Mamma is generous with her stories. They come replete with humour, something she has always relied on to keep things in control, perhaps to hide the more painful moments; now I assume the humour is simply a ploy to conceal the things that have gone to sleep forever in her head.

Which burnished gem shall I remove from its faded velvet bed? Are they not equally valuable? For some unknown reason, I find myself directing curiosity towards what is left of her romantic heart. I have a craving to rummage in places where Mamma and I have never been together before. Places that at one time did not seem appropriate. Perhaps time removes the stigma attached to certain subjects, and sex and romance no longer feel like forbidden territories. I ask Mamma about her wedding day, and as I listen to her she takes me back to a time and place I can only imagine, and her words become a living story.

In the medieval town of Ceprano, in the region of Latium, just above the calf of Italy's boot, on a quiet country road lined with umbrella pines, a black car waited. The sun almost directly over-head in the sky indicated the midday hour. A man sat behind the steering wheel, his face obscured by the wide bent brim of his hat. The sun reflecting on the murky glass made him almost invisible. He sat motionless, waiting. Soon she would appear. Soon she would be walking home after a morning spent working in the fields. It was the month of May, and the sun was bright. The countryside was a shade of green that could only come from spring rain and warm days. The mimosa trees were still full with yellow flowers. It was a perfect day, the kind of day that only the month of May, the month of our Blessed Mother, could deliver. The man stepped out of the car and paced up and down the length of it until he noticed the slight figure in the distance. As it approached slowly and rhythmically, it began to take shape. He fumbled with his hat nervously as he waited for the figure to come closer. She was the one he was waiting for. He recognized the pulse of her movements, the length of her loose dark hair, the cadence of her voice humming the familiar tune of "Giovinezza." With each approaching step, her cotton print dress swimming about her hips and legs, she became real. The man lit a cigarette to keep his nervous fingers busy. With each lungful of air he felt his heart expand. She stopped a short distance from where he was standing, and her intense, shadowy eyes settled on him and seemed to penetrate into his skin. He flicked the cigarette to the ground and crushed it beneath his heel as he walked towards her. He stopped when his face was a breath away from hers, his lips tremulous. All that escaped from his parched throat was her name.

"Marianna."

For a moment the silence between them was louder than bells. Marianna's inquisitive eyes did not move. This had happened before. He had been waiting for her before, many other times, and each time she had repeated the same words.

"I am promised to someone else; you know that. Please leave me in peace."

Her screams were muffled. There was no one around in the midday hour to hear her. Everyone was at home, in their kitchens, enjoying their daily meal. Two men jumped out of nowhere, took hold of her arms and forced her into the car, while the man in the hat positioned himself in the driver's seat. They sped away along the country road towards the hill as the sunlight flickered through the expansive branches of the tall umbrella pines. The man in the hat was my father. He kidnapped the woman he loved on a sunny spring day two years before my birth. On a country road less than a mile away from a small town cradled in the arms of sloping hills, beneath a blue and secretive Mediterranean sky, my father committed his one passionate crime.

This unscrupulous act was not an uncommon practice in small, desperate towns devastated by the Second World War in Italy. At times it was a consensual agreement between two lovers who could not afford the cost of a wedding. On other occasions it was because the intended bride had no dowry, her family too poor to provide the respected endowments that went along with marrying a daughter, so the couple resorted to the dramatic pretense. Eloping or being stolen by a boyfriend or fiancé became a practised and practical alternative. Occasionally a young, beautiful girl became the victim of a young man's obsession, a young man who could not have her any other way and resorted to kidnapping. Of course, people in the towns always assumed, or believed, it was all pre-arranged by the two individuals involved, and even if there had been no physical violation it was understood that the woman now belonged to her captor.

My father had known my mother all his life. They had grown up together in the same town, had gone to school together as children. He had loved my mother from the time they were old enough to play the childish games of romance, and had claimed

283

her as his when he was twelve and she was only nine. He announced to his friends and any potential suitor that Marianna would one day be his wife. Although my mother was fond of him, considered him a friend and even found him charming and attractive, she was not in love with him. Papa stole the woman he wanted, without her consent, and changed the course of her life on a bright, warm day in the month of May.

Mamma married my father in the month of September, when the season is ripe with colours and the sweet taste of fruits. September, when the grape becomes the new wine and the sun begins to slowly cool in the sky. She agreed to love and honour on a Thursday afternoon in the church of Saint Rocco, in the centre of the town's piazza. She married my father not in a long white gown with flowing lace but in a pale blue suit with an ivory collar. The straight skirt stopped below her knees and had a slit in the back. The pearl buttons on the jacket came to her waist, and a white lace kerchief draped freely on her loose curls landed on her shoulders. Her bouquet was of wild autumn flowers from the open fields. On her feet were shiny black leather shoes, high-heeled shoes, the new style, with a tiny bow made of deep crimson velvet on the pointed tips. A matching handbag and gloves had been bought in Rome and sent to her by her great-aunt. Her twenty-two years were her dowry. Mamma stood compliant—her five-foot frame, her pallid skin, her hazelnut eyes unforgiving—next to the man who had chosen her wedding suit, chosen her shoes, chosen the month and the day she would become a bride.

Mamma and I sit at the kitchen table on late Saturday evenings; it is a habit now, and we have long conversations. The month of May is a sour memory.

"Only prostitutes marry in May." Mamma laughs out loud, taking in a deep mouthful of air. "No respectable woman would steal the light of the Blessed Mother and get married in the month of May; it belongs to her. Besides, in May everyone is busy in the fields, planting, working. Your father chose the wrong month to commit his crime, but then he never relied on sense—he was a romantic, like you. He always acted with his heart, not his head, and that will get you in trouble."

Mamma's face turns away from me; perhaps some things are best not remembered, not shared. I cannot help but be her husband's daughter for a while and indulge my romantic heart.

"Did you ever love Papa at all?" I ask her. She fumbles with her wedding ring as if she is channelling the correct answer.

"You learn to love a person over the years; it makes it easier. You have children with a man, you find a way to love him."

"Papa loved *you*, he adored *you*, all those years, and right till the end I could see it in his face, in the way he looked at you, the way he spoke to you, always with warmth, respect. You were still that young girl on that spring day. He loved you," I tell her.

"I know . . . I know he did. That's the tragedy, isn't it: I could never love him back the same way . . ." Mamma opens the cupboard door, pulls out the espresso pot and begins preparing the coffee.

"How did you feel when you had to sleep with him?" I ask her.

The cupboard door slams shut.

"Sleep with him? Oh no. No, no, no. I knew I had to marry him because people would believe we had been together—my reputation was ruined—but I wouldn't sleep with him until we got married. I lived with his parents, your grandparents, until the wedding day. He never touched me, never, until after we got married." Mamma counts the spoonfuls of coffee and places them into the pot, patting the coffee down with the spoon to make sure the flavour will be strong.

"Why didn't you wear a wedding dress, then, a long white wedding dress instead of the suit?" My tongue stumbles over the question.

"A stolen woman is not worthy of white, no longer the lily-pure virgin of the month of May. In those days, if someone stole you, then you were used goods, you were considered spoiled; you couldn't wear a white gown whether you were innocent or not."

More than sadness, I see resignation in her eyes.

"But I married in church without sin. God knows and I know; that's enough for me."

Mamma places the espresso pot on the element and switches it on to high, a sign that she wants it to boil quickly.

"I did have a wedding dress, a beautiful one your grandmother made for me. The dress I was supposed to wear when I got married. But your father changed all that. After your father stole me, the boy I was in love with left and went to Germany. I never saw him again. I suppose he got married and had a family. I hope so."

"What was he like, the man you loved?" I fold my arms and rest them on the table.

Mamma waits. She lifts the lid of the pot to see if the coffee has started to rise up the little spout. It is too soon.

"Oh, he was so handsome—curly hair, black, not too tall. His name was Vito." She places the sugar bowl on the counter. "He was so gentle, a sweet boy. A shoemaker. A very good *artigiano* he was. He worked with leather, a real craftsman. He once made me a pair of sandals with long strings that wrapped around your legs, like the Romans used to wear. We called them *ciocie* in our dialect. They were very fashionable at the time. He was a good man." Mamma's smile comes easily.

"The wedding dress, tell me about the dress you didn't get to wear."

"It was a dress like any wedding dress—beautiful. Your grandma hand-stitched and embroidered the veil; the lace came from Sicily. It was really beautiful. I kept it for a long time, thinking, *I will have daughters someday who will like to wear my dress,* but you and your sister, you two would never have fit into it. I knew that by the time you girls were six years old. Both of you came out so big, and then coming here to this cold country, growing up in this Canadian air, it must have worked like yeast. I don't know, but not even those elastic girdles would have helped you girls get into that dress."

The laughter dances in Mamma's chest. I enjoy listening to the pleasure in her voice and seeing the delight that comes over her face as she remembers those restrictive girdles my sister and I were forced to wear. Remembering how we fought with such determination against having to wear them.

"You were always a big girl," Mamma assures me. "You were almost eleven pounds when you were born, the longest baby anyone had seen in our *quartiere.* I fought for almost two days to get you out of my belly, and my right leg and my back have never been normal since."

Mamma's lightness of spirit in describing my beginnings is a sure sign that there are things about me she is not aware of. I have battled with the issue of weight all my life, and it seems to have completely escaped her.

"Your grandmother was so amazed that I could give birth to you, such a big baby, that she walked to town in the middle of the night in a freezing January to wake the priest out of his nice warm bed and make him come out to the farm to bless both of us." She breaks into a chuckle, and I cannot help but join in. "How she managed to get Father Bernardo out there in the middle of the night in January, I just don't know, but your grandmother had her ways."

My grandmother Mariangela had given birth to seven children of her own, my mother being her last baby. I was her baby's first-born, and my grandma reserved a special place in her heart for this huge, dark, long child who had erupted from her daughter's small and aching womb. By the time my own wedding became a possibility, my grandmother had died. She had waited patiently for her tall, defiant granddaughter to find a husband, had wanted to embroider my veil, to see me in a wedding dress, but at ninety-one she was tired of waiting for my feminist ideas to move aside long enough to make space for a groom, for a church, a priest. I was too involved in the New World, the pursuit of the dream and the books of Germaine Greer. I was trying to find and understand my own identity before becoming somebody's wife. Grandma couldn't wait for all that.

I married at thirty-two. At thirty-two my grandmother had had five children. I felt old. I had always felt old with the weight of my Italian history, the lack of confidence that most Italian immigrant girls seemed to be victims of. The cultural ties to my Italian roots and sensibilities were powerful and strong. The expected practice of certain traditions, the religious fears and the guilt associated with wanting something different or wanting to be different caused a constant struggle in my head and heart. I was caught between two worlds, and I couldn't decide which one I belonged to, which one would make me happy. I married a man whose background was new to me, and very exciting. A man who had grown up in New Zealand, whose ancestors had settled there from Scotland four generations before. I decided my wedding dress should reflect the mature, serious and intelligent woman I believed I was. I knew my future husband had little interest in the theatrical pageantry of large Italian-Canadian weddings, and I believed I had moved beyond such frivolous spectacles myself. We decided on a small and tasteful celebration with family and friends.

My dressmaker, Maria, who had been shaping material around my bountiful body since my teenage years, offered to sew the dress for me. I went shopping for the perfect fabric. I went alone, having opted out of the tradition of half a dozen brides-maids wearing mustard chiffon dresses with silly bouffant hairstyles. My best friend, Emilia, was my maid of honour, and she would end up sewing her own lovely blue dress. I shopped for days, trying to find the appropriate textile in the appropriate shade. I settled on an ivory silk crepe. Maria's talents created a dress whose soft A-line skirt rested on my knees. The sleeves were three-quarter length, and the V-neck line hinted at cleavage. My long black hair was pulled back in a flamenco dancer's bun, with a fresh lily inserted at the side. I wore pearl

earrings and one string of white pearls around my neck, ivory open-toed sandals and a small cream purse I had found in a second-hand store. I was elegant and conservative, unlike the rebellious feminist I thought I had been all my life.

＝

"You never wanted a traditional wedding dress. You and those women's liberation ideas." Mamma pours a cup of coffee and dunks the amaretto cookie deep into the little cup. "Look at your wedding picture on the wall." Her head turns towards my wedding photograph, positioned just above my sister's wedding photo, both of them prominently displayed on the wall next to the refrigerator, so no one can ever open the fridge door to remove a beer or a piece of cheese without being reminded that Mamma has two married daughters. My beautiful twenty-three-year-old sister stands arm in arm with her handsome husband, she in a white turban with a long veil that stops at her ankles, a soft georgette skirt and a lace bodice covered in rows of endless pearls.

"You thought you were too old at thirty-two, too old to wear a long white dress, so you decided to wear something mature . . . mature . . . that's what you said . . . right?"

"Yes, that's what I said. I felt old. I thought I'd look stupid in a wedding dress with lace and frills. I wasn't a kid anymore; I didn't want to look like some Barbie doll princess. I really believed that back then," I explain.

"We are always in jail with what we think we believe, what other people think of us. Just like me: I should have walked away, not married your father, but where would I go? What would I do? There was nothing for me back then. It is different now." Mamma shakes her head and starts to play with the coffee spoon, round and round in her cup. "Stupid world, stupid ideas, stupid people.

I see a young, pretty girl in that picture. That's what I see. A girl a little scared, maybe, in a dress too grown-up for her. You would have looked like an angel in a long white dress with lots of lace, but somehow you didn't think you deserved it. Did you?"

"Never mind my dress. I decided what I wanted to wear; wrong or right, I decided."

"Did you really?" Mamma rolls her eyes.

"Yes, I did. And yes, I do regret it a little. Is that what you want to know?"

Her face fills with sympathy. "Sometimes we make the wrong choice for the right reasons. Now your grandma, well, she got married in one of those traditional costumes—you know, the ones you see in the postcards. *La Ciociara.* She had a long colourful skirt with the white apron and the cotton blouse with waves of ruffles and the black corset that holds up your breasts. She had three strings of coral beads around her neck, the most beautiful necklace you ever saw. Her earrings were coral too. She had a white linen handkerchief folded in a triangle on her head. Your aunt Concetta has a picture. Your grandma had left the coral beads to the first three daughters, one string each for your aunts, but Mussolini took it all during the war. Women were expected to give up their gold, anything valuable like coral, for the war effort. Mussolini even took your grandma's wedding band. I would have liked those earrings."

"What happened to your dress, the one Grandma made for you?" I ask her.

Mamma's face softens. She turns, stares at the kitchen window and walks over, pulling aside the thin veil curtain. I look to see what has captured her attention, but there is only the faint grey-white light of the late evening, hanging like an old, fading drape. Without turning her head she answers, "I gave it away."

She continues to stand still, her eyes fixed on the pane.

"Who did you give it to?"

Mamma turns and walks slowly towards the table. She sits again, facing me, and picks up my hand. "Your hands are so large. You have your grandfather's hands, worker's hands, not like your father; he had long, thin fingers like an artist or musician, but he only played cards with those hands. He was a bad gambler." She takes in a breath that settles deep in her chest.

"I am the gambler's daughter, Mamma, even if our hands are different," I say.

"He was a bad gambler, your father, but he wasn't bad. No, he wasn't bad."

"That dress was not meant for a bride. Not for me, or you or your sister. I gave it away years ago to a woman who needed it."

"So someone did wear it for their wedding, then?" I am almost pleased.

"No. She . . . she didn't wear it for her wedding, she wore it for her funeral."

My espresso cup hits the saucer. I reach for the tea towel and begin to wipe up the coffee spilled on the table. Mamma walks over to the window again and looks out at the tree in the yard, its branches beginning to sprout little green splotches, like splashes of paint from a child's reckless paintbrush.

"What did you say?" I ask.

"She wore it for her funeral," Mamma repeats. "She was just seventeen, not a woman at all, just a child, really. Her mother and me, we worked together in the same factory. Remember where I worked? We made toys at the factory down the east side of the city, near Carlaw Avenue."

I did remember; I still had some of the discarded, rejected toys she would bring home to my sister and me, the ones that had not passed inspection and could not be sold. The dolls with crooked eyeballs or missing fingers, rubber balls with smudged designs. Some of them were still in boxes in the basement.

"We worked side by side on that assembly line, painting faces on those little dolls, dressing them in little dresses with little plastic shoes, day after day in that dark building without windows, me and Cristina, day after day, year after year." Mamma's eyes begin to moisten. She pulls out a handkerchief from her pocket and brushes it across her face. "Cristina was my friend. She had two daughters a little older than you and your sister. One of her daughters died back in the sixties. I can't remember the exact year." She begins shaking her head, as if to jumble the pictures in her brain. "That poor woman needed help. She had no money; she would have gone into debt to buy her daughter a white wedding dress to bury her in. That's what they did then, for young virgin girls who hadn't had a chance to be brides—they buried them in wedding gowns. So I gave her mine. It was an honour to have her child wear it. I didn't need it anymore."

My mother's words "It was an honour" chime in my head. What meaning do we attach to white lace and satin and silk? Maybe our hearts and souls have a preference for fabric, or colour, or tex-ture, and culture and values are recognizable only by the costumes we wear. What sentiment, what need is anchored in my closet, where my own wedding dress hangs clean, pressed and covered by plastic. Why is it still there? My conservative dress, four sizes too small for me now and way too large for my own beautiful daughter, who has grown to embrace her father's Scottish genes and not my Italian ones. I look up at the wedding photos of my sister and me and realize how much they are a part of my mother's daily rituals, how they are there with her morning coffee, with her evening meals, how they comfort her, how they validate the time and experiences of her life. I realize how much we are the traditions we try to bury inside ourselves or run away from.

Mamma pours herself another espresso and refills my cup. There are no words between us as we drink the thick, black, sugary solution. The evening has turned to night. There is no light from the window. The tree has vanished into the darkness. Mamma and I sit together in silence. Words are unnecessary. I stretch my large hand and rest it on hers. I feel the warm beating flow of her full veins. Suddenly I have an irresistible desire to go out and buy her a new pair of earrings. Perhaps I will give her a coral pair of mine.

GIANNA PATRIARCA is a teacher, poet and writer. She lives in Toronto with her husband, her daughter and her mother. She has published five books of poetry and one children's book and is currently working on a novel entitled *The Sicilian's Bride*. She continues to be fascinated by life, love and people's stories. She enjoys fine Italian cooking and long ago threw away the restrictive girdle.

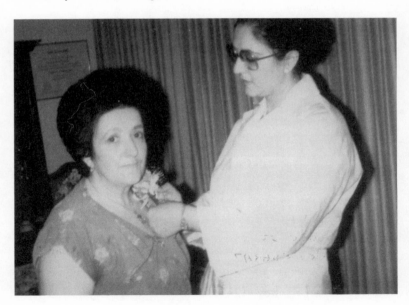

Dark Water

My mother's wedding dress, a rich, blue-black velvet, flowed from her shoulders to just above her ankles. It had weight to it and a soft nap that invited you to touch and hold it like a liquid shadow in your hands. As a child, I used to climb inside her closet, where it hung in the back, and rub my cheek against it. By the time I was old enough to understand the word *vintage* and ask if I could wear it, Mom had cut it up and turned it into two cushion covers. It seemed a sacrilege. Throughout my childhood, it had been the most beautiful article of clothing in the house.

For years I thought my mother's ruination of the dress was simply an example of her thrift and practicality, though the cushions didn't stay long on the couch. She hadn't taken the time to sew a smooth seam, and rather than buy proper stuffing, she'd used two old pillows that were too big and had to be bent and folded into the corners. The cushions didn't lie flat; nor did the colour match the couch or the room. Now I wonder if she had other reasons. Was she sick of the dress and what it stood for? Or with rare but understandable selfishness did she want to prevent it from being worn by anyone else on any other day than October 26, 1938, the date two young people from Saskatchewan farms pledged their love, honour and obedience to one another?

By 1938, Saskatchewan had suffered eight years of drought. The fields were blowing away, there were relief lines at the CPR station, yet with her mother, my mom as a young bride-to-be caught the train to Swift Current to look for a gown at Kling's Ladies' Wear on Central Avenue. The small city was thirty miles away from Success. This would be a first—at twenty years old Mom had never owned a store-bought dress. My grandmother had sewn her three daughters' clothes, some of them from flour sacks, but for this occasion she'd somehow scraped together enough money, perhaps from the scarce eggs and cream produced in that dry year, to purchase a modestly priced gown. She didn't know if she and her Singer machine could handle a material fancier than they were used to, and besides, her middle daughter deserved something special.

Mom had sent home the little money she'd earned helping her future mother-in-law do her spring cleaning and cook for the men on the threshing machine bringing in the thin fall crop. To pay for a perm, Grandma contributed a duck and a chicken Mom could sell to the Chinese café in town. The chicken died on the way, and Emerson, the man who would become my father, gave his betrothed the extra twenty-five cents she'd need to pay the hairdresser to create her curls.

Dust would have been blowing on my parents' wedding day. I imagine my mother running her hands over the blue-black velvet, brushing it clean in the foyer of the church before she walked down the aisle. She and Dad were going to live in a small grey shack abandoned by a homesteader and across the road from his parents' farm. The reception would be held in their new place, and that morning she'd peeled potatoes and turnips, made stuffing for the turkey and baked three raisin pies. Her older sister would put the roaster in the wood stove just before the wedding started. Her father had bought some beer, enough for the ten or so men who'd be crowded into the one-room shack. Just before the wedding party arrived from the church, both the bride's and the groom's younger brothers found the stash of bottles in the root cellar and downed every one. It was before my father's drinking days, so it wasn't a tragedy to him, but my grandfather was ready to take his horsewhip to their hides.

What a contrast on the wedding day between the luxuriousness of the dress and the starkness of that shack! In its small space, I imagine the guests shoulder to shoulder, wanting to brush against the bride. She is so beautiful in the pictures, and I hope she knew it for that one autumn day in 1938, because she has denied her beauty all her life. During the reception, her new husband must have loved to rest his arm around her, feeling the texture of the cloth, and later to slide his hands over the rich smoothness of her hips and down her legs. The velvet, the colour of pooled ink, must have drawn the moonlight into its folds and dewlaps as it lay draped on a chair by the bed, the couple young and naked in one another's arms, their lives together stretching in front of them, full of promise like the gifts they'd unwrapped earlier that day, bright with newness and good cheer in that hand-me-down, make-do time of drought and failure.

The morning after the wedding night, Mom shook the dust out of the bedding and hung the dress on a wooden hanger on one of the nails pounded into the wall. She then walked to the nearby town to buy a big bottle of formaldehyde from the general store. I don't know where my father was, maybe back at work fixing some machine on his family's farm. At her new home, in the biggest pot my mother could find, probably the turkey roaster used for the reception, she boiled the formaldehyde for hours on the back of the stove. The night before, the shack had been alive with bedbugs. The deadly home remedy killed the biting insects, and for the next few days, she and my father had only mice to deal with. When Mom tells me now about the effectiveness of the embalming fluid, I ask, "But what did it do to you?" Eighty-eight years old, she says, "I'm still here."

The velvet would have soaked up the funeral-home scent; it would have overpowered whatever perfume my mother's neck and shoulders had brushed into the fabric. By the time I buried my face in its softness, that mortuary odour was gone. The dress had taken on the more delicate smells of time passing: traces of meals cooked in different kitchens; the musty closeness of moth-balls; the scent of lilacs from the ubiquitous mauve bushes blooming in prairie yards; years of dust from the fields, the gravel roads and the grassless backyard of the rented house in Swift Current where I grew up. No female scent was left from the hours the dress graced my mother's body, no smell of my father's sun-browned hands remained in the fabric, no whiff of the physical love that made my brother and then made me. As a child, I went back to its dark presence in the back of the closet not for its smell but for its texture, for the midnight opulence of its blue, for the memory it held of my mother's young beauty, her hope-fulness, her pride, her small flight into a better life. When she tried it on in the store, it was the first time she'd seen herself in a full-length mirror, turning to the left, then the right, standing on her toes and looking over her shoulder at the waterfall of velvet spilling down her back, almost touching the floor. It was like something from the movies. In those years of drought, it was a dark, heavy cloud blessed with rain.

There's a strange synchronicity surrounding my first marriage and my mother's. Like her, I was twenty. She's thirty years older than me, and my marriage took place in 1968, exactly thirty years after hers. By that time no bride wore anything but white. My dress, which I'd picked out with Mom from the same store she'd gone to all those years ago, though its name and owners had changed, was a sleeveless, straight gown with a princess waist and a long matching jacket. I thought it elegant and classy in its simplicity. It had no lace, beads, sequins or frills. Its material was satin-like and puckered as if someone had pinched the fabric with her thumbs as you do a pie crust to make the scalloped edge. Although my fiancé and I were paying for our small, no-frills wedding, like her mother my mom insisted on buying my dress. No longer on the farm, she didn't have eggs or cream to sell, but for years she'd cleaned houses to buy groceries and have some spending money of her own.

Both Mom and I weighed 118 pounds on our wedding days. I didn't have to cook the reception dinner as she had done, but the two settings where the guests gathered had much in common. Although my parents had long ago moved out of their country shack to the city of Swift Current, the rented house where we moved when I was fourteen was almost as small and derelict. The toilet and bathtub sat in a cellar with dirt walls and a dirt floor covered by a sheet of cracked linoleum. There was no sink; we had to wash our hands upstairs in the kitchen. Against the northern wall, where it was cool, Dad had pounded together a big bin to hold the potatoes dug from the garden. To get to the toilet or the tub, separated from one another by salvaged plywood Mom had whitewashed to brighten things up, you had to navigate past the wringer washer and a backless wooden chair that held the big tin laundry tub. The stairway down was dark and narrow, and though Mom was a spit-and-polish housekeeper, no one could make the cellar look clean. Because she worried about my white dress brushing the steps and floor every time I needed the toilet, she'd arranged for me to use our neighbour's house to change into my finery.

The Stuarts, who lived across the street and who made their place available on my wedding day, owned our house. The city accountant, Harry Stuart, along with his wife, had bought for close to nothing and rented out several rundown buildings in our town. Mom had mixed feelings about them. On the one hand, Harry was a hearty, friendly man; Maria, an immigrant from Germany, was hard-working and unassuming. And though they had three daughters of their own, they'd offered to lend me money for my first year at university. They'd done this anonymously through my school principal. Over the years we lived across from them, I was unaware that they'd watched my father's slide into alcoholism and the effects of his drinking on Mom and me. They'd also followed my high school successes in the local paper, had gone to my school plays and, I think now, had concluded I was capable of rising above my station. Their generous gesture opened a door for me that couldn't be closed.

On the other hand, when Mom would ask them to pay for a gallon of paint so she could brighten up the kitchen, or requested that a light be installed in the cellar stairwell because she was afraid one of us would stumble in the dark and fall, they expressed anger at her temerity and refused. The fence around the yard was falling down, one of the front steps had caved in, the insulation was so bad that the north side of my bedroom wall was furred with frost in the winter mornings. With no help from the landlords, my parents fixed what they could without spending money they didn't have.

The afternoon I stood on the pale carpet in their big upstairs guest room with its dormer window full of light and pulled on my wedding dress, I could pretend this was my family home. I stared at my tall, chic self in the long mirror on the closet door. The straight lines of the dress and the bun that tamed my curls and sat on top of my head added inches to my five-foot-three frame. The dress was also pristine and cool as if it had been made from snow dimpled by the wind. I wore white satin shoes and the string of cultured pearls my fiancé had given me the night before. He was a working-class kid like me, and I knew he'd chosen the most exotic and refined thing he could imagine. They'd come in a black velvet box shaped like a flattened scallop shell, and a tiny diamond chip shone in the centre of the clasp.

No one looking at me would have said I didn't belong in this beautiful house, this large, sun-filled room with its tulle curtains and pale yellow bedspread with four, not two, pillows, an abundance I'd never seen before. I floated pearled, pale and untouchable down the hall to the gleaming bathroom, turned a many-faceted glass doorknob and stood in front of a three-sided mirror above the sink, the three fixtures shining and pink. There were white matching towels and washcloths by the tub and pink roses from the garden on the counter. The soap in its own little dish was shaped like a fully opened rose. I knew Mrs. Stuart had done her best to make her house pretty on my wedding day. I bent to smell the blossoms. For reasons I didn't understand then, the beauty made me feel like weeping, as if I'd inhaled the thorns, not the perfume.

When I look at the studio photograph of me now, I'm amazed at how young I was. I'm even more amazed at how I don't look like me. I was trying so hard to escape who I was and where I'd come from, to be classy and aloof, to love with all my heart the man I'd chosen. The conventionality of the dress says a lot about me.

I wanted to fit in, to do what all my friends were doing, to be "a good girl," not a fallen one from the wrong side of the tracks. I didn't want to be poor or gaudy or bad.

For my generation, and probably for my mother's, the worst thing that could happen to a family was an out-of-wedlock pregnancy. If the girl's parents could afford it, she was sent to a home, though everyone pretended she was "visiting an aunt" in the city. If there was no extra money to pay for room and board in Regina or Saskatoon, her shame grew with her belly if she dared to show herself in the streets. I'd hung on to my virginity as if it were a magic talisman, as if its loss would brand me with a scarlet letter everyone could see. With two more years of university to go before I could start teaching, one of the reasons I was getting married was to break my maidenly state. I was tired of saying "no." My mother was relieved she didn't have to worry about an unwed daughter's pregnancy anymore, and she could see that the honour-roll young man I'd met at university had two things strongly in his favour: he wasn't a drinker like my dad, and he had a steady job teaching high school math and physics.

I don't know if my mother and I had virginity in common on our wedding nights. We've never talked about that. Perhaps the biggest difference between our marriages lies not in the dissimilarity of our dresses but in the duration of our commitment to our vows. On the living-room wall of the cozy house she and Dad moved into in their early sixties, long after I'd left home, hangs a petit point square, a gift from one of my cousins. Flowers delicately scroll the four margins, and in the centre three lines are stitched with fine red thread:

Emerson and Margaret Crozier
Golden Wedding Anniversary
October 28, 1938–1988

In spite of the problems alcohol creates in a marriage, Mom and Dad were together until his death two years after their fiftieth anniversary. My marriage didn't last. Even while I was walking down the aisle in my white gown, I knew I was doing something wrong, something untrue to myself, though I couldn't have told you who that self was or would turn out to be. It took me ten years to figure that out and to find the courage to leave. After all, my husband was a good man, his teaching salary helped put me through my last two years of school, and we had much in common, including a love of books, dogs and cross-country skiing. My friends called him a feminist. If I wasn't happy, what was wrong with me? Who did I think I was? When I was able to see myself more clearly, I realized the last thing I wanted in my twenties was goodness. I wanted sparks and conflagration. I wanted to strike big wooden matches and burn my fingers. If I'd bought a dress to leave the marriage as I'd bought one to go into it, it would have been bright red with a long, wide skirt that swished and swirled when I strode away.

Though I clearly recall my mother's cushion covers, I don't remember what I did with my wedding dress. The material, unlike her velvet, didn't invite you to touch it, rub your face against it or run it through your fingers. It was stiff, and though I can't come up with the exact name of the fabric, there was something artificial about it. It wouldn't have drawn a child to its folds. Its narrow, rigid skirt reined in my usual long stride, and I rustled down the aisle with mincing steps that, even then, didn't suit me. They were made worse by high heels I wasn't used to, though my dad, who'd kept his promise to stay sober, gave me a steady arm.

Since I didn't inherit my mother's and grandmother's ability with handiwork, or their pragmatism, I didn't cut the dress up years later then stitch it together for another use. Surely I didn't leave it behind in the old blue metal trunk Mom bought me when I turned eighteen and left home for university. Surely it didn't sit in the basement of the house I'd owned with my husband, waiting for him and his new wife to find it. He'd met her at the high school where we both once worked. She taught home ec and designed and sewed her gown by hand. People said it was a masterpiece, nothing like it in the stores. I'd like to think I threw mine into a burning barrel and pushed it into the fire with a long stick, but that wish shows a bitterness I don't deserve to feel. After all, I was the one who left, who ran off with another man, flamboyantly and seemingly without a care for anyone but myself.

My husband did one thing that made my parents understand at least some part of why I'd had to leave him. I headed down the road with my new love in July. At the end of September, they drove out to the acreage my husband and I had bought together and where he still lived. They'd come to dig up the potatoes we'd let them plant that spring. It was a huge plot of earth, and as they pulled up to it in their car, they saw that the whole thing had been rototilled, the potatoes split into small pieces by the spinning blades. There was nothing left to harvest. For two farm people who'd survived the years of drought, there couldn't have been a surer sign of bad character. It would have been different had he dug up the potatoes and used them for himself. They'd never encountered such a waste.

The advantage always lies with the person who tells the story. It's possible I've exaggerated the fluidity and beauty of my mother's dress and the stiffness of mine. Maybe she regretted the colour and would call it sooty if I asked her. Maybe the inside lining made her itch. It could have been a hot day, the shack sweltering as the turkey cooked in the wood stove, the dress, close and heavy, clinging to her skin. With the perspective of distance, I can see my own gown as an outward sign of the rigidity that came from my fierce attempt to hold in what I was and what I feared to be. I shouldn't be so hard on its design and fabric. At the time, it was a costume of purity and good taste. As I walked down the aisle, it announced, "This is a regular twenty-year-old bride who will lead a regular domestic life." I didn't know that my family's poverty, my father's drinking and my cultural ignorance had narrowed me. I didn't know enough to free myself of my own limited expectations of what a woman's life could be. I was not ready to be reckless.

I saw my mother's dress through a young girl's eyes, not a grown woman's, but I think I've described it as truly as I can. She's bought others since, of course, mainly from catalogues, but this was the best, and I like to believe it had an effect on me when she wore it, though it was just for one day. If there's any truth to the belief that our spirits exist pre-birth in some kind of ether, looking down, I chose my mother when I saw her in that dress. In spite of the harshness of the setting, the failed crops and dust, I picked the prairies as my home because she lived there; I opened my eyes to the unmediated light pouring around her as she stood on the church's top step. Just before she walked through the door to stand by my father, did she look up and meet my gaze? Did she sense me then and draw me to her? From the day of her wedding, I waited for my time to live inside her, the velvet she had chosen the same colour as the dark water that would hold me ten years later in her womb.

LORNA CROZIER is a Distinguished Professor at the University of Victoria, where she chairs the Department of Writing. In 2001, after living together for twenty-three years, she and Patrick Lane got married in their garden. Patrick says they had a long engagement; Lorna says they were never engaged. Once again, she didn't like her wedding dress. Perhaps because she was in marriage denial, she put off shopping until a few days before the event. It was the end of August, and all that was left in the stores were the on-sale items that no one else had chosen to take home. She'd wanted to wear red but ended up with the only suitable dress she could find, a long white cotton with a flirty hem. It made her look fat. She and Patrick, one year sober, stood under the apple tree weighted with fruit, their two cats brushing against their legs. A small group of friends listened to the exchange of vows. Though the dress was wrong, everything else was right, especially Patrick, especially the fifty-three-year-old woman she'd become.

Two Suits and a Closet

The voice at the other end of the line asked for a piece about my wedding dress.

"I didn't have one. It was a suit."

"Write about your suit, then."

How absolutely uninteresting, I thought.

The eager voice continued. "It will have emotion attached to it. All wedding dresses, I mean suits, do."

"Do you want the wedding in England years ago, or the one in Toronto that a couple of friends boycotted last June?"

"I wasn't sure if you'd be comfortable with it, but if you are, that would be wonderful. What did you wear?"

I told her.

"*Great,* so either, or both. Anyway, think about it, eh?"

I didn't want to. I struggled to hold it at bay, but it chased me like a sniffing dog. *Get away,* I told him, *I can't remember a thing about it.*

Reluctantly, I nudged my memory on that first one, but I could remember only the jacket. It was a fine dark tweed, with padded shoulders and a nipped-in waist. Was the whole thing a pantsuit? It couldn't have been, not in 1946. I don't think women wore pantsuits then, let alone to their weddings, and certainly not if you were a parson's daughter in England, where I grew up.

In desperation I hunted for a wedding photo. At last I found a couple in an ancient album my old nurse had given to me. The last time I had looked through it was on my visit to England shortly before she died, in the early seventies.

The slender young bride looks out at me tensely, more diffident than her older husband, handsome in a naval uniform. She wears a "costume," as we called them, and although its frugal appearance echoes the war, the skirt has two pleats in front (and in the back, as I recall), and I was very proud of it. Those kick pleats were supposed to give women a beginning sense of freedom after the war. What a mirage. I had yet to learn that willow-figured brides can put on weight too, and in my case would

outgrow the marriage along with the costume. (My friend on the phone was right. There *is* emotion tied up in this thing: emotion I want to resist, but already it is tugging me in.)

How did Duncan and I get together in the first place?

He was my first cousin, fourteen years older, and a professional actor, so I had always known about him, but he lived far away and didn't impinge on my child's world. That ended during a fateful day in the fall of 1937 when his touring company came to play for a week in our city.

I had already picked theatre as my number one choice from my sister's book of careers. The idea that a faraway actor cousin was coming to our town, staying in our house for a week, made my heart race. I didn't expect for a second that he would take notice of a scrawny thirteen-year-old.

Our family attended opening night. I thought I would burst with excitement. The play was *The Zeal of Thy House* by Dorothy Sayers, and it thrilled me with its medieval staging, deep male voices and a sexy love scene somewhere near the end. During the intermission, our family visited Duncan in the green room. To my amazement, this tall, robust man with a deeply furrowed brow and a shock of dark, wavy hair, fixed me with his intense blue eyes and asked my opinion of the play as if it mattered to him. I felt awkward when he presented me with a few slender stalks of red berries and told me their names, though I was almost sure my sister looked piqued. When we returned to our seats, my mother hissed: "Cousins don't marry." I have never known if her words put the idea in my head, or found it there.

One day during the following week, I found my cousin in my room looking at my homework. I was both annoyed and fascinated. When he saw me standing there, he drew me in and slowly, almost reverently, kissed me on the mouth. (For weeks I relived this kiss, which felt like an electric shock up my spine.)

310

Several times he asked me to go on walks with him. He talked expertly about theatre, plants, architecture: grown-up talk that left me tongue-tied. After his visit, he wrote me a long letter expressing in a poetic manner how much I meant to him. It frightened me, and I showed it to my mother. She wrote to him in no uncertain terms and asked him to desist. For the time being, he did.

I was sixteen when he joined the navy. During leaves he would often seek me out, whether I was at home or at boarding school, and always with a small gift or a bunch of flowers. I continued to feel the same turmoil: I wanted him; I wanted him gone forever. Outwardly I put on an assured air. My mother gave up trying to interfere.

By the time he returned from the war, I was in my early twenties. On the rebound from someone else, I craved a family and was ready to marry. Duncan, fighting malaria, dragged his heels.

Had he outgrown his Lolita complex? I wondered. Or did I no longer fit his dream? Maybe he was merely bound by a sense of loyalty to continue what he had begun.

All this the wedding outfit has brought back.

How did we come to buy it? Initially, a little bird of hope had fanned a flame in this young bride's heart.

"Can we get a long white dress, Duncan?"

"It's not practical. Why spend a pack of money we haven't got on something you'll never wear again?"

"I could have it cut down—as a party dress?"

He laughed. "I'm no good at partying and dances."

I knew that. The little bird died.

There was still my mother.

"Why don't you buy a wedding gown, darling? People will expect it. Besides, it will look good with his naval uniform."

"No, Mummy, we can't afford something I'll never wear again."

"You could have it cut down—"

"How many people are coming?"

"Around a hundred."

"A *hundred?* We wanted it small." *Registry office small,* I thought, but that was unthinkable, even for me, as the daughter of an Anglican minister.

"I know, but you left the invitations to us. There were a lot of people we couldn't leave out."

"You've just moved here. How can you know them all?"

"We don't, but thanks to you, we can start right now."

The wedding was mounted for us, but it wasn't ours. It was a heaven-sent opportunity for my parents to welcome their new parishioners. Living in London now, I knew none of them.

We duly bought the wedding costume, and agreed quite quickly on the dark tweed. He said it looked good with my height and fair hair. Privately I wondered how it would match with his uniform, but I told myself it was patriotic to avoid unnecessary expense so soon after the war. My eye fell on a wide-brimmed hat with white trim that cost the earth; I tried it on and gazed winningly at him. He softened, and carefully doled out the pounds from his wallet.

Today, my heart tears at the thought of his six years in the navy, the last two as a commissioned officer, of the danger his unit faced checking the landing beaches for bombs, of the small pill ready for ingestion (standard navy provision: death preferred to being captured and tortured for vital information), of the time he went missing in Malaysia for three months. I wonder how he felt having to buy a young woman's frivolous hat with money earned at such a price.

All I managed at the time was to push away financial worry now that he was returning to the precarious life of the theatre.

=

The two outfits hang side by side in my mind, swinging and whis-
pering together.

The fine dark tweed [FT] has a peevish voice. The cream pantsuit
with reddish pinstripes [RP] narrowly keeps its patience.

FT   I don't know why you're here at all.

RP   How d'you mean? I have just as much right as you have.
In fact, more. I'm more recent by a long shot.

FT   Ha! Some people wouldn't even recognize you as a
wedding garment.

RP   Why? Because I'm a pantsuit?

FT   (*sarcastically*) No. You know what I mean.

RP   Your ideas are as old-fashioned as you are.

FT   Excuse me, I was the height of fashion right after the war.
I was, in fact, only one year short of the New Look.

RP   Rings a bell.

FT   Well, if you can still remember Deanna Durbin's films . . .

RP   I'll crank my memory.

FT   Think of her tight bodices, full light skirts, foaming petticoats. That was the New Look, created by Dior in Paris in 1947.

RP   Still, it made sense not to postpone the wedding for
something not yet in the stores.

FT   (*missing the irony*) Anyway, my bride jolly well wouldn't
have chosen a pantsuit for herself.

RP   In those days, she'd have been lucky to find one—well,
maybe in pink polyester.

[*PAUSE*]

What are you thinking?

FT   Nothing.

RP   I bet.

313

FT   Okay, then: I was just wondering if you will have the same fate as me.

RP   What's that?

FT   To be outgrown so fast.

RP   (*laughing*) Not likely. I'm a good deal larger—

FT   It wasn't size I meant.

RP   I didn't think so.

[*LONG PAUSE*]

FT   I hung in the cupboard for ages, even when she couldn't get into me anymore. But finally, she gave me away . . .

[*FT'S VOICE SOUNDS FAINTER AND FAINTER TILL FINALLY IT DISAPPEARS*]

RP   Where are you, Tweed? Tweed? Answer me.

[*SILENCE*]

We moved into a little apartment in London, and Duncan found a job in repertory. I accompanied him for one week to a nearby town, where we lived in a B & B. I began to see my life mapped out in digs like these, or scrimping at home when work was scarce. The idea of raising a family began to recede.

A colourful Canadian poster intended to encourage emigration hung on the door. From such slight chances momentous decisions spring. As we gazed at the wheat fields of Alberta, we began to yearn for the limitless spaces of this great country.

In 1948 we left England for Edmonton, where our two children were born. We were welcomed into a community of amateur theatre enthusiasts, and our early years there were happy and productive. In time, Duncan was able to switch from construction work to an interesting classical music job at the university radio station, but his original vocation still tugged at him. Nine years later, we made a final move to Toronto, the mecca of professional theatre at that time. But it was too late.

By then, would-be actors were applying in droves for the few available jobs. Our money ran low; discouraged, Duncan settled for a steady occupation as a props specialist with CBC-TV. Struggling against a sense of stagnation, I began to pursue my second choice from that career book of so long ago: social work. I found a job as an untrained worker and was accepted at university, to work towards my degree.

The power in our relationship shifted from one partner to the other; our mutual love was not strong enough to survive the imbalance. My requests to seek counselling met a wall. Ever stoical, intensely private, Duncan pronounced that we must "carry on."

For what? I wondered.

The breakup was so quiet when it came. Duncan went to work as usual that day, our son to high school; our daughter had already moved out. Everyone knew Mother would not be living at home after that day. Of the furniture, I would leave everything except for my piano, which would be moved within a week.

We had recently allowed ourselves the luxury of a cleaning lady. It was her regular day.

"I'm moving out, leaving home," I told her as gently as I could.

Her face widened with shock. "You leave? Oh no, Missus, don't go. No good, leave husband . . . kids. Oh, Missus, please, *don't go.*"

No doubt we seemed a nice family in a nice home, so why would Missus break it up? Her broken phrases touched me but did not change my mind. I could not explain that the marriage had been dying on its feet for years. Most of all I could not tell her that I was in love, especially not with a woman.

How did I meet Kay?

Two years earlier, to help with my expenses, I had applied for a part-time job at a small counselling agency, unaware of the turn my life was about to take . . .

315

I am waiting in the office. Kay, the director, walks in.

It is as if a blinding light hits me across the eyes. We shake hands, but my voice won't work. I have the sensation I have always known her. To my utter surprise, I am wholly in love. From that second on, Kay is constantly on my mind and in my heart.

Two years later, I moved in with her.

My mother wrote from England: *Darling, after twenty-two years, it's going to be very hard for all of you. Oh dear, I keep asking myself, Was it my fault? Something I did or said that made you this way?* I assured her she was not responsible; I was what I was.

My father wrote: *Take a three-month break, old thing. You've had a trying time, working such long hours. Then go back to him.*

To Duncan he wrote: *Win her back at all costs.*

"It's no good trying to win you back, is it?" Duncan asked me.

"I'm afraid not."

We were actually able to laugh over this notion of "winning back"—like some knight his lady.

My old nurse wrote simply: *You were unequally yoked.* Her insightful acceptance, expressed in scriptural parable, comforted me.

In time, my parents, too, accepted the loving relationship between Kay and me, and came over to visit us one year. We were much luckier than many in this.

Over the early years of my new relationship, we both had to bear the inevitable deaths of parents. The most grievous trial of all was the serious mental illness of my son, which led him to make an unsuccessful attempt on his life in 1974. Although he survived, he was disabled for life. Throughout it all, Kay and I supported each other. In time, my sense of guilt receded and joy returned.

═

Fast-forward to summer 2003. Kay's younger nephew is visiting from Vancouver. We talk about the fact that our two provinces have recently recognized gay marriage.

"So when are you two going to get married?" We hear the inno-cent mischief in his tone and laugh.

"What? In our eighties?"

"Why not?"

"Well, we've certainly talked about it."

He turns serious. "If you do decide on it, I'd feel honoured to be invited."

"You mean that?"

"I certainly do."

After he has left, we talk some more.

"I want to marry you," she says, "but I don't want a wedding."

"What's bad about a wedding?"

"Feels like a party. As a kid I'd run a mile rather than go to a party."

"No different now?"

She shrugs. "Can't stand to be the centre of attention."

"You'd have to share it with me."

She laughs, but I know she would dread it.

Echoes of my first marriage: dislike of parties. But this is differ-ent. For one thing, she understands why, and I don't have to feel responsible. I'm more patient, too; I can wait. After thirty-four years of living together, I've learned to give her time, and space.

It is the next year before we really swing into action. Her nephew says he is coming here in June, which spurs us to set the date.

The next day I say, "If one nephew is coming, then we want the other one too."

"Yes, of course."

"And I wouldn't like to leave out my nieces and their families—"

"And at the very least five or six of our friends." She is running out of fingers. "That could be over twenty."

"Yes."

She sighs. "There's no end to it." As in: *I'm resigned.*

After a pause, she asks, "Do you think you could find out about wedding licences?"

"Good idea," I respond, in a casual tone.

I start by calling Toronto City Hall, which seems reasonably safe from North York, where we live. I blush, even though the woman can't see me.

"I would like some information about arranging a wedding."

"Yes, for what date?"

I tell her: June the sixth.

"A lovely time of year. You know your licence will last for three months—"

"It's a same-sex marriage," I blurt out, as though she will try to stop it.

"Fine," she says. "Is there anything else you would like to know?"

She answers all my queries and is both efficient and considerate. She tells us June is a popular month and advises us to get our licence in good time. Her attitude helps me take the first step towards coming out publicly. It scares me, but feels good.

On March the tenth we apply for the licence at the North York Civic Centre. I tell myself I do not have two heads and neither does my partner. The male registrant is equally pleasant and matter-of-fact. We thank our lucky stars we live in Ontario.

I am first asked for my divorce papers, which I have brought with me. This, more than anything, confirms for me that it is a legal marriage contract we are undertaking.

We sit on a bench and fill out the rough draft of our marriage licence. The monikers Groom and Bride make us giggle. We cross

318

them out and substitute Spouse under each. When we return the completed form, the registrant explains it is the only document they have at this time, and he cannot alter it. We glance at each other; I give her a slight nod, and she tells him she'll be Groom. (*Lavender's blue, dilly, dilly, lavender's green / When you are King, dilly, dilly, I shall be queen.*)

After a few moments he gives us the final typed copy. The designations stir up unpleasant memories of inequality but bear no relevance here.

After we reserve the date, Kay suggests we book our reception at a nearby hotel. I can hardly believe it. My love, who hated (still hates) a party. The young woman who takes the reservation seems genuinely thrilled and congratulates us. I feel more normal by the hour.

Later, I ask Kay what she will wear.

"Nothing new," she says. "I've got plenty of summer pantsuits."

She brings them out, but decides they won't fit the occasion.

We go shopping. It doesn't take me long to decide on a creamy suit with reddish pinstripes and a top to match the stripes. Kay dislikes shopping for clothes (books are a different matter). She trails her frustration up and down the aisles, pulling out this, touching that. Finally, she finds a light beige fitted jacket and an orange top, which she decides to mix and match with a favourite pair of brown silky-textured pants that I gave her last year.

Slowly I move her forward on ideas she at first resisted: cake, speeches, flowers on the tables. My daughter is thrilled to stand up for us, along with Kay's nephew. We tell him he is our Cupid. Kay's elder nephew is Master of Ceremonies. My sixteen-year-old grandson looks after the CD of music we have chosen for the ceremony. He is able to sit with his dad, who managed to fly here for the ceremony. We decide we cannot tell my son, who is now in long-term care, personally sustained by a religion that frowns on homosexuality. I am sad it has to be this way, because he invariably welcomes our visits, relies as deeply on Kay as on me, but we have no doubt at all that he would suffer unnecessary distress at the thought of our marriage.

Two of our invited friends genuinely regret that they will be away; another three decline to attend our wedding. It is a painful reminder that, even though the majority of our friends accept our relationship without question, some are nevertheless opposed to gay marriage. We are grateful that five others accept.

At final count we are twenty, including our officiant. She was the only woman on the chapel's list of a dozen officiants of varying denominations, and one of only two officiants who agreed to marry a same-sex couple. She is both experienced and helpful; at our request, she provides us with her framework for a non-religious service, which is exactly right for us, and leaves us free to alter or substitute as we see fit. We incorporate most of her material, though for the readings we choose only one of hers and we set out to find another one. The search leads us to think and talk about our relationship more deeply than ever before, and look unsuccessfully for a piece that feels even more personal. Kay says we'll have to write it.

One evening, when I am out at a meeting, she puts her thoughts on paper. Knowing her to be outwardly undemonstrative, the expressive words touch me even more. Nothing needs to be changed. We decide to use them as a frontispiece on the leaflet I am developing:

LOVE IN OUR EIGHTIES

Love is the steady centre of our lives, the joy and strength on which we draw.

Built on friendship, shared laughter and sorrow, pain and

rejoicing, common and differing interests, it gives us space to be separate and the longed-for pleasure of coming together.

It is trust and a place of safety— weaknesses and foibles are known, and love continues—a miracle which nurtures, encourages and supports.

Our Love is the sustaining happiness that fills our days, and is the very ground of our being.

It is dated and signed with our two names.

When the great day arrives, Kay is tense, and I am tense because she is. Our officiant guides us through the service and helps us to relax. After planning and typing for weeks, I'm sure I know the words by heart, but we follow the leaflet to calm our nerves. The love and support from family and friends is palpable.

The service proceeds through readings, the exchange of vows (*I accept you as my partner in marriage / I promise to share my life openly with you / I promise to care for you / I promise to encourage you in the fulfilment of your dreams / throughout the changes in our lives*) and then the exchange of rings.

It reaches its pinnacle when the officiant declares us to be "partners in marriage." I grab Kay's hand, and she gives me a small, tense smile.

After the closing words comes the kiss. This is the part she dreads, because we have never kissed in public. To have been lesbian all your life in a small town, as Kay was, meant that you lived hidden. I feel her shaking, and the kiss is brief, but by the time we sign the register we are able to laugh again.

The officiant presents us to the gathering, and everyone spontaneously bursts into applause. It is a wonderful and unexpected moment.

My grandson starts up Handel's music at the designated spot, and in time we all troop over to the nearby hotel. There we promise our guests just one public kiss at the reception; they loyally honour our request: there is no tinkling of cutlery on glasses. After the meal and the speeches, my daughter reminds us that they have waited patiently.

We rise and respond with a lingering, beautiful exchange: a public avowal of our mutual commitment. Even the presence of our enthralled waiter cannot inhibit us. It is entirely different from the peck in the chapel, and the whole gathering is delighted.

After the reception, Kay is more alert than I: she dashes around the tables, gathering up the half-dozen yellow roses for our informal photos. Now she can't stop smiling. She tells me later: "It was lovely, sweetheart. Thank you for persisting."

Surrounded by family and friends, we are relaxed in our photos, a gift from relatives who are professional photographers. Later on, I send a selection to those who live far away. One niece in England describes the look of "serene joy" on our faces.

Now, as I gaze at the photos from both weddings, the difference in apparel and mood hits me for the first time: formal and stiff in the first wedding; relaxed and joyous in the second. It's very true that wedding garb reveals the emotions hidden deep within the ritual.

ROSEMARY HOOD belonged to a group of children's writers over most of the past decade and produced many tales of her English childhood. "Two Suits and a Closet" is the story of her two weddings—one in the old world, the other in the new. For the purpose of this story, she assigned a pseudonym to each of her spouses. Because of the sensitive nature of the material with regard to her son, she asked for the greatest discretion should identification, by chance, be made.

Rosemary Hood lived in Toronto with her partner and three cats until her death in September 2006. Writing this memoir meant a great deal to her we feel very lucky to be able to include Rosemary's story in the anthology.

S. W. and A. L. C.

Afterword

In 2004, a man named Larry found his ex-wife's wedding dress in the attic. Instead of burning it, his first impulse, he put the dress up for sale on eBay. "One Slightly Used Size-12 Wedding Gown. Only worn twice: Once at the wedding and once for these pictures." The photographs, which became famous around the world, show Larry, a tattooed man in a baseball cap and black T-shirt, wearing a white beaded halter-top gown with a train. In the auction listing, the former groom reveals that he paid US$1,200 for the gown. Though he writes with vitriol about his ex, he's nicer about the dress. "I gotta say it did make me feel very pretty. So if it can make me feel pretty, it can make you feel pretty, especially on the most important day of your life, right?" he writes. "Ladies, you won't regret this. You may regret the dude you marry but not the dress." After 17 million hits on the eBay ad, the dress sold for US$3,850.

Who bought Larry's dress, and why, remains a mystery. For now. Perhaps the worldwide fame of that particular gown outweighed its unhappy history and made someone feel, indeed, very pretty. Perhaps it was bought by a group of divorced men who wanted Larry to get his money back. But whatever its current journey, that dress has a most spectacular history. The resounding success of Larry's eBay ad lies in the compelling story of a wedding dress. There's always something interesting hiding behind the buttons. I remember first seeing my mother's dress, folded with care in a trunk in our basement. I begged for the story: "Where did you meet Dad?" "How did he propose?" "Did you feel beautiful?" More than any other piece of clothing we possess, this dress promises a rosy future—a chance at love; it is freedom, a leap of faith. And over the years, this same tulle/silk/satin/chiffon costume holds our history—the good, the bad, the ugly. Revealing the secrets of their dresses, these contributors have proved that no matter the length of the train or the intricacy of the embroidery, woven into the very fabric of this particular outfit are emotions that range from fear to exhilaration, indifference to joy, sadness to hope.

There are as many wedding dress tales as there are gowns hanging in bridal boutiques around the world. And almost every story begins with the hunt for perfection. Picking through samples bunched on racks in the bridal boutique. Rummaging through a friend's closet. Glancing into a small store on the walk home. A bride yanks one frothy number over her head, and a new vision of her life is revealed. *We will be happy and have four children,* the dress sings. *I'm not sure,* whispers another. *We will not become our parents.* Hunting for The Dress—even if it is a tailored suit or a friend's sundress on loan—is a rite of passage. No woman forgets how she found her dress. No woman is indifferent to the power of memory stitched into that fabric.

The story of my dress begins in the summer of 2005. We had four months to plan our wedding. John proposed in May, and we decided to hold the wedding on September 10, the day before my parents' fortieth wedding anniversary. Initially, I was very Zen about the whole thing. *It's a nice time of year,* I thought, *and what's there to plan? We've thrown parties before.* I had no idea. Before long, I was juggling hundreds of details, all requiring an immediate decision. A month into the planning, I hadn't had time to think about what I would wear. In an effort to reduce my stress level, I decided two things: let the experts *be* the experts, and everyone must have fun. Including me. In the end, however, what I wore proved not to be the biggest clothing hurdle.

A wedding is the only time a woman will ever have veto over what her best friends wear. Though many former bridesmaids—especially those forced into slipless, clingy purple silk with elbow-length gloves in dusty peach—believe that the sole purpose of matching bridesmaid gowns is to make the bride look better by comparison, the real reason brides choose their maids is that they love them. For years, I confided in these wonderful women, cried on their shoulders, despaired of ever finding love and was bolstered by their constant friendship. They tether me to reality when I'm losing my grip. They are smart, confident, funny and warm. They love me without conditions. And in that spirit, my five bridesmaids said they would wear anything. A big pink synthetic pouf? Bring it on! Crinolines and a jaunty cap? No problem! To be honest, I had forgotten that I was supposed to pick their outfits. I had no idea what they would wear, and within minutes of my friends saying "yes" to my request that they stand up for me, worries about weight, size and style came to light. Dealing with the body issues of one woman is difficult, but balancing the fat thighs/short waist/lank hair/double chin issues of a group of my closest friends is near impossible. In addition, only one of the five lives in my hometown—the rest are scattered across the country. Mix in that one friend was pregnant, two were carrying "baby weight" (their words, *not* mine), my oldest friend had never worn a dress and my sister is tiny, and you have a mess of bridesmaid dress issues.

I decided to be bold. I instructed my friends to choose their own outfits (for the pants-only friend, I suggested a suit similar to those of the groomsmen). It seemed easier—they are experts on their own bodies, and they could have fun picking something out. "Wear whatever you like," I said. Patting myself on the back for such a mature and relaxed decision, I sat back to plan my own outfit with the same requirements. I had about three minutes before their panic began: "What colour? What length? I want to wear what *you* want me to wear." It took ten minutes before the real concerns burst forth: "What if I can't get it made like everyone else? What if I look like the dumpy country mouse next to four city bombshells? What if I'm the fattest woman there?"

After several long-distance phone calls and urgent emails, I decided on a course of action. I chose a colour for the bridesmaids—pink. And then, over the next three months, I bought yards of buttery silk and flowing chiffon to send across the country. I emailed photographs of shades of pink and dresses hanging in the windows of Toronto stores. I spent hours surfing websites, with my friends directing me by phone. I looked at shoes, purses, wraps, earrings, hairstyles and even facial blotting paper for my friends. By the time the wedding rolled around, I'd spent an enormous amount of time on bridesmaid dresses—ten times more than I spent on my own.

I'd never had a dream dress. I'd always known it had to be a V-neck (to accent my smallish boobs) and it had to be long (I'm 5'9"). But the rest of the details were hazy. White? The feminist in me, who lost her virginity years ago, wouldn't allow it. Sleeves? Only if they weren't puffy. A big frothy skirt with a bustle? Depended on the groom—if he was a hefty man, I could balance out the overall effect with a bigger dress. "That couple, well, they're just larger than life!" our guests would murmur. Well, the man I chose to marry is 6'4" and weighs about ninety pounds. There would be no big fat dress for me.

I knew what I didn't want, but I had to find ideas for what would work. I'm not much of a shopper—the false compliments of sales staff working on commission and the struggle to find clothes that hide my thighs and highlight my ass make me irritable. With Mum living in Israel for a few months and my sister on vacation, I was dreading the whole process. But on a steaming Tuesday afternoon, I found myself in the wedding dress district and decided to browse. The dresses in the windows made me itch just looking at them— layers of stiff underskirts, enormous trains, sweetheart necklines and tight three-quarter-length sleeves. Entering one store, I was alone except for two eager saleswomen who shadowed my every move. When they heard that the wedding was only three months away, one grimaced while the other announced that there would be at least a $2,000 rush fee. "Or," she said, eyeballing my grubby flip-flops and tattered purse, "you can have one off the rack. If you find one that fits."

Running my hands through the fabric, I tried to imagine myself in any of the gowns. Some were dismissed on contact— too stiff, too beady, too much pouf. Others made me cringe—too Princess Di, too tarty, too mature bride. One modest dress caught my eye, and I pulled it from the hanger. Looking it over, I noticed a smudge of mascara on its lacy neck. I pulled another gown down. It, too, had a smear of makeup. All of the samples were steeped in nervous sweat, sweet perfume, lipstick and a million girls' tears. Dodging the saleswomen holding out the gaudy and grotesque, I raced from the store. I wasn't going to find my dress, or start my story, in a place that reeked of women's panic and endless body issues.

Nine months after our wedding, The Dress hangs on my study door. It is stained at the hem and the train is filthy, the signs of a good party. For some reason, I can't try it on. I can't even bear to look at it very often—my eyes fill with tears and my heart aches for that once-in-a-lifetime evening. *I will never experience that magic again,* I think. And in spite of the wonderful memories of that day, every time I look at my gorgeous dress I mourn for what has passed. The dress served its purpose well, but I can't imagine it against my flesh again. It would be a huge disappointment when there's no aisle to walk down with skirts swishing, no guests to sigh over its tailored perfection, no music for dancing.

My mother, whose own wedding dress story graces the front pages of this book, would tell me to get a grip. She's probably right. Mothers are good for that: stepping in before high emotions rocket us into the Bridezilla stratosphere. It's striking, and yet not surprising, that the majority of these wedding dress stories include our mothers, or mother figures such as an adored aunt or grandmother. Maybe we all remember the first time we saw their wedding dress pulled from storage, or maybe it's simply that our mothers represent what we hope to become, or will strive to avoid, in our marriages.

The same holds true for my story—in my wedding dress tale, Mum is the hero. After the icky experience at the bridal boutique, I put off looking for a dress. I didn't want anyone else's panic swooping me up, so I lied to friends. "I'm having it made," I said. "It's gorgeous." The only three people who knew the truth were my mother, my sister and John. "I'm going naked," I cried one evening. "I can't deal with it."

Mum, bless her heart, unearthed North American wedding

magazines in Jerusalem. She pored over the pages and found a pretty, pale pink dress she thought I'd like. "Look at their ad in the magazine, p. 37, the right-hand side," she emailed me from Israel. "Hair is very much like yours will be; body same shape. It is really lovely. It is a V-neck over the shoulders, with a very slightly gathered midriff, all pulled to one side over the hip with a rose and then the organdy or whatever it is draped back across the skirt in folds over a silk underskirt."

I found the magazine and Mum was right. I'd found my dress. It was breathtaking. Romantic yet not frivolous. Seductive without being slutty. The only thing I worried about was the rose. I don't need any more padding on my hips. "Hi darling," Mum wrote again. "The moment I saw it, I thought . . . Amy. I love the two-way diagonal look. You have the body for this dress. As for the rose on the hip, I think it could be a flat one or nothing, but you are definitely slim enough to have the whole thing. You'll notice there is no necklace. I like that, but you would need some very elegant earrings—pearl drops with diamond base or something. Just looked at the picture. Pearl drops."

It took me years but I now accept that my mother is always right.

I found an excellent designer, who assured me that making the dress in two months was no problem. A talented guy but a little loose with planning, he sketched a copy of the gown on his pad of paper, agreed that pale pink chiffon would do nicely and told me to come back a week or so before the wedding. Consumed with bridesmaid dresses, I didn't think much more about my gown.

330

When I think about my wedding dress story, it is really the story of dressing my bridesmaids that comes to mind. In the time since our friendships were cemented, our worlds have grown heavy with jobs, children, illness, partners and physical distance. And so the effort spent planning the perfect outfit with each of my dearest friends was worth more than any gift. Two hours before the wedding, my bridesmaids, readers and female ushers gathered in my old bedroom at my parents' house. The room was filled with women in different shades of pink with varying necklines, skirt shapes and lengths and hairstyles. Even my bridesmaid who had never worn a dress, not even to our high school prom, was in pink. Two days before the wedding, she decided on a flirty strapless dress and added a feather boa to the ensemble. She had kept her outfit a surprise. And seeing her, looking at all of them dressed so beautifully in honour of me, I burst into tears. I will never forget the precious time spent blathering about clothes, a frivolity we don't often allow ourselves now.

I also think of my mother in my wedding dress story. How vital she is in my life. No one else will listen as carefully to my worries or concerns or dreams. She supports my decisions, fights for me when I'm weak and is inspired by events in my life. Without her, this particular story would have a very different ending.

When I went in to try on The Dress four days before our wedding, it was awful. No magic. No romance. No seduction. Instead, my hips looked enormous. My chest was lost inside the chiffon. I'd decided to be the hands-off bride, and now I was paying for it. Once again, Mum stepped in. There is no fiercer love than that of a mother for her daughter, especially when she sees her child fighting back tears while trying on her wedding dress. "All wrong," she said to the designer, snapping photos of my sad face (ever the reporter, my mother). "We need more swoop, more movement. A more delicate neckline, and the rose isn't right. Maybe we need another one or two."

Taking me aside, Mum gathered me into a tight hug. "I will *not* have my daughter wearing anything but her dream dress on her wedding day," she whispered. "I don't care how much it costs, this is going to be perfect."

And in the end, it worked out. My mother was right, again, and the designer performed miracles. The day before my wedding, my dream dress was ready.

A wedding dress is just a dress—a skirt, a top, a silk lining and some buttons. There might be French lace or Asian beading or a linen handkerchief that belonged to an ancestor sewed into the cuff, but it's just a dress. Why is it, then, that we weigh it down with all of our hopes and hang-ups? With this dress, I thee wed. My every dream will come true. Granted, it is worn on a day that is heavy with meaning—the most important day of a bride's life. For this reason, the wedding dress is a symbol of commitment, innocence and tradition. It's just a dress, but it's also a symbol of the hope we put into our decision to marry. And after the night is over, after the dancing and feasting and kissing and crying, we put it in the closet and forget that it's there. But the memories we have of our younger, more innocent self never fade—it's clear from all of these wonderful stories that just a glimpse of our gown will immediately bring us back to that day when we leapt through the fire, filled with hope.

I finally tried on my pretty pink dress today and I felt . . . nothing. Maybe it's too soon, maybe I worked myself up, maybe an overcast Tuesday afternoon wasn't the right time. But I wasn't emotional. I wasn't sad. I fingered the three beautiful chiffon roses on my hip and adjusted the straps. I twirled around, the soft skirt floating around my legs, and there it was—a tiny stir of sadness for a perfect evening that ended much too soon.

John caught sight of me in the hall and smiled.

"You look gorgeous," he said.

"I'm glad it still fits," I replied, twirling around again.

John peered at the bright pink plastic gardening shoes I was wearing under the hem of the dress and we started laughing. In that moment, the teary emotion was gone. I'd created a new moment with John. It is a dress that needs an audience, true, but now I'm fine with that audience being made up of one.

I don't know yet how my wedding dress story ends. But the beginning of the tale is filled with love, and hope, and floating on air in pale pink chiffon.

AMY CAMERON is an award-winning journalist. Before getting married, in September 2005, she had gone on so many terrible dates that she wrote the non-fiction short story collection *Playing with Matches: Misadventures in Dating* (Anchor, 2005). Though trained in painting and fashion design, she fell into journalism after university, working as the crime and Aboriginal affairs reporter for *The New Brunswick Telegraph Journal* and then on the arts and entertainment beat at *Maclean's* magazine. Now based in Toronto, Amy is a freelance journalist and screenwriter.

ACKNOWLEDGMENTS

It is with gratitude and great respect that thanks are given to the following people: Deirdre Molina, editor at Knopf Canada/Vintage Canada, whose enthusiasm, support and expertise added great joy to the whole experience; Craig Carter, who gave many hours of his time and expertise to navigate the legal waves for us; Francis Corrigan, who took over when good computer karma was needed. And the following people need to be named for their generosity in helping to contact writers and their overall encouragement in bringing this book to birth: Rebecca Cunningham, Marie Howe, Mary Jo Leddy, Deborah Murphy, Jacquelyn Ryan, Lauretta Santarosa, Barry and Lorraine White.

Contributors' Credits

P. xii: Stevie Cameron with husband, David. Credit: Courtesy of the author.

P. 13: Anita Rau Badami. Credit: Courtesy of the author.

P. 26: Alisa Gordaneer. Credit: Courtesy of the author.

P. 41: Joanne Arnott's wedding dress and Nick's wedding suit. Credit: Nick Zenthoefer.

P. 49: Elyse Pomeranz with husband, Amnon. Credit: Courtesy of the author.

P. 58: "The Wedding Party." Credit: Maggie Garrard.

P. 71 and p. 77: Anne Laurel Carter with husband, Craig. Credit: Courtesy of the author.

P. 87: Ilana Stanger-Ross with mother. Credit: Ellen Dubin Photography.

P. 93: Jane Munro with father and mother. Credit: Courtesy of the author.

P. 101: Jane Munro with husband Bob. Credit: "ORAF."

P. 111: Kerri Sakamoto with husband, Daniel. Credit: Courtesy of the author.

P. 119: Rebecca Cunningham with husband, John. Credit: Nadia Petrei.

P. 122: Susan Whelehan's parents. Credit: Courtesy of the author.

P. 126: Wedding button. Credit: Courtesy of the author.

P. 129: Susan Whelehan with husband, Francis. Credit: Courtesy of the author.

P. 139: Jenny Manzer with father. Credit: Stephanie Cole.

P. 149: Kathleen Boyle Hatcher with mother. Credit: Courtesy of the author.

P. 153: Edeet Ravel with ex-husband, Yaron. Credit: Courtesy of the author.

P. 165: Edeet Ravel on wedding day in front of "Shalom" sign. Credit: Courtesy of the author.

P. 181: Laurie Elmquist. Credit: Elizabeth Simpson.

P. 207: Sandra Campbell (maid of honour) with sister, Di. Credit: Horsdal Photography Studio.

P. 213: Sandra Campbell. Credit: Horsdal Photography Studio.

P. 223: Michele Landsberg with husband, Stephen. Credit: Courtesy of the author.

P. 229: Adwoa Badoe. Credit: Courtesy of the author.

P. 235: Adwoa Badoe with husband, Fulé. Credit: Courtesy of the author.

P. 245: Margaret Goudie Parsons with husband, Lee. Credit: Courtesy of the author.

P. 254: Jamie Zeppa with ex-husband, Tshewang, and family. Credit: Courtesy of the author.

P. 269: Darla Tenold. Credit: Hamada Bekhit.

P. 279: Ami McKay's wedding dress hanging on the clothesline. Credit: Ian McKay.

P. 289: Gianna Patriarca with best friend, Emilia Chiocca. Credit: Courtesy of the author.

P. 294: Gianna Patriarca with mother, Antonietta. Credit: Courtesy of the author.

P. 309: Rosemary Hood with ex-husband, Duncan. Credit: Courtesy of the author.

P. 323: Rosemary Hood (on right) with partner, Kay. Credit: David Govan.

P. 333: Amy Cameron with husband, John. Credit: Andrew Adams Photography.